Adolf Neubauer, Arthur Ernest Cowley

The Original Hebrew of a Portion of Ecclesiasticus (XXXIX. 15 to XLIX. 11)

Adolf Neubauer, Arthur Ernest Cowley

The Original Hebrew of a Portion of Ecclesiasticus (XXXIX. 15 to XLIX. 11)

ISBN/EAN: 9783337415389

Printed in Europe, USA, Canada, Australia, Japan

Cover: Foto ©Thomas Meinert / pixelio.de

More available books at **www.hansebooks.com**

THE ORIGINAL HEBREW

OF A PORTION OF

ECCLESIASTICUS

(XXXIX. 15 TO XLIX. 11)

TOGETHER WITH

THE EARLY VERSIONS AND AN ENGLISH TRANSLATION

FOLLOWED BY

THE QUOTATIONS FROM BEN SIRA IN
RABBINICAL LITERATURE

EDITED BY

A. E. COWLEY, M.A., AND AD. NEUBAUER, M.A.

WITH TWO FACSIMILES

OXFORD
AT THE CLARENDON PRESS
M DCCC XCVII

DEDICATED

TO

PROFESSOR A. H. SAYCE

CONTENTS.

PREFACE.

In editing the recently discovered Hebrew fragments of the book of Ben Sira, we have limited our aim to presenting the original text with as little delay as possible, and at the same time giving in a convenient form the materials for further study. A full commentary, as well as a detailed comparison of the versions, must be left for the future. We shall therefore not discuss the author's full name, or the date of his composition or of the Greek and Syriac translations [1]. For the literature on these points the reader is referred to Schürer's admirable work on 'The History of the Jewish People in the time of Jesus Christ [2].' In what follows we shall confine ourselves to some remarks on what is known, from Jewish sources, of Ben Sira and his writings.

It is now generally admitted that Jesus, son of Sirach (Σειράχ, סירא [3]), of Jerusalem, wrote his ethical work (usually quoted as 'the book of Ben Sira [4]'), in Hebrew, between 200 and 170 B.C. in Jerusalem. It was translated into Greek by his grandson, as stated in the prologue, from which we also gather that the version was made from the Hebrew, in the year 132 B.C.[5] The Hebrew of the present fragment is (with the exceptions referred to below, p. xiii) *classical*, not Rabbinical: still less is it an Aramaic dialect, such as that of several of the passages quoted in both Talmuds (the Palestinian [6] as well as the Babylonian), in the Midrashim, and in later Hebrew writings.

---

[1] On this subject, see E. Hatch, *Essays in Biblical Greek*, vii. p. 254 seq.

[2] English translation, 2nd division, vol. iii. p. 23 seqq. (Clark, Edinburgh, 1886); and later, his article on 'Apocryphen des Alten Testaments' in the *Realencyclopädie für protestantische Theologie und Kirche*, vol. i. p. 650 seqq. (3rd ed., Leipzig, 1896).

[3] Schürer, op. cit., p. 25, explains the name to mean 'coat of mail.' In the Hebrew Josippon (Pseudo-Josephus) the form שירך is a transliteration from the Latin; v. Zunz, *Die gottesdienstlichen Vorträge der Juden*, 2nd ed., 1892, p. 107, note *h*. He was not, as sometimes stated, a priest; Zunz, ibid., p. 106.

[4] So most frequently in early Rabbinic literature. S. Jerome (see p. x, note 5) says that it was called *Parabolae* (משלים) in Hebrew: cf. Ecclus. l. 27, and the use of משל (p. xxvi) and מתלא (p. xx) in the quotations. According to Seadyah (ספר הגלוי, ed. Harkavy, p. 151, lines 11 and 12) Ben Sira wrote a *book of instruction* (كتاب اداب, ספר מוסר? see our text, p. 10, l. 8) similar in character to the book of Proverbs.

[5] The many passages in which the translator has misunderstood his original, written only some sixty years before his own time, may perhaps serve as a warning to those scholars who are inclined to overrate the authority of the LXX version of the Old Testament.

[6] It is remarkable that only five quotations are found in the Palestinian Talmud; see below, p. xix seqq. (Nos. I. *b*, XVII, XXVI, XXXII, LIV).

In early times the book seems to have hovered on the verge of the canon, or to have been included among the כתובים (Hagiographa, see p. xxii below), since quotations from it are introduced by שנאמר (*as it is said*), a phrase applied only to the sacred writings. Although afterwards excluded from the canon by the Rabbis, it continued to live and to be appreciated both in the Palestinian and the Babylonian schools, as is proved by the fact that the text was constantly quoted either in the original or in a Rabbinical or Aramaic form. The Rabbis who lived before the destruction of the Temple used it without acknowledgement in the 'Sentences of the Fathers' (פרקי אבות, the earliest production of Rabbinical literature), while others quote from it either expressly under the name of Ben Sira, or anonymously, or else base their maxims upon it[1]. Rabbi Akiba and Ben Azai borrowed from it *verbatim*[2], and there is reason to believe that some apocryphal books were influenced by it[3]. Thus the official exclusion from the canon did not involve destruction, as in the case of some Christian uncanonical Gospels and Acts: the book of Sirach was allowed to be freely read, but it was regarded merely as literature and not as sacred[4]. Passing on to the later history of the book, we find that S. Jerome[5] (fourth century A. D.) possessed a Hebrew copy, although he did not translate it. That the book continued to be known, to individuals at least if not generally, is proved by the passages quoted from it (in a language already debased), by the Rabbis of the fifth and sixth centuries, in the later Midrashim of the seventh and eighth centuries (as the Tanḥuma), and in the sayings collected by R. Nathan in the ninth century[6]. Zunz (op. cit., p. 108, end of note c) believes that the early liturgist, R. Eleazar haq-Qalir, borrowed from Sirach (l. 5–8) in his liturgy for the day of Atonement, in praise of the High Priest. Simultaneously some of the sayings of Sirach are quoted by the Babylonian doctors in an Aramaic form[7].

For the tenth century we are on even firmer ground as to the existence of the book in its original language. R. Seadyah (סעדיה) Gaon, of Bagdad (920 A. D.), and of the Fayyum in Egypt, was blamed by the Qaraites[8] for sending out

---

[1] The quotations were first collected by Asaria de Rossi. For a list of them, see below, pp. xix to xxviii, and, for the literature dealing with them, Zunz, op. cit., pp. 108, 109, and notes.

[2] Bacher, *Die Agada der Tannaiten*, i. p. 277, note 2; p. 417, notes 1 and 2.

[3] See e. g. the list of parallel passages cited by Mr. Charles in *The Book of the Secrets of Enoch* (Oxford, 1896), p. 96, Index I; and Ryle and James, *The Psalms of Solomon* (Cambridge, 1891), p. lxiii seq.

[4] הקורא בחן בקורא באינרת, J. T. Synhedrin x. 5.

[5] The well-known passage in his preface to the translation of the books of Solomon is as follows: 'Fertur et πανάρετος Jesu filii Sirach liber et alius ψευδεπίγραφος,. qui Sapientia Salomonis inscribitur. Quorum priorem Hebraicum repperi, non Ecclesiasticum ut apud Latinos, sed Parabolas praenotatum, cui juncti erant Ecclesiastes et Canticum Canticorum, ut similitudinem Salomonis non solum librorum numero, sed etiam materiarum genere coaequaret.' S. Jerome simply adopted the old Latin version of the book; see pp. xxxvii to xlvii.

[6] Critically re-edited by S. Schechter, Vindobonae, 1887.

[7] Dalman, *Grammatik*, p. 29.

[8] A Jewish sect which sprang up in the eighth century under Anan (ענן), and denied the authority of oral tradition. See Harkavy in *Grätz Geschichte d. Juden*, 3rd ed., vol. v. p. 413 (note 17).

missives written in Hebrew provided with vowel-points and accents. They reproached him with endeavouring to give to his correspondence an appearance of holiness equal to that of the Biblical text, since the vowel-points and accents were supposed, according to tradition, to have been given with the Law on Mount Sinai. In answer to this accusation Sᵉadyah[1] states that these additions to the text are found also in copies of Ben Sira, in the book of the Wisdom of Eleazar ben Irai (Iri[2]), and in the scroll of the Hasmoneans[3]. In the course of his defence he quotes seven (or rather eight, see note 2 below) genuine sayings of Sirach[4] in classical Hebrew, so that it may be concluded that the book was at his disposal in the tenth century. The mentions of Ben Sira after this date are scanty and uncertain. R. Nissim ben Jacob (eleventh century) of Kairowân, in Tunisia, makes a quotation, which however he may have derived from Sᵉadyah. In the eleventh century, according to Reifmann[5], signs of Sirach's influence appear in the collection of sayings entitled מבחר הפנינים (Choice of Pearls), attributed to the famous poet and philosopher Solomon ben Gabirol[6] (Avicebron). The same scholar[7] also finds traces of the influence of Sirach (ii. 18) in the Jewish daily prayer[8], and (xlix. 10 and 11) in the hymn[9] for the outgoing of the Sabbath. He contends further that Sirach has an allusion (i. 2) to Aristotle and the doctrine of the eternity of matter, and that even Spinoza was perhaps influenced by Sirach (xliv. 34). These suggestions, as well as the inference (from the Aramaic form of the proverb, No. LIV below), that he was an Essene, are, to say the least, not convincing. There is no direct trace of the existence of the Hebrew Sirach in Spain, Provence, or among the Rabbis of France, the Rhine-land, and Germany. Rashi[10], the authors of the glosses on the Talmud (תוספות), and even Maimonides[11], did not possess the book; and later Rabbis, who mention sentences from it, most probably quoted second-hand from

---

[1] ספר הגלוי, p. 162.

[2] עיראי or עירי. It is curious to note that the saying . . . במופלא ממך (p. xix), ascribed in the Talmud to Ben Sira and found in the Greek version, is quoted by Sᵉadyah (op. cit., p. 178, l. 18) as belonging to the Wisdom of Ben Irai. Of this Eleazar b. Irai, Sᵉadyah also quotes two other sentences in classical Hebrew, but not in so easy a style as most of Sirach. He says Ben Irai's book of Wisdom is analogous to Ecclesiastes, while Ben Sira resembles the book of Proverbs. Of this enigmatical Eleazar ben Irai nothing further is known. Perhaps he is identical with the R. Eleazar who often reports sayings בשם בן סירא (see p. xix). Bacher (*Die Agada d. Palästinischen Amoräer*, ii. 1896, p. 11, note 5) identifies him, not very plausibly, with Eleazar ben Pedath.

[3] Edited by Dr. M. Gaster; see Notice in *Jewish Quarterly Review*, vi. p. 570.

[4] See pp. xix to xxiii.

[5] In the Hebrew periodical האסיף, iii. p. 250.

[6] See Steinschneider, *Die Hebräischen Uebersetzungen*, p. 382 seqq. (§ 221).

[7] In the essay on Ben Sira in his ארבעה חרשים (Prag, 1860), p. 3 seqq.

[8] See the Authorised Daily Prayer Book, with a new translation by the Rev. S. Singer, p. 62, נפלה נא ביד יהוה כי רבים רחמיו וגו׳.

[9] Beginning אליהו הנביא. It is not included in the English Authorised Daily Prayer Book.

[10] See p. xx (No. XI).

[11] The Sira he quotes in his Commentary on the Mishna (Sanh. xi. 1) must be, to judge from his low opinion of him, the compiler of the Alphabet; cf. Reifmann, האסיף, iii. p. 251.

older authorities[1]. No doubt it might be said, though the supposition is not very probable, that all the quotations from Sirach were made from memory, and that they were derived from oral tradition. Recent discoveries however have removed all uncertainty on this point.

Mrs. Lewis, who brought to light the now famous codex of the Syriac Gospels in the convent on Mount Sinai, some time ago acquired some manuscript fragments in the East[2], among which Mr. S. Schechter, Reader in Talmudic in the University of Cambridge, recognized one leaf as containing a fragment of Sirach (xxxix. 15 to xl. 7) in Hebrew, which he published with English translation, introduction, and notes in the *Expositor* for July 1896, (p. 1 seqq.). Through the kindness of the owner we have since been allowed to make a fresh examination of the leaf, and have found reason to alter some of the readings accepted by Mr. Schechter (see the Hebrew text, pp. 2 and 4). Although the leaf is mutilated in places, the parts which are still intact are abundantly sufficient to show the character and style of the composition, and to convince critics that the text is original and not a translation. After pointing this out, Mr. Schechter rightly adds: 'Its correspondence with the versions changes almost in every line, agreeing in some places with the Greek, in others with the Syriac. In other places, again, it agrees with *neither* of these versions, omitting whole clauses which are to be found both in the Greek and in the Syriac, or offering new readings which have been either misunderstood or misread by the translators. Certain clauses, again, are to be found in our MS. which are wanting in *both* versions, or are only reproduced by a very short paraphrase. There cannot, therefore, be even the shadow of a doubt that our text represents nothing else but the original. Even the marginal glosses testify to this fact. Such differences of *plena* and *defectiva* as צורך and צרך, or such fine variants as פי and פיהו, cannot possibly have been suggested by any translation, and could only have been made from some other copy of the original.'

Almost simultaneously the Bodleian Library acquired, through Professor Sayce, a box of Hebrew and Arabic fragments, among which we recognized another portion of the same text of Sirach, consisting of nine leaves, and forming the continuation of Mrs. Lewis' leaf, from chapter xl. 9 to xlix. 11. These fragments cannot be part of the copy mentioned by S'adyah, since they are not provided with vowel-points or accents, and also because the writing is not of the tenth century, but of the end of the eleventh[3] at the earliest, as may be seen from the facsimiles. The MS. does not seem to us to have been written by a Qaraite. There are in both fragments marginal notes[4] giving the variants of another copy of Sirach, or more probably of two other copies. These copies were however

---

[1] As e.g. Joseph ben Nahmias, *Jewish Quarterly Review*, iv. p. 164.

[2] See *Jewish Quarterly Review*, ix. p. 115 seqq.

[3] Mr. Schechter (ibid., p. 4) considers it 'certainly not later than the beginning of the twelfth century.'

[4] These are indicated in the MS. by a small circle ° over the word in the text, which we reproduce.

incomplete, the marginal notes giving their variants only as far as chapter xlv. 8 (see note in loco), and on xlvii. 8 and 9. In the Bodleian fragment there are also at least two Persian glosses (ff. 1 and 5^b), which point to its having been written in Bagdad or Persia, possibly transcribed from Sadyah's copy. The MS. is written on oriental paper, and is arranged in lines, eighteen to the page (in Mrs. Lewis' leaf one line is cut off), and the lines are divided into hemistichs. There is no indication of chapters, but a line is left blank occasionally, as shown in our printed text. The MS. is unfortunately damaged in many places, which we have marked by dots, showing approximately the number of letters missing, and by [ ] when letters are supplied. Our object being however to give the text of Sirach as we found it, we have carefully restricted conjecture to its narrowest limits. In some cases we have preferred to leave a lacuna, where either the space in the MS. did not allow of what seemed the obvious word, or some letter such as ל, ן, or ק was excluded; see e.g. xlv. 13^b. In every case a letter about which we felt there could be any reasonable doubt, has been marked with a horizontal stroke, thus א̄. On some orthographical peculiarities of the MS. see the note appended to the glossary, p. xxxvi. As regards the translation again, we have deemed it our duty as editors of a unique manuscript, to express the text faithfully, and not to adopt conjectural readings, except where the text yielded absolutely no sense. Usually, indeed, the meaning is clear; but passages occur which, from whatever cause, are obscure, and we cannot feel confident that we have seized the sense of all of them. A (?) in the translation indicates doubt either as to the reading or the rendering. There are sufficient indications that the text is not everywhere in its original purity, and we do not doubt that (as in many parts of the O. T.) cases will be found in which a purer reading has been preserved by one or other of the early versions; but a detailed comparison of the Hebrew text and the versions, and a discussion of their comparative merits, must, we think, be left to a commentary, as well as to a time when, we may hope, more of the original shall have been recovered. We have noted, lastly, the more important places in which the language is coloured by reminiscences of the Old Testament.

The language, as already observed, is classical Hebrew, the syntax displaying no traces of the peculiar New-Hebrew constructions, such as occur, for instance, so frequently in Ecclesiastes[1], though the vocabulary has an admixture of late or Aramaic words or expressions, such as might be expected from the date at which the author wrote. The latter, together with other words not occurring in Biblical Hebrew, will be found collected in the glossary (p. xxxi). The style is occasionally a little heavy, but this may sometimes be due to corruption of the text. Otherwise (especially chap. xliv. ff.) it is remarkably easy and flowing. It stands throughout on an altogether higher level than that, for instance, of Chronicles, Ecclesiastes, or the Hebrew

[1] The relative שׁ never occurs; the imperfect with ו consecutive occurs frequently; the perfect with ו consecutive in 42, 1^c. 8^c. 11^c; the perfect with simple ו only in 39, 32. 44, 2. 16. 20^b. 48, 11. 12^d.

parts of Daniel. We know from Ecclesiastes that the New-Hebrew idiom was in process of formation at this time, and it is evident that both New-Hebrew and Aramaic[1] words were current in the Hebrew with which the author was familiar; but the predominant character of his style is nevertheless pure and classical. The marginal readings are often interesting: the variations which they indicate are frequently considerably greater than those noted by the Massorites in the O. T., and resemble rather the various readings often presupposed by the LXX, while at other times they are noticeable as giving an Aramaic equivalent for a Hebrew word in the text. Sirach's position with regard to the New-Hebrew would no doubt be made clearer by the discovery of the originals of other apocryphal books, such as Judith, Maccabees i, Enoch, and the Psalms of Solomon. Finally the theory that he wrote his proverbs in metre is not supported by the newly-recovered text: the lines are very variable in length, and there is no indication that the author sought to adapt them to a uniform metrical scheme.

In the present edition we give:—(*a*) The Hebrew text, with the marginal notes and glosses arranged as in the MS. (*b*) The English translation of the Hebrew, adopting as far as possible the diction of the revised version of the O. T. (*c*) The Syriac version (which was made from the Hebrew), according to Lagarde's edition, a blank space indicating that the translator, or copyist, omitted a passage. (*d*) The Greek translation, according to Dr. Swete's edition, the blanks again indicating such omissions. The uncertain condition of the Greek text is well illustrated by Hatch[2], and will strike the reader on even a slight examination. Its value for comparative purposes is further lessened by the translator's tendency to paraphrase, as is the case also with the Syriac. (*e*) At the end, the Old Latin, according to Lagarde's edition of the Codex Amiatinus. For more convenient reference we have in all five texts numbered the chapters and verses as in Dr. Swete's edition, and indicated the hemistichs by letters of the alphabet in order. The Syriac, Greek, and Latin texts are reproduced exactly as in the editions followed. It did not fall within our plan to give the variants of these versions. (*f*) A glossary of noticeable words and expressions. (*g*) A list of proverbs attributed to Sirach in Talmudic and Rabbinical literature, with a translation, arranged in the order of the Greek version. Here again we resolved not to add the various readings, since the Talmudic dialect is not the original language of Sirach, and moreover, all the new Talmudic fragments found within the last two years have not yet been collated. For completeness sake we have added the so-called 'Alphabets' of Ben Sira, a late composition—probably of the eleventh century or perhaps even later, but containing some genuine proverbs of Sirach, both in the first and second parts[3]. The stories given after each proverb in part i. are mostly indecent, and

[1] The strong Syriasms which sometimes occur, deserve notice, as מגרמין (41, 5^c) and חסתויר (42, 12^b).

[2] Op. cit., p. 258 seqq.

[3] In the Bodleian MS. No. 1466 the order is reversed.

written in mockery of Jewish literature. We reproduce the first אב (MS. second), with a translation: for the second (MS. first), we only refer to the numbers in our list of proverbs with which it agrees, ignoring the rest as alien to Sirach. The Alphabets[1], though a late and unedifying compilation[2], survived, whilst Ecclesiasticus was completely neglected. A Persian text of them was lately acquired by the British Museum (MS. Or. 4731), and another copy has just been brought by Mr. E. N. Adler from Persia, probably translated from the Constantinople edition (see below, p. xxix). (*h*) Some specimens of attempted restorations of the original Hebrew by modern scholars confronted with our text. The comparison will, we think, justify the caution and reservation which must be observed in attempting to restore lost works on the basis of ancient translations[3]. In the present instance, for example, both versions prove to be much freer than was assumed to be the case by those who so used them.

In conclusion, we have great pleasure in acknowledging the help of friends who have enabled us to carry through the work in a short time in spite of difficulties. Mr. J. F. Stenning, of Wadham College, rendered valuable aid in deciphering the difficult parts of the MS., including the Cambridge leaf, and in all doubtful places he concurs in the readings which we have adopted in our text. He also revised the Syriac. Mr. E. N. Bennett, of Hertford College, read the Greek: Rev. F. E. Brightman, Librarian of the Pusey House, read the Latin. Professor D. S. Margoliouth has also shown an interest in the work in various ways. We feel, however, specially grateful to the Regius Professor of Hebrew, Dr. Driver. He revised the translation throughout, besides being entirely responsible for the glossary, with the note appended, and almost every page of the book owes something to the judgement and accuracy which he has been always ready to expend upon it.

---

[1] The *Editio princeps* is that of Constantinople, 1519. (The Bodleian copy is defective.) For the other editions, see Steinschneider's *Catalogus Librorum Hebraeorum in Bibliotheca Bodleiana*, Berolini, 1852–1860; and Zedner's *Catalogue of Hebrew Books in the British Museum* (London, 1867), with Van Straalen's *Supplement* (1894).

[2] See Reifmann, Hakarmel ii. p. 124 seq.

[3] Cf. Driver in *The Oxford Magazine*, vol. viii (1890), no. 11, p. 182, and no. 12, p. 190 seq.

A LIST OF WORKS USED.

Bacher (W.), Die Agada der babylonischen Amoräer. Strassburg, 1878.

——— Die Agada der Tannaiten. Strassburg, 1884.

Ball (C. J.), The Ecclesiastical or Deutero-Canonical Books of the Old Testament, commonly called the Apocrypha, edited with various renderings and readings from the best Authorities. [The Variorum Bible], Eyre and Spottiswoode, London, n. d.

Ben Seeb (Wolfsohn, Jehuda Loeb), . . . חכמת יהושע בן סירא נעתק בלשון עברי. Wien, 1814.

Bickell (G.), Die Strophik des Ecclesiasticus, in the Vienna Oriental Journal, vi. (1892), p. 87. Compare his restoration of the alphabetical poem (51, 13–20) in the Zeitschrift für Katholische Theologie, 1882, p. 326 seqq.

Coronel (N. N.), חמשה קונטרסים (for the Baraitha Kallah). Vindobonae, 1864.

Dalman (G.), Grammatik des Jüdisch-Palästinischen Aramäisch. Leipzig, 1894.

Driver (S. R.) in the Oxford Magazine, vol. viii. no. 11 (p. 182), and no. 12 (p. 190). Oxford, 1890.

Dukes (L.), Zur rabbinischen Spruchkunde. Wien, 1851.

——— Rabbinische Blumenlese. Leipzig, 1844.

Edersheim (A.) in the Holy Bible . . . . . with an explanatory and critical commentary, &c. Apocrypha, edited by Henry Wace, D. D., vol. ii. London (Murray), 1888.

Eichhorn, Bibliothek. Leipzig, 1787 &c. (vol. ii. p. 691 seqq.).

Fränkel (S. I.), כתובים אחרונים, Hagiographa posteriora . . . in linguam Hebraicam convertit . . . S. Isaac Fränkel. Lipsiae, 1830.

Fritzsche (O. F.), Libri Apocryphi Veteris Testamenti. Lipsiae, 1871.

Gabirol (R. Salomon ibn), ספר מבחר הפנינים, A Choice of Pearls, originally compiled from the Arabic . . . translated into Hebrew by R. Jehuda ibn Tibbon, the Hebrew text . . . accompanied by a faithful English translation by the Rev. B. H. Ascher. London (Trübner), 5619–1859.

Geiger (A.) in the Zeitschrift der Deutschen Morgenländischen Gesellschaft, vol. xii. (p. 536 seqq.).

Grätz (H.), Geschichte der Juden. Leipzig, 1874.

Hamburger (J.), Real-Encyclopädie für Bibel und Talmud. Supplement, Band i. p. 77 seqq. (art. Jesus Sohn Sirach). Leipzig, 1886.

Harkavy (A.), Studien u. Mittheilungen aus der Kaiserlichen Oeffentlichen Bibliothek zu St. Petersburg: fünfter Theil, erstes Heft. St. Petersburg, 1891.

Hatch (E.), Essays in Biblical Greek (p. 246 seqq.). Oxford, 1889.

Horowitz (J.) in the Monatsschrift für Geschichte u. Wissenschaft des Judenthums, vol. xiv. (p. 101 seqq., p. 136 seqq., p. 178 seqq.).

Kohut (A.), Aruch completum. Viennae, 1878–1892.

Lagarde (P. A. de), Libri Veteris Testamenti Apocryphi Syriace. Lipsiae, 1861.

——— Mittheilungen. Göttingen, 1884 (p. 285 seqq.).

LAMBERT (M.), Commentaire sur le Séfer Yesira . . . par le Gaon Saadya. Paris, 1891.
MARGOLIOUTH (D. S.) in the Expositor, April and May, 1890.
MIDRASH TANḤUMA, ed. Warsaw, 1879.
——— RABBA. Frankfurt, 1705.
NEUBAUER (Ad.) in the Jewish Quarterly Review, vol. iv. (p. 162 seqq.).
——— Catalogue of Hebrew MSS. in the Bodleian Library. Oxford, 1886.
RAPOPORT (S. J.) in the Hebrew periodical בכורי העתים, x. p. 116 seqq. (on Qalir). Wien, 1829.
REIFMANN (J.) in the periodical האסיף, vol. iii. Warsaw, 1886.
——— מאמר ארבעה חרשים. Prag, 1860.
——— in the periodical הכרמל, ii. p. 124 seqq. Wilna, 1873.
DE ROSSI (Asaria), מאור עינים, section אמרי בינה (p. 29 seqq.). Mantua, 1574.
SCHECHTER (S.) in the Jewish Quarterly Review, vol. iii. no. 12 (July, 1891).
——— in the Expositor, 5th series, no. xix. (July, 1896).
——— Aboth de Rabbi Nathan. Vindobonae, 1887.
SCHÜRER (E.) in the English translation, A History of the Jewish People in the time of Jesus Christ, 2nd division, vol. iii. Edinburgh, 1886.
——— in the Realencyclopädie für protestantische Theologie und Kirche, 3rd ed. Leipzig, 1896 (art. Apocryphen des Alten Testaments).
SeADYAH, ספר הגלוי, in Studien u. Mittheilungen aus der Kaiserlichen Oeffentlichen Bibliothek zu St. Petersburg, von Dr. A. Harkavy: fünfter Theil, erstes Heft. St. Petersburg, 1891.
SINGER (S.), The Authorised Daily Prayer Book. London, 5655–1895.
STEINSCHNEIDER (M.), אלפאביתא דבן סירא, Alphabetum Siracidis utrumque. Berolini, 1858.
——— Die Hebräischen Uebersetzungen des Mittelalters. Berlin, 1893.
——— Catalogus Librorum Hebraeorum in Bibliotheca Bodleiana. Berolini, 1852–1860.
STRAALEN (S. van), Catalogue of Hebrew Books in the British Museum. (London), 1894.
SWETE (H. B., D.D.), The Old Testament in Greek according to the LXX, vol. ii. Cambridge, 1891.
TALMUD, the Jerusalem. Krotoschin, 1866.
——— the Babylonian. Frankfurt a. M., 1721.
TAWROGI (A. J.), Derech Erez Sutta. Königsberg, 1885.
TAYLOR (C.), Sayings of the Jewish Fathers, comprising Pirqe Aboth and Pereq R. Meir. Cambridge, 1877.
WOLFSOHN, see Ben Seeb.
YETSIRA (Sepher), see Lambert.
ZEDNER, Catalogue of Hebrew Books in the Library of the British Museum. (London), 1867.
ZOHAR, ed. Lublin, 1882.
ZUNZ (L.), Die gottesdienstlichen Vorträge der Juden . . . zweite . . . Auflage . . . herausgegeben von Dr. N. Brüll. Frankfurt a. M., 1892.

SOME ATTEMPTS AT RECONSTRUCTING THE ORIGINAL OF SIRACH, CONFRONTED WITH OUR TEXT.

Sir. 40, 14[b].

Ball.	Sirach.
So shall transgressors come to nought.. [*Heb. perhaps*, therefore (al-ken *for* ken).]	כי פתאם לנצח יתם :

Sir. 40, 19.

Edersheim (Margoliouth).	Fränkel.	Benzeeb (41, 20).	Sirach.
Sons and daughters (בנין ובנות) continue a man's name, &c. ('...the Syriac shows us that πόλεως is a gloss').	בנים ובוני־עיר מקימי־שם המה :	כבוד ויקר יתנו שם :	ילד ועיר יעמידו שם :

Sir. 44, 22. 23.

Bickell.	Fränkel.	Benzeeb (45, 14. 15).	Sirach.
ובן ביצחק הקים למען אביו: ברכת כל אדם ובריתו: ובראש יעקב הניחו: בברכותיו יכירנו: וינחל יחלק חלקיו: שבטים שני עשר יחצם :	ובעבור אברהם אביו הקים בריתו את־יצחק ויתנהו לברכה בארץ: ויעמידה ליעקב לחוק ויברכהו לרשת נחלה ויבדילה לשנים־עשר שבט:	אף ליצחק נשבע בעבור אברהם אביו וברכות אבותיו שם על ראש ישראל אשר קרא בני בכורי: ויקם בריתו אתו לרשת ארץ מגורו ויתנהו אב לשנים עשר שבט :	וגם ליצחק הקים בן (כן .M) בעבור אברהם אביו : ברית כל ראשון נתנו וברכה נחה על ראש ישראל: ויכוננהו בברכה (ויכנהו בבכורה .M) ויתן לו נחלתו: [ו]יציבהו לשבטים לחלק שנים עשר :

Sir. 45, 25.

Fritzsche.	Fränkel (45, 29).	Benzeeb (46, 18).	Sirach.
ואת־הברית לדוד בן־ישי למטה יהודה נחלת המלכות לבן מבן לבדו :	וכאשר נשבע לדוד בן־ישי לבלתי הסר שבט מיהודה כן הנחיל משמרת הכהנה לאהרן ולזרעו וגו	כאשר נשבע לדוד בן ישי לבלתי הסיר שבט מזרעו כן נתן לאהרן כהנה לו ולזרעו :	וגם בריתו עם דוד בן ישי למטה יהודה נחלת אש לפני כבודו נחלת אהרן לכל זרעו:

Sir. 49, 9.

Geiger.	Fränkel.	Benzeeb (49, 34).	Sirach.
גם את איוב זכר בסערה לגמל דרכי ישרו :	ברמיון גשם שטף חוה על חוי־שוא ולהולכי בתמים בשר תנחומים :	ועל איוב אמר כי כל ארחותיו ישרים :	וגם הזכיר את איוב המכלכל כל ד[רכי צ]דק :

BEN SIRA'S PROVERBS PRESERVED IN TALMUDIC AND RABBINIC LITERATURE[1].

I.

Sir. 3, 21. *χαλεπώτερά σου μὴ ζήτει,*
καὶ ἰσχυρότερά σου μὴ ἐξέταζε.
22. *ἃ προσετάγη σοι, ταῦτα διανοοῦ·*
οὐ γάρ ἐστίν σοι χρεία τῶν κρυπτῶν.

a.

Sᵉadyah in ס"ה הגלוי (ed. Harkavy), p. 178, l. 18, quotes as an extract from the Wisdom of Elcazar ben Irai (see Preface, p. xi) the following:

במופלא ממך אל תדרש. במכוסה ממך אל תחקר.
באשר הרשיתה התבונן. לא יש לך עסק בנסתרות

This seems to be the original text of Ben Sira.

Inquire not into that which is too difficult for thee;
and that which is concealed from thee search not out.
Attend to that which is permitted to thee:
thou hast no business with hidden things.

b.

*רבי לעזר (אלעזר i. e.) בשם בר סירה: פליאה ממך מה תדע. עמוקה משאול מה תחקור. במה שהורשיתה התבונן. אין לך עסק בנסתרות

J. T. Ḥaghigah, ii. (fol. 77ª).

That which is too difficult for thee, why shouldest thou know?
that which is deeper than Sheol, why shouldest thou search out?
Attend to that which is permitted to thee;
thou hast no business with hidden things.

c.

*כתוב בספר בן סירא בגדול ממך אל תדרוש. בחזק ממך אל תחקור. במופלא ממך בל תדע. במכוסה ממך בל תשאל. במה שהרשית התבונן ואין לך עסק בנסתרות

B. T. Ḥaghigah, fol. 13ª.

Inquire not into that which is too great for thee;
and that which is too hard for thee, search not out.
That which is too difficult for thee do not know;
and that which is concealed from thee do not ask.
Attend to that which is permitted to thee;
thou hast no business with hidden things.

d.

*ר' אליעזר אֹמ׳ בשם בֿסֿ (בן סירא i. e.) בגדול ממך אל תדרוש בחזק ממך אל תחקור במופלא ממך בל תדע במכוסה ממך בל תשאל במה שהרשית התבונן אין לך עסק בנסתרות

Midrash Rabba בראשית, viii. (MS. vii, see Bodl. New Heb. Cat., No. 147, fol. 1גᵇ).

II.

Sir. 4, 30. *μὴ ἴσθι ὡς λέων ἐν τῷ οἴκῳ σου.*

לעולם אל יטיל אדם אימה יתירה בתוך ביתו

B. T. Gittin, fol. 6ᵇ.

Let a man never bring excessive terror into his house.

III.

Sir. 5, 4.

Μὴ εἴπῃς· ἥμαρτον, καὶ τί μοι ἐγένετο;
ὁ γὰρ κύριός ἐστιν μακρόθυμος.

אם יאמר לך יצר הרע חטוא והקבה מוחל אל תאמן

B. T. Ḥaghigah, fol. 16ª.

If the evil propensity say to thee, Sin, for the Holy One (blessed be he!) excuseth, do not believe.

IV.

Sir. 5, 5.

περὶ ἐξιλασμοῦ μὴ ἄφοβος γίνου,
προσθεῖναι ἁμαρτίαν ἐφ' ἁμαρτίαις·
καὶ μὴ εἴπῃς Ὁ οἰκτειρμὸς αὐτοῦ πολύς,
τὸ πλῆθος τῶν ἁμαρτιῶν μου ἐξιλάσεται·
ἔλεος γὰρ καὶ ὀργὴ παρ' αὐτοῦ,
καὶ ἐπὶ ἁμαρτωλοὺς καταπαύσει ὁ θυμὸς αὐτοῦ.

[1] The proverbs marked with an asterisk are mentioned with the name of Sirach.

*ואל סליחה אל תבטח להוסיף עון על עון. ואמרתה רחמיו רבים לרוב עונותי יסלח. כי רחמים ואף עמו ועל רשעים ינוח עזו

Saadyah, p. 176, l. 19.

And be not confident of pardon,
to add iniquity to iniquity,
or say, His mercies are great,
he will pardon the multitude of my iniquities;
for mercy and wrath are with him,
and his might resteth upon the wicked.

V.

Sir. 5, 7. *μὴ ἀνάμενε ἐπιστρέψαι πρὸς κύριον,*
καὶ μὴ ὑπερβάλλου ἡμέραν ἐξ ἡμέρας.

שוב יום אחד לפני מיתתך

B. T. Shabbath, fol. 153ª.

Repent one day before thy death.

VI.

Sir. 5, 15. *ἐν μεγάλῳ καὶ ἐν μικρῷ μὴ ἀγνόει.*

Syriac ܣܓܝ ܘܙܥܘܪ ܠܐ ܬܡܣܪܘܚ

Great and small do not injure.

אל תהי בז לכל אדם

Aboth, iv. 6.

Despise not any man.

VII.

Sir. 6, 6. *οἱ εἰρηνεύοντές σοι ἔστωσαν πολλοί,*
οἱ δὲ σύμβουλοί σου εἷς ἀπὸ χιλίων.

*רבים יהיו אנשי שלומיך גלה סודך לאחד מני אלף

Saadyah, op. cit., p. 178, l. 1; also B. T. Yebamoth, fol. 63ᵇ, and Synhedrin, fol. 100ᵇ, where the words of Micha 7, 5, משוכבת חיקך שמור פתחי פיך, follow.

Let those that are at peace with thee be many,
but reveal thy secret to one of a thousand
[keep the doors of thy mouth from her that lieth in thy bosom].

VIII.

Sir. 6, 7. *εἰ κτᾶσαι φίλον, ἐν πειρασμῷ κτῆσαι αὐτόν,*
καὶ μὴ ταχὺ ἐμπιστεύσῃς αὐτῷ.
8. *ἔστιν γὰρ φίλος ἐν καιρῷ αὐτοῦ,*
καὶ οὐ μὴ παραμείνῃ ἐν ἡμέρᾳ θλίψεώς σου.

*קנית אוהב במסה קנהו ואל תמהר לבטח עליו. כי יש אוהב כפי עת ולא יעמד ביום צרה

Saadyah, p. 178, l. 3.

If thou gettest a friend, get him by proving,
and be not hasty to trust in him;
for there is a friend according to the occasion;
and he will not abide in the day of adversity.

IX.

Sir. 6, 13. *ἀπὸ τῶν ἐχθρῶν σου διαχωρίσθητι,*
καὶ ἀπὸ τῶν φίλων σου πρόσεχε.

*משנאיך הבדל ומאוהביך הזהר

Saadyah, p. 178, l. 8.

Separate thyself from them that hate thee,
and be careful of thy friends.

X.

Sir. 7, 1. *μὴ ποίει κακά, καὶ οὐ μή σε καταλάβῃ κακόν.*

Cf. 12, 2.

*מתלא אמר בן סירא. טב לביש לא תעבד וביש לא ימטי לך

Bereshith R., p. 44ª; Midrash Qobeleth v; Midrash Tanḥuma חקת § 1.

Ben Sira said the proverb: Do not good to the evil, and evil will not befall thee.

See Schechter, *J. Q. R.* iii. p. 694, No. 17 and note.

XI.

Sir. 7, 10. *μὴ ὀλιγοψυχήσῃς ἐν τῇ προσευχῇ σου.*

אמר רב כל שאין דעתו מיושבת עליו אל יתפלל משום שנאמר בצר אל יורה[1]

B. T. Erubin, fol. 65ª.

[1] Text has יורה 'to teach.' Rashi (Solomon of Troyes) says: I have searched to find this verse in the Hagiographa, but did not succeed. Perhaps it is in Sirach.

Rab said: Let not a man pray whose mind is not at rest within him, because it is said: In adversity who shall give thanks?

Perhaps a reminiscence of Ps. 6, 6.

XII.

Sir. 7, 17. *ταπείνωσον σφόδρα τὴν ψυχήν σου.*
ὅτι ἐκδίκησις ἀσεβοῦς πῦρ καὶ σκώληξ.

[So ℵA arrange the lines.]

מאד מאד הוי שפל רוח שתקות אנוש רמה ובן אדם תולעה

Aboth, iv. 7.

Cf. No. LVI below.

Be humble exceedingly in spirit;
for the hope of man is a worm, and the son of man is a maggot (cf. Job 25, 6).

XIII.

Sir. 8, 5.
μὴ ὀνείδιζε ἄνθρωπον ἀποστρέφοντα ἀπὸ ἁμαρτίας·
μνήσθητι ὅτι πάντες ἐσμὲν ἐν ἐπιτίμοις.

אם היה בעל תשובה לא יאמר לו זכור מעשיך הראשונים

Mishnah Baba Metsia, iv. 10.

If a man repents, one does not say to him,
Remember thy former doings.

XIV.

Sir. 8, 8. *μὴ παρίδῃς διήγημα σοφῶν,*
καὶ ἐν ταῖς παροιμίαις αὐτῶν ἀναστρέφου·
ὅτι παρ' αὐτῶν μαθήσῃ παιδείαν
καὶ λειτουργῆσαι μεγιστᾶσιν.

אמר רב אפילו שיחת חולין של תלמידי חכמים צריכה למוד

B. T. Sukkah, fol. 21b, and Abodah Zarah, fol. 19b.

Rab said: Even the ordinary conversation of the wise requires learning.

XV.

Sir. 8, 18. *ἐνώπιον ἀλλοτρίου μὴ ποιήσῃς κρυπτόν.*

ששה דברים נאמרו בעמי הארץ . . . ואין מגלין לו סוד

B. T. Pesaḥim, fol. 49b.

Six things are said of the people of the land (the unlearned) . . .; and they reveal not to him a secret.

XVI.

Sir. 9, 8.
ἀπόστρεψον ὀφθαλμὸν ἀπὸ γυναικὸς εὐμόρφου, . . .
ἐν κάλλει γυναικὸς πολλοὶ ἐπλανήθησαν . . .
9. *μετὰ ὑπάνδρου γυναικὸς μὴ κάθου τὸ σύνολον,*
καὶ μὴ συμβολοκοπήσῃς μετ' αὐτῆς ἐν οἴνῳ.

*העלם עיניך מאשת חן פן תלכד במצודתה. אל תט אצלה[1] למסוך עמה[1] יין ושכר. כי בתואר אשה יפה רבים הושחתו ועצומים כל הרוגיה:

B. T. Synhedrin, fol. 100b; Yebamoth, fol. 63b.

[1] So Rashi (ap. Schechter, ibid., p. 700, note 36), ed. אצל בעלה למסך עמו.

Hide thine eyes from a comely woman,
lest thou be caught in her snares[2];

[2] Cf. 9, 3b: *μή ποτε ἐμπέσῃς εἰς τὰς παγίδας αὐτῆς.*

turn not aside to her, to mingle wine and strong drink with her.:
for through the beauty of a fair woman many have been destroyed,
and 'all her slain are a mighty host' (Prov. 7, 26).

XVII.

Sir. 11, 1. *σοφία ταπεινοῦ ἀνύψωσεν κεφαλήν,*
καὶ ἐν μέσῳ μεγιστάνων καθίσει αὐτόν.

*בסיפרא דבן סירא כתיב
סלסלה ותרוממך (Prov. 4, 8)
ובין נגידים תושיבך

So in J. T. Berakhoth, vii. 2, and in Midrashim: the B. T. Berakhoth, fol. 48a, quotes Proverbs 4, 8, entire, omitting the last three words of the saying. See Reifmann's essay on Ben Sira in האסיף iii. p. 248, 3.

In the book of Ben Sira it is written:
Exalt her and she shall lift thee up (Prov. 4, 8),
and set thee among princes.

XVIII.

Sir. 11, 8. *πρὶν ἢ ἀκοῦσαι μὴ ἀποκρίνου,*
καὶ ἐν μέσῳ λόγων μὴ παρεμβάλλου.

שבעה דברים בגולם ושבעה בחכם . . . ואינו נכנס לתוך דברי חבירו ואינו נבהל להשיב

Aboth, v. 10.

Seven things are in a clod, and seven in a wise man. (The wise man) . . . does not interrupt the words of his companion; and is not hasty to reply . . .

Cf. Prov. 18, 13. Monatsschrift, 1865, p. 186, note 8.

XIX.

Sir. 11, 9.
περὶ πράγματος οὗ οὐκ ἔστιν σοι χρεία μὴ ἔριζε.

שנתעסק בדברים שלא היה לו צורך בהן

Midrash Tanḥuma (p. 73a) וארא, ה.

For he was busied with matters whereof he had no need.

XX.

Sir. 11, 28. *πρὸ τελευτῆς μὴ μακάριζε μηδένα,*
καὶ ἐν τέκνοις αὐτοῦ γνωσθήσεται ἀνήρ.

*לפני מות אל תאשר כי באחריתו יתנכר איש

Seadyah, p. 178, l. 6.

Call no one happy before (his) death,
for by his end shall a man be known.

XXI.

Sir. 11, 29.

μὴ πάντα ἄνθρωπον εἴσαγε εἰς τὸν οἶκόν σου.

*מנע רבים מתוך ביתך ולא הכל תביא ביתך

B. T. Synhedrin, fol. 100b; Yebamoth, fol. 63b.

Keep away many from the midst of thy house,
and bring not every man into thy house.

XXII.

Sir. 13, 2.

ἰσχυροτέρῳ σου καὶ πλουσιωτέρῳ μὴ κοινώνει.
4. *ἐὰν χρησιμεύσῃς, ἐργᾶται ἐν σοί·*
καὶ ἐὰν ὑστερήσῃς, καταλείψει σε.

הוו זהירים ברשות שאין מקרבין לאדם אלא לצורך עצמן ונראין כאוהבין בשעת הנאתן ואין עומדין לאדם בשעת דחקו:

Aboth, ii. 3.

Be cautious with (those in) authority,
for they let not a man approach them but for their own purposes;
and they appear like friends when it is to their advantage,
and stand not by a man in the hour of his need.

Monatsschrift, 1865, p. 186, note 8.

XXIII.

Sir. 13, 11b. *ἐκ πολλῆς γὰρ λαλιᾶς πειράσει σε,*
καὶ ὡς προσγελῶν ἐξετάσει σε.

*כי ברב שיח מנסה אותך ושחק לך וחקרך

S'adyah, p. 178, l. 15.

For with much talk will he try thee,
and will laugh at thee, and search thee out.

Cf. No. XXXIV below.

XXIV.

Sir. 13, 16.

πᾶσα σὰρξ κατὰ γένος συνάγεται,
καὶ τῷ ὁμοίῳ αὐτοῦ προσκολληθήσεται ἀνήρ.

Cf. 27, 9. *πετεινὰ πρὸς τὰ ὅμοια αὐτοῖς καταλύσει.*

ומשולש בכתובים דכתיב כל עוף למינו ישכון ובן אדם לדומה לו

B. T. Baba Qama, fol. 92b.

Thirdly, in the Hagiographa; as it is written:
Every bird dwelleth according to his kind,
and (so doth) man according to his like.

XXV.

Sir. 13, 25.

καρδία ἀνθρώπου ἀλλοιοῖ τὸ πρόσωπον αὐτοῦ,
ἐάν εἰς ἀγαθὰ ἐάν τε εἰς κακά.

לב אדם ישנה פניו בין לטוב בין לרע

Ber. Rabba, fol. 64b.

The heart of a man changeth his countenance,
whether for good or for evil.

XXVI.

Sir. 14, 5. *ὁ πονηρὸς ἑαυτῷ τίνι ἀγαθὸς ἔσται;*

כל מי שהוא צריך ליטול ואינו נוטל הרי זה שופך דמים ואסור להתרחם עליו על נפשיה לא חיים על חורנין לא כל שכן

J. T. end of Peah.

Every one who needs to receive (alms) and refuses to take them, is (like) a shedder of blood, and it is forbidden to have compassion on him. If he has no pity on himself, how much less will he have pity on others?

XXVII.

Sir. 14, 11.

Τέκνον, καθὼς ἐὰν ἔχῃς εὖ ποίει σεαυτόν.
17. *ὅτι οὐκ ἔστιν ἐν ᾅδου ζητῆσαι τρυφήν.*
ἡ γὰρ διαθήκη ἀπ' αἰῶνος θανάτῳ ἀποθανῇ.
18. *ὡς φύλλον θάλλον ἐπὶ δένδρου δασέος,*
τὰ μὲν καταβάλλει, ἄλλα δὲ φύει.
οὕτως καὶ γενεὰ σαρκὸς καὶ αἵματος·
ἡ μὲν τελευτᾷ, ἑτέρα δὲ γεννᾶται.

אל רב לרב המנונא: בני. אם יש לך היטיב לך שאין בשאול תענג. ואין למות התמהמה. ואם תאמר לבני (ולבנותי[1]) חק בשאול מי יגיד לך: בני אדם דומים לעשבי השדה. הללו נוצצין והללו נובלין

B. T. Erubin, fol. 54a.

[1] See Kohut, *Aruch* s. v. הק (i).

Rab said to his son Hamnuna:
My son, if thou hast aught, do good unto thyself,
for there is no pleasure in Sheol, and death tarries not.
And if thou sayest, It is for my sons and for my daughters,
who shall declare to thee the law in Sheol?
The sons of men are like the herbs of the field,
some flourish, and others fade.

XXVIII.

Sir. 16, 17.

μὴ εἴπῃς ὅτι Ἀπὸ Κυρίου κρυβήσομαι·
μὴ ἐξ ὕψους τις μου μνησθήσεται;
ἐν λαῷ πλείονι οὐ μὴ μνησθῶ,
τίς γὰρ ἡ ψυχή μου ἐν ἀμετρήτῳ κτίσει;

*אל תאמר מאל נסתרתי ובמרום מי יזכרני. בעם כבד
לא אודע או מי נפשי בקצות רוחות

S'adyah, p. 178, l. 12.

Say not, I am hidden from God,
and in the height who shall remember me?
Among a numerous people I shall not be known,
or what is my soul among the multitude of spirits?

XXIX.

Cf. Sir. 18, 16, &c.

οὐχὶ καύσωνα ἀναπαύσει δρόσος;
οὕτως κρείσσων λόγος ἢ δόσις.

כל הנותן פרוטה לעני מתברך בששה ברכות
והמפייסו בדברים מתברך בי״א ברכות

B. T. Baba Bathra, fol. 9b.

He who gives a farthing to a poor man is blessed with six blessings, &c.:
but he who comforts him with words is blessed with eleven blessings.

XXX.

Sir. 18, 23.

πρὶν εὔξασθαι ἑτοίμασον σεαυτόν, (τὴν εὐχήν σου ℵ^{c.a})
καὶ μὴ γίνου ὡς ἄνθρωπος πειράζων τὸν κύριον.

*אמר בן סירא בטרם תדור הכן נדרך בל תהיה כמתעה

Midrash Tanḥuma וישלח § 8.

Ben Sira said:
Before thou vowest, make ready thy vows:
be not like a deceiver.

XXXI.

Sir. 20, 9. *ἔστιν εὐοδία ἐν κακοῖς ἀνδρί,*
καὶ ἔστιν εὕρεμα εἰς ἐλάττωσιν.

מברך על הרעה מעין הטובה. ועל הטובה מעין הרעה

Mishnah Berakhoth, ix. 3.

A man gives thanks for evil which results in good,
and for good which results in evil.

XXXII.

Sir. 20, 15. *ὀλίγα δώσει καὶ πολλὰ ὀνειδίσει.*

ואל תמסור מזונותינו בידי בשר ודם שמתנתם מעוטה
וחרפתם מרובה

J. T. Berakhoth, iv. 2.

Deliver not our livelihood into the hands of men (*lit.* flesh and blood),
for their giving is small, and their reproaching great.

XXXIII.

Sir. 21, 11.

ὁ φυλάσσων νόμον κατακρατεῖ τοῦ ἐννοήματος αὐτοῦ.
καὶ συντέλεια τοῦ φόβου Κυρίου σοφία.

בראתי יצר הרע ובראתי לו תורה תבלין. ואם אתם
עוסקים בתורה אין אתם נמסרים בידו

B. T. Qiddushin, fol. 30b.

I created the evil propensity:
I created against it the Law as a safeguard (*lit.* a seasoning).
If ye are occupied in the Law,
ye shall not be delivered into its hand.

XXXIV.

Sir. 21, 20.

μωρὸς ἐν γέλωτι ἀνυψοῖ φωνὴν αὐτοῦ,
ἀνὴρ δὲ πανοῦργος μόλις ἡσυχῇ μειδιάσει.

Cf. also 19, 30.

בשלשה דברים אדם ניכר. בכיסו ובכוסו ובכעסו
ואמרי ליה אף בשחקו

B. T. Erubin, fol. 65b.

By three things a man is known, by his purse, by the wine-cup, and by his vexation. They say to him: By his laughter also.

Compare Aboth N., p. 86a:

בשלשה דברים בודקין את האדם. במשא ומתן וברוב
יין וברוב שיחה

By three things do men test a man,
by trading (*lit.* giving and taking), and by much wine, and by much talking.

XXXV.

Cf. Sir. 21, 22. *ποὺς μωροῦ ταχὺς εἰς οἰκίαν.*

Also verse 23.

*כתיב בספר בן סירא שלשה שנאתי וארבעה לא
אהבתי. שר הנרגל בבית המשתאות. ואמרי לה שער
הנרגן. (ואמרי לה שר הנרגז.) והמשיב שבת במרומי קרת.
והאוחז באמה ומשתין מים. והנכנס לבית חבירו פתאום

B. T. Niddah, 16b.

Three things I hate, and four I do not love: (1) a prince who frequents the house of banqueting; (2) . . . .; (3) . . . .; (4) the man that enters suddenly the house of his neighbour.

XXXVI.

Sir. 21, 22.

ποὺς μωροῦ ταχὺς εἰς οἰκίαν,
ἄνθρωπος δὲ πολύπειρος αἰσχυνθήσεται ἀπὸ προσώπου.

23. *ἄφρων ἀπὸ θύρας παρακύπτει εἰς οἰκίαν,*
ἀνὴρ δὲ πεπαιδευμένος ἔξω στήσεται.

*ולעולם אל ימהר אדם לבית חבירו שכך כתו׳ בספר בן סירא: רגל נבל מהרה אל בית ואיש מזימות יכניע רבים: לעולם אל יסתכל אדם לשער חבירו שכן בספר בן סירא: אויל מפתח יביט אל בית וכבוד לאיש בבית עמיו

פרקא דרבינו הקדוש, 14ᵃ, ed. Schönblum; see Schechter, *J. Q. R.* iii. p. 695, No. 21.

Let a man never hasten into the house of his neighbour; for thus it is written in the book of Ben Sira:

The foot of a senseless man hastens to (another's) house,
but a prudent man will subdue many.

Let a man never look in at the door of his neighbour; for thus (it is written) in the book of Ben Sira:

A foolish man gazes from the door into (another's) house,
but a man's honour is in the house of his own kinsmen.

XXXVII.

Sir. 25, 2.

τρία δὲ εἴδη ἐμίσησεν ἡ ψυχή μου . . . .
πτωχὸν ὑπερήφανον, καὶ πλούσιον ψεύστην,
γέροντα μοιχὸν ἐλαττούμενον συνέσει.

ארבעה אין הדעת סובלתן. אלו הן: דל גאה. ועשיר מכחש וזקן מנאף. [ופרנס מתגאה על הצבור[1]]

B. T. Pesaḥim, fol. 113ᵇ.

There are four things that the mind cannot bear. They are these:
A poor man that is proud, a rich man that is a liar,
an old man that is an adulterer,
and a ruler that exalts himself above the multitude.

[1] The last clause is not in Sirach.

XXXVIII.

Sir. 25, 3. *ἐν νεότητι οὐ συναγείοχας,*
καὶ πῶς ἂν εὕροις ἐν τῷ γήρᾳ σου;

וכן מתלא אמר: אם בנערותיך לא חפצתם איך תשיגם בזקנותיך

Aboth N., ch. 24 (p. 78).

Thus says the proverb:
If in thy youth thou hast had no delight in them,
how wilt thou attain them in thy old age?

XXXIX.

Sir. 25, 13.

πᾶσαν πληγήν, καὶ μὴ πληγὴν καρδίας·
καὶ πᾶσαν πονηρίαν, καὶ μὴ πονηρίαν γυναικός.

אמר רב כל חולי ולא חולי מעים כל כאב ולא כאב לב כל מיחוש ולא מיחוש ראש כל רעה ולא אשה רעה

B. T. Shabbath, fol. 11ᵃ.

Rab said: Any sickness, but not sickness of the bowels;
any pain, but not the pain of the heart;
any ache, but not the aching of the head;
any evil, but not an evil woman.

XL.

Sir. 26, 1.

γυναικὸς ἀγαθῆς μακάριος ὁ ἀνήρ,
καὶ ἀριθμὸς τῶν ἡμερῶν αὐτοῦ διπλάσιος.

*אשה יפה אשרי בעלה מספר ימיו כפלים

B. T. Yebamoth, fol. 63ᵇ.

Happy is the husband of a beautiful woman:
the number of his days is doubled.

XLI.

Sir. 26, 3. *γυνὴ ἀγαθὴ μερὶς ἀγαθή,*
ἐν μερίδι φοβουμένων Κύριον δοθήσεται.

*כתוב בספר בן סירא אשה טובה מתנה טובה בחיק ירא אלהים תנתן. [אשה רעה צרעת לבעלה מאי תקנתיה יגרשנה מביתו ויתרפא מצרעתה][1]

B. T. Synhedrin, fol. 100ᵇ; cf. Yebamoth, fol. 63ᵇ.

It is written in the book of Ben Sira:
A good wife is a good gift;
she shall be given into the bosom of him that feareth God.
An evil wife is a plague (*lit.* a leprosy) to her husband.
What is the remedy? Let him drive her from his house (i. e. divorce her),
and he shall be healed from the plague of her (*lit.* from her leprosy).

[1] The second part not in Sirach.

XLII.

Sir. 28, 12. *ἐὰν φυσήσῃς σπινθῆρα ἐκκαήσεται,*
καὶ ἐὰν πτύσῃς ἐπ᾿ αὐτὸν σβεσθήσεται.

*בר סירא אומר היתה לפניו גחלת נפח בה ויבערה. רקק בה וכבתה

M. Rabbah, Leviticus, fol. 153; and anonymously in Yalkut, Levit., § 460; Psalm, § 767; Job, § 501.

Bar Sira says:
There was a live coal before a man: he blew upon it and it flamed;
he spit upon it and it was extinguished.

XLIII.

Sir. 30, 23.
ἀγάπα τὴν ψυχήν σου καὶ παρακάλει τὴν καρδίαν σου,
καὶ λύπην μακρὰν ἀπόστησον ἀπὸ σοῦ·
πολλοὺς γὰρ ἀπέκτεινεν ἡ λύπη,
καὶ οὐκ ἔστιν ὠφελία ἐν αὐτῇ.

*אל תצר צרת מחר כי לא תדע מה ילד יום שמא מחר ואיננו נמצא מצטער על עולם שאין שלו

B. T. Yebamoth, fol. 63b.

Be not troubled for the trouble of the morrow,
for 'thou knowest not what a day may bring forth' (Prov. 27, 1).
Perhaps on the morrow he will be no more,
and be found grieving over a world that is not his.

XLIV.

Sir. 30 (33), 33.
ἄρτος καὶ παιδεία καὶ ἔργον οἰκέτῃ.
34. *ἔργασαι ἐν παιδί, καὶ εὑρήσεις ἀνάπαυσιν.*

דניחא ליה דלא נסתרי עבדיה

B. T. Baba Metsia, fol. 65a.

For it is better for him that his servant should not become an idler.

So Rashi; cf. Kohut, *Aruch* s. v. נתר (ii).

XLV.

Sir. 31 (34), 26.
φονεύων τὸν πλησίον ὁ ἀφαιρούμενος συμβίωσιν,
καὶ ἐκχέων αἷμα ὁ ἀποστερῶν μισθὸν μισθίου.

וא"ר יוחנן כל הגוזל שוה פרוטה מחבירו כאלו נוטל נשמתו ממנו

Midrash Tanḥuma (p. 12b) נח, ד.

Rabbi Joḥanan said: Any one who steals the worth of a farthing from his neighbour is as though he took away his life.

XLVI.

Sir. 31 (34), 27.
καὶ ἐκχέων αἷμα ὁ ἀποστερῶν μισθὸν μισθίου.

כל הכובש שכר שכיר כאלו נוטל נפשו ממנו

B. T. Baba Metsia, fol. 112a.

Every one who suppresses the hire of an hireling is as though he took from him his life.

XLVII.

Sir. 32 (35), 21. *προσευχὴ ταπεινοῦ νεφέλας διῆλθε.*

ההיא מלתא סלקא ובקע רקיען

Zohar, Levit. יג (3, p. 62).

That word mounts up, and cleaves the firmaments.

XLVIII.

Sir. 34 (31), 28.
ἀγαλλίαμα καρδίας καὶ εὐφροσύνη ψυχῆς
οἶνος πινόμενος ἐν καιρῷ αὐτάρκης.

Cf. the Syriac (31, 28).

זכה משמחו לא זכה משממו

B. T. Yoma, fol. 76b.

If he acts rightly, (i. e. drinks in moderation, Rashi,) it (wine) gladdens him; if he does not act rightly, (i. e. drinks to excess,) it ruins him.

XLIX.

Sir. 34 (31), 28. 29.
ἀγαλλίαμα καρδίας καὶ εὐφροσύνη ψυχῆς
οἶνος πινόμενος ἐν καιρῷ αὐτάρκης·
πικρία ψυχῆς οἶνος πινόμενος πολὺς κ.τ.λ.

אלא שירותא דחמרא חדוותא סופיה עציבו

Zohar, Levit. שמיני (3, p. 77).

But the beginning of wine is gladness, and the end thereof sorrow.

L.

Sir. 35 (32), 4. *ὅπου ἀκρόαμα μὴ ἐκχέῃς λαλίαν.*

אין מסיחין בסעודה

B. T. Taanith, fol. 5b.

Men should not talk much at a meal.

LI.

Sir. 36 (33), 7.
διὰ τί ἡμέρα ἡμέρας ὑπερέχει,
καὶ πᾶν φῶς ἡμέρας ἐνιαυτοῦ ἀφ' ἡλίου;
8. ἐν γνώσει Κυρίου διεχωρίσθησαν,
καὶ ἠλλοίωσεν καιροὺς καὶ ἑορτάς.

שאלה זו שאל טורנוס רופוס את ר׳ עקיבא אמר לו ומה יום מיומים. אמר לו ומה גבר מגוברין. אמר לו דמרי צבי. שבת נמי דמרי צבי

B. T. Synhedrin, fol. 65^b; Midrash Tanḥuma, Exodus תרומה, ג (p. 109^b).

Turnus Rufus asked this question of R. Akiba, and said to him,
Why is one day different from another?
He said to him, And why is one man different from another?
He said to him, Because the Lord wills;
and the Sabbath also is because the Lord wills.

LII.

Cf. Sir. 36, 26. πάντα ἄρρενα ἐπιδέξεται γυνή.

אמר ריש לקיש טב למיתב טן דו מלמיתב ארמלו

B. T. Kethuboth, fol. 75^a.

It is better to dwell two together, than to dwell a widow.

LIII.

Sir. 36, 30^b.
καὶ οὗ οὐκ ἔστιν γυνή, στενάξει πλανώμενος.

שמחת לב אשה

B. T. Shabbath, fol. 152^a.

The joy of the heart is a wife.

כל אדם שאין לו אשה שרוי בלא שמחה

B. T. Yebamoth, fol. 62^b.

Every man who has no wife, dwells without joy.

LIV.

Sir. 38, 1.
τίμα ἰατρὸν πρὸς τὰς χρείας τιμαῖς αὐτοῦ.

המשל אומר כבד את רופאיך עד שלא תצטרך לו

Midrash Rabba, Exodus, c. xxi.

(The proverb says): Honour thy physician before thou hast need of him.

The proverb also occurs in an Aramaic form:

אמר ר׳ לעזר אוקיר לאסייך עד דלא תצטרך ליה:

J. T. Taanith, iii. 6.

In Midrash Tanḥuma, Gen. מקץ, § 10 (p. 51^b), it is introduced with the words:

אר׳ לעזר כתוב בספר בן סירא

See Schechter, *J. Q. R.* iii. p. 694, No. 16, and note 79.

LV.

Sir. 38, 4.
Κύριος ἔκτισεν ἐκ γῆς φάρμακα·
7. ἐν αὐτοῖς ἐθεράπευσεν καὶ ἦρεν τὸν πόνον αὐτοῦ,
8. μυρεψὸς ἐν τούτοις ποιήσει μίγμα.

אלוה העלה סמים מן הארץ. בהם הרופא מרפא את המכה ומהם הרוקח מרקח את המרקחת

Midr. Rabba, Genesis, viii; Midr. Yalkut, Job, § 501.

God causes spices to spring up out of the earth:
With them the physician heals the stroke,
and of them the perfumer compounds the perfume.

LVI.

Sir. 38, 24.
καὶ ὁ ἐλασσούμενος πράξει αὐτοῦ σοφισθήσεται.

הוי ממעט בעסק ועסוק בתורה וזריז למצות והוי נוהג בשפלות רוח עם כל אדם

Aboth N., cap. 33, p. 73^b (cf. also Aboth, iv. 14).

Have little business, but be busied in the Law,
and eager for the commandments;
and behave thyself in humbleness of spirit with every man.

LVII.

Sir. 39, 25. ἀγαθὰ τοῖς ἀγαθοῖς ἔκτισται ἀπ' ἀρχῆς,
οὕτως τοῖς ἁμαρτωλοῖς κακά.

טובה שמורה לטובים ורע שמורה לרעים

Sepher Yetsira, p. 102, note 1.

Good is kept for the good,
and evil is kept for the evil.

LVIII.

Sir. 40, 19.
τέκνα καὶ οἰκοδομὴ πόλεως στηρίζουσιν ὄνομα,
καὶ ὑπὲρ ἀμφότερα γυνὴ ἄμωμος λογίζεται·

שלשה מרחיבין דעתו של אדם. אלו הן. דירה נאה. ואשה נאה. ובלים נאים

B. T. Berakhoth, fol. 57[b].

Three things enlarge the understanding of a man. They are these:
a comely dwelling, a comely wife, and comely furniture.

Sir. 40, 25.

LIX.

χρύσιον καὶ ἀργύριον ἐπιστήσουσιν πόδα.

ואת כל היקום אשר ברגליהם. א״ר אלעזר זה ממונו של אדם שמעמידו על רגליו

B. T. Pesaḥim, fol. 119[a].

'And every (living) substance that followed them' (Deut. 11, 6, *lit.* that was at their feet). R. Eleazar says: This means the wealth of a man, which makes him stand firm upon his feet.

Sir. 40, 29.

LX.

ἀνὴρ βλέπων εἰς τράπεζαν ἀλλοτρίαν,
οὐκ ἔστιν αὐτοῦ ὁ βίος ἐν λογισμῷ ζωῆς.

שלשה חייהן אינם חיים. ואלו הן המצפה לשלחן חברו ומי שאשתו מושלת עליו ומי שיסורין מושלין בגופו:

B. T. Betsah, fol. 32[b].

There are three men whose life is no life. They are these:
The man who watches the table of his neighbour,
the man whose wife rules over him,
and the man whose body is ruled by pains.

LXI.

Sir. 42, 9. *θυγάτηρ πατρὶ ἀπόκρυφος ἀγρυπνία,*
καὶ ἡ μέριμνα αὐτῆς ἀφιστᾷ ὕπνον.
10. *ἐν παρθενείᾳ μή ποτε βεβηλωθῇ ....*
καὶ συνῳκηκυῖα μή ποτε στειρώσῃ.

בת לאביה מטמונת שוא. מפחדה לא יישן: בקטנותה שמא תתפתה. בנערותה שמא תזנה. בגרה שמא לא תנשא. נשאת שמא לא יהיו לה בנים. הזקינה שמא תעשה כשפים.

B. T. Synhedrin, fol. 100[b].

A daughter is a vain treasure to her father:
for fear about her, he does not sleep;
in her youth, lest she be seduced;
in her maidenhood, lest she play the harlot;
when she is marriageable, lest she be not married;
when she is married, lest she have no sons;
when she is old, lest she practise sorcery.

LXII.

Sir. 9, 12 (Syriac).

ܥܡ ܐܢܬܬ ܓܒܪܐ ܠܐ ܬܣܓܐ ܡܡܠܠܐ

אל תרבה שיחה עם האשה

Aboth, i. 5; Geiger in *ZDMG.* xii. p. 537.

And prolong not converse with a woman.

The following proverbs, ascribed to Ben Sira, are not found in the Greek or Syriac versions.

LXIII.

*הדר אלהים בני אדם. הדר בני אדם כסותן (בסותו *or,*)

End of Derekh Erets Zuta (anonymous); Tanya, No. 10 (with the introductory words בן סירא אומר). See Schechter, *J. Q. R.* iii. p. 695, No. 19.

The glory of God is the sons of men;
the glory of the sons of men is their clothing.

LXIV.

*כדכתיב בספר בן סירא: הכל שקלתי בכף מאזנים ולא מצאתי קל מסובין. וקל מסובין חתן הדר בבית חמיו. וקל מחתן אורח מכניס אורח. וקל מאורח משיב דבר בטרם ישמע

B. T. Baba Bathra, fol. 98[b]; Yalqut Proverbs, § 956.

As it is written in the book of Ben Sira:
I have weighed all things in the balance,
and have found nothing lighter than bran;
but lighter than bran is the bridegroom who dwells in the house of his father-in-law,
and lighter than the bridegroom is a guest (*lit.* traveller) who introduces another guest,
and lighter than the guest is 'he that giveth answer before he heareth' (Prov. 18, 13).

LXV.

*כתוב בספר בן סירא: זכור את יום אסיפתך ואסוף חרפה וקבץ זכיות כי ביום אסיפת האדם אין מלוהו הון ורב כח כי המעשה נבון ילך לפניו וצדקתו תאיר עיניו

Baraitha Kallah, ed. Coronel, 7[b]. See Schechter, *J. Q. R.* iii. p. 697, No. 23.

It is written in the book of Ben Sira:
Remember the day of thy being gathered (in death);
withdraw (*lit.* gather in) reproach and acquire virtue (*lit.* merits);
for in the day of a man's being gathered,

neither riches nor great strength accompany him; for his work is prepared, it will go before him, and his righteousness shall lighten his eyes.

LXVI.

*כל ימי עני רעים בן סירא אומר אף לילות בשפל גגים גגו ובמרום הרים כרמו ממטר גגים לגגו ומעפר כרמו לכרמים :

B. T. Synhedrin, fol. 100[b].

See marginal note to Sir. 40, 22, in the Hebrew text.

All the days of the poor are evil. Ben Sira says, the nights also. His roof is the lowest of roofs, and his vineyard is in the height of the mountains: the rain of other roofs falls on his roof, and the earth of his vineyard falls on other vineyards.

LXVII.

*דכת[י]ב זלדקן קורטמן עבדקן סכסן :

B. T. Synhedrin, 100[b].

As it is written: The thin-bearded is cunning and the thick-bearded is a fool.

This proverb is also found in the second Alphabet (see below, p. xxix).

LXVIII.

*מפרש בספר בן סירא : לכך קורא מקום להקב״ה לפי שהוא מקומו של עולם ואין העולם מקומו

It is explained in the book of Ben Sira, that the Holy One (blessed be he!) is called 'place'[1],' because he is the place of (i.e. contains) the world, and the world is not his place.

See Schechter (*J. Q. R.* iii. p. 697, No. 24, and p. 706, note 109), who points out that the passage is probably taken from Bereshith Rabba (ב״ר), not from Ben Sira (ב״ס). See No. I. *d.*

[1] A common Rabbinical designation of God. Cf. τόπος in Philo (e.g. de Somniis, i. § 11, ed. Mangey, i. 630).

LXIX.

*כתיב בספר בן סירא : הוי רחים לשלמא. דעליה קם עלמא. רחים כל עמה וג׳

Baraitha Kallah, ed. Coronel, 7[b].

It is written in the book of Ben Sira: Love peace, for on it the world is stayed. Love all people, &c.

The rest of the passage is very corrupt, and cannot be translated without resorting to violent emendations. See Schechter, ibid., p. 696, and p. 705 for Reifmann's reconstruction.

The next two passages have been quoted as belonging to Ben Sira, but on insufficient grounds.

LXX.

לפום גמלא שיחנא

B. T. Sota, 13[b]; Bereshith R., § 19, beginning.

According to the camel, so is the burden.

LXXI.

במגלת חסידים מצאו כתוב. יום תעזבני יומים אעזבך

J. T. Berakhoth, end.

In the scroll of the Ḥasidim it was found written:

For one day thou didst desert me,
and for two days will I desert thee.

LXXII.

The Alphabet of Ben Sira (*see above,* p. xiv).

אוקיר לאסיא עד דלא תצטריך ליה

Honour the physician before thou hast need of him.

Cf. above, No. LIV.

בר דלא בר (סבר .Reifmann conj) שבקיה על אפי מיא וישם

The son who is not clear-witted, leave him upon the surface of the water and let him swim (trade).

גרמא דנפיל בחולקך בין טב או ביש גרריה

The bone that has fallen to thy lot, whether it be good or evil, gnaw it.

דהבא צריך לקמצאה ועולימא להלקאה

Gold must be hammered, and a child must be beaten.

הוי טב וחולקיך מן טבתא לא תמנע

Be good, and thy portion of goodness do not refuse.

ווי ליה לבישא ווי להון לדבוקיהו

Woe to the wicked, and woe to them that consort with him.

זרוק לחמך על אפי מיא ואת משכח ליה בסוף יומיא

Cast thy bread upon the waters, for thou shalt find it at the end of the days.

Eccles. 11, 1.

הזית חמר אוכם לא אוכם ולא חיור

Hast thou seen white (l. חיור) and black (combined)? It (the result) is neither black nor white.

The readings are uncertain.

טב לביש לא תעביד ובישא לא ימטי לך

Do not good to the evil, and evil shall not befall thee.

Cf. above, No. X.

ירך מן טיבותא לא תמנע

Restrain not thy hand from doing good.

The Bodleian MS. (New Hebrew Catalogue, No. 1466) has ירך מן נגרא לטלמא לא תמנע, never restrain thy hand from chastising a child.

כלתא עלת לגנונא ולא ידעת מה מטי לה

The bride goes into the canopy, and knows not what is coming upon her.

לחכימא ברמזא לשטיא בכורמיזא (MS. חוטרא)

For a wise man with a sign, for a fool with the fist.

מוקיר מבסרוהי דמה לחמרא

He who honours a man that despises him, is like an ass.

נור דליק מוקיד גדישין סניאין

A fire when it is kindled (? l. קליל a little fire) burns many sheaves.

Cf. Ep. of S. James 3, 5.

סבא בביתא סימנא טבא בביתא

An old man in a house is a good sign in the house.

ערבא טבא מאה צפרין ובישא אלף אלפין

A good surety is for a hundred days, but an evil surety is for a thousand thousand.

פתור פתורה פריש מחלוקת

Make clear the explanation, and remove differences.

צריך את למיסב ולמיתן יהא חולקך עם בר טבין

If thou must trade, let thy lot be with the lucky.

קריבא סחורתא אכלתיה מריה ורחיקא אכלא למריה

Stock that is near at hand its owner consumes, but that which is far off consumes its owner.

רחימא קדמאה לית את כפר ביה

An old friend do not thou repudiate.

MS. Bodl. רחימך קדמאה לא תתכפר ביה ובדיקנא ליה את נבר:

שיתין מליכין יהוון לך ומליכות נפשך לא תשבוק

Take sixty counsellors, but the counsel of thy heart do not abandon.

Cf. above, No. VII.

תתיהב לך ידא כי הות שביעא ולא דהות כפינא

Let the hand be given to thee when it is satisfied, but not when it is hungry.

MS. Bodl. התן לך ידא דהוה שביעא ולא דהוה בפיו ושבעת:

LXXIII.

With regard to the second Alphabet, see the Preface, p. xiv.

The first line (letter א) is similar to No. XLIII in our list of proverbs. Lines 2 (ב), 5 (ה), 16 (פ), 17 (צ) are from No. XVI in our list. Line 3 (ג) is from No. VII. Line 7 (ז) is from No. LXVII. Lines 9 (ט), 10 (י), and 11 (כ) from No. LXI.

The rest is not worth reprinting.

The Persian translation mentioned above (p. xv) (British Museum MS. Or. 4731) begins as follows:

בשם שרי בורא עלם באמירה. אהחיל לכתוב ספר בר סירא. אלפא ביהא לבן סירא

כתיב עושה גדולות עד אין חוקר ונפלאות עד אין מספר. נישתה אסת כונאי בוזרגי הא הא כה נישת שמארי ועגאייב הא תא כה נישת נהאייתי

(In Persian characters: نوشته است كوناي بزورگيها تا كه نيست شماري وعجايبها تا كه نيست نهايتي.)

The following sayings found in the work מבחר הפנינים, *ascribed to Solomon ibn Gabirol (see above, p. xi), are cited by Reifmann* (Haasyf, iii. p. 250) *as showing the influence of Sirach. The translation, which is from Ascher's edition, is rather free.*

LXXIV.

Sir. 19, 10. *Ἀκήκοας λόγον; συναποθανέτω σοι· θάρσει, οὐ μή σε ῥήξει.*

ושאלו לחכם אזהו הסתרת הסוד. אמר שמתי לבי קברו

מבחר הפנינים, No. 318.

The sage was asked the surest means of keeping a secret. Said he, I make my heart its tomb.

LXXV.

Sir. 20, 18.

Ὀλίσθημα ἀπὸ ἐδάφους, μᾶλλον ἢ ἀπὸ γλώσσης.

אמר מות האדם בכשלון לשונו. ולא מות בכשלח רגלו. כי בכשלק לשונו יסיר ראשו וכשלח רגלו ירפא לזמן מעט

Ibid. 357.

He was wont to say, A slip of the tongue is more dangerous than the slip of the foot, for the slip of the tongue may cost thy head, whilst the slip of the foot may easily be cured.

LXXVI.

Sir. 20, 30 (and 41, 14).

Σοφία κεκρυμμένη καὶ θησαυρὸς ἀφανής,
τίς ὠφέλεια ἐν ἀμφοτέροις;

ואמר כל חכמה שלא ידובר בה, כמטמן שאין מוציאן ממנו

Ibid. 58.

Wisdom lying dormant is like an unproductive treasure.

LXXVII.

Sir. 26, 28.

Ἐπὶ δυσὶ λελύπηται ἡ καρδία μου,
καὶ ἐπὶ τῷ τρίτῳ θυμός μοι ἐπῆλθεν·
ἀνὴρ πολεμιστὴς ὑστερῶν δι' ἔνδειαν,
καὶ ἄνδρες συνετοὶ ἐὰν σκυβαλισθῶσιν,
ἐπανάγων ἀπὸ δικαιοσύνης ἐπὶ ἁμαρτίαν.

ואמר חמלו על נכבד שנקל. ועל עשיר שנורש. ועל חכם שנפל בין הפתאים: ואמר אין מי שצריך לחמול עליו. כחכם שנפל עליו דין כסיל

Ibid. 66, 67.

The sage observed, Pity the noble-hearted who has fallen; the rich that has become reduced; and the wise whose lot is cast amongst the fools. None deserves our pity more than the wise who has become subjected to the judgement of fools.

LXXVIII.

Sir. 30, 16.

Οὐκ ἔστιν πλοῦτος βελτίων ὑγείας σώματος,
καὶ οὐκ ἔστιν εὐφροσύνη ὑπὲρ χαρὰν καρδίας.

אין עושר כבריאות ולא נעימות כלב טוב

Ibid. 457.

There is no greater riches than health, no greater pleasure than a cheerful heart.

LXXIX.

Sir. 40, 28. *Τέκνον, ζωὴν ἐπαιτήσεως μὴ βιώσῃς· κρεῖσσον ἀποθανεῖν ἢ ἐπαιτεῖν.*

ואמר הקבר ולא הרש

Ibid. 564.

Better the grave than a fall to poverty.

GLOSSARY OF WORDS

*not found in the Hebrew of the Old Testament, or found in it only in the passages quoted, or referred to. The words marked * are either themselves common, or closely resemble words which are common, in New-Hebrew or Aramaic.*

*אִכְפָּה *pressure, distress,* בְּאִכְפָּה לְ 46, 5 *when there was distress to* . . . (Talm.: cf. אָכַף *to press upon,* Prov. 16, 26; אֶכֶף *pressure,* Job 33, 7; ܐܟܦ ܠ *to be a care to,* ܐܟܦܐ *care*).

אָסוֹן *bodily injury* or *mishap,* 41, 9 (Gen. 42, 4. 38. 44, 29. Ex. 21, 22. 23).

אַפַּיִם *face,* 41, 21ª (si vera l.: v. marg.) in a *general* sense, as in Aram. (with 𝔊 cf. 1 Ki. 2, 17 𝔗 לא יתיב ית אפיך, 20. In O. T. אפים is confined to two or three particular phrases).

אַצִּיל *joint,* viz. of the upper arm, i.e. either the *shoulder-joint* or the *elbow* (𝔊 ἀγκών: cf. 9, 9 𝔖 ܐܨܝܠܐ *elbow*), 41, 19 (אַצִּלוֹת ידיך Jer. 38, 12; [ם]אַצִּילֵי ידי Ez. 13, 18; אַצִּילָה Ez. 41, 8 ?).

אָצַל *to set apart, separate,* Nif. 46, 8 (Gen. 27, 36. Num. 11, 17. 25. Qoh. 2, 10); *to be withdrawn, diminished,* 42, 21ᶜ (Ez. 42, 6).

*אִשּׁוֹת *fires,* 48, 3 (NH. pl. of אֵשׁ).

בֵּית 42, 12 perhaps *among,* cf. 𝔊 (contr. from בֵּינַת: so Ez. 41, 9ᵇ, and perhaps Prov. 8, 2 𝔊 𝔗 𝔙, Job 8, 17 𝔊. Syr. ܒܝܬ).

*גְּהַר (conj. for נהה) *to blind, dazzle,* 43, 4 (Syr. ܓܗܪ, ܐܬܓܗܪ *to blind,* said of the sun).

*גּוּר *to commit adultery,* 42, 9.

*גְּמַר (or גַּמֵּר) *to bring to an end,* 43, 4 (O. T. גָּמַר *to come to an end,* Ps. 7, 10. 12, 2. 77, 9; *to complete,* si vera l., 57, 3. 138, 8).

*גִּפָּה *side, bank,* 40, 16 (cf. *j.* Targ. גִּיף, גַּף *bank; j.* Aram. ܓܦܐ *side*).

דְּבִיר *hindmost part* (cf. دُبُر), viz. of a temple, *inmost temple* (i.e. the Holy of holies), 45, 9 (15 times in 1 Ki. 6–8, 2 Chr. 3–5; Ps. 28, 2; and probably 2 Ki. 10, 25 for עִיר).

*דּוֹפִי *spot, fault,* 44, 19 *marg.* (Talm.: דֳּפִי Ps. 50, 20).

*דָּחַף *to urge on, impel,* partcp. [דָּ]חוּף perhaps 40, 6ᵈ (Est. 3, 15. 8, 14; נִדְחַף 6, 12. 2 Chr. 26, 20: cf. מַדְחֵפֹת *thrusts,* Ps. 140, 12. Also Targ.).

*דֵּעַת *state of mind, thought,* 40, 5ᵈ (NH. *mind, opinion, view,* cf. p. xx, No. XI; p. xxiv, No. XXXVII. In O. T. only in the objective sense of *knowledge*).

הוֹדוֹת *thanksgiving,* 47, 8 נָתַן הוֹדוֹת (unless תּוֹדוֹת should be read, prob. an extension of the substantival use of the inf. הוֹדוֹת found in Neh. 12, 46, cf. 1 Chr. 25, 3. Ezra 3, 11).

הָמוֹן *multitude* (in a weakened sense, of *inanimate* things), 45, 9 (so in late Heb., 1 Chr. 29, 16. 2 Chr. 31, 10).

זֶבֶד *bestowal, gift,* 40, 29ᶜ *marg.* (Gen. 30, 30; Syr. ܙܒܕ, spec. of a *dowry*).

*הִזְהִיר *to shine,* 43, 9 (Dan. 12, 3: usually in O. T. *to warn*).

*זְהִירָה *shining,* 43, 8 (cf. ܙܗܪ, Targ. זֵיהוֹר: זֹהַר Ez. 8, 2. Dan. 12, 3).

*זָהִיר *warned, well-advised,* 42, 8ᶜ (NH. (*Aboth* 1, 9); Targ., Syr., Aram. of Ezra 4, 22).

*זוּעַ *to quake,* 48, 12 (Est. 5, 9. Qoh. 12, 3; Aram. of Dan. 5, 19. 6, 27. The Pilpel also Hab. 2, 7).

*זִיקוֹת *sparks, flashes,* 43, 13. זִיקִים *marg.* (Is. 50, 11; cf. זִקִּים Prov. 26, 18 *fiery missiles:* ܙܝܩܐ *shooting-star*).

*זְמָן *time,* 43, 7 (Qoh. 3, 1. Neh. 2, 6. Est. 9, 27. 31; and often in the Aram. of Dan., Ezra).

*זַן, pl. זְנִים, *kind,* 49, 8 (Ps. 144, 13. 2 Chr. 16, 14; Aram. of Dan. 3, 5. 7. 10. 15).

הִתְעִים *to make indignant*, 43, 17 *marg.* (זָעַם in Qal, Ps. 7, 12 *al.*; but ? יָזִיעַ *shaketh*, Ps. 29, 8 𝔖 for Heb. יָחִיל, Is. 23, 11 𝔗).

זָרָא *loathsomeness*, 39, 27 (from Num. 11, 20).

*חִוָּה *to declare*, 42, 19 (Ps. 19, 3, and prob. 52, 11 אַחְוַת for אַמְנַת, Job 15, 17. 32, 10. 17. 36, 2, and Aram. of Dan.; cf. אַחֲוָה *declaration*, Job 13, 17).

חַיַּת שֵׁן *beast of tooth*, 39, 30 (for the *combination*, cf. the common Syr. expression ܚܝܘܬܐ ܫܢܐ, Deut. 32, 24 [for Heb. שֶׁן־בְּהֵמֹת]; Rev. 13, 1, &c.: PS. col. 1255. Cf. Sir. 12, 13 𝔖).

חֲלִיפוֹת *things that have passed away*, *the past*, 42, 19 (cf. חָלַף *to pass away*, Is. 2, 18. Cant. 2, 11. Job 9, 26. Ps. 102, 27; *to pass away from*, *escape*, Sir. 42, 20).

*חֵלֶף *for the sake of*, 42, 25 (Num. 18, 21. 31: Targ. חֲלָף, Syr. ܚܠܦ).

*חֶסֶד *reproach*, 41, 22ᶜ *marg.*, perhaps also 41, 6 (see the note), and certainly (note the same difference between 𝔖 and 𝔊) 31, 31 (Lev. 20, 17. Prov. 14, 34: חִסֵּד *to reproach*, Prov. 25, 10. Syr. ܚܣܕ; Targ. חִסּוּד).

חָסַם *to close up firmly*, *stop up*, 48, 17ᵈ (Deut. 25, 4 *to muzzle*; Ez. 39, 11 MT. *to stop* persons passing through[1]).

חָשַׂף *to lay bare* (a secret), 42, 1 (O. T. חָשַׂף Jer. 49, 10 *al.*).

*חֵפֶץ *business*, 43, 7 (late sense: Prov. 31, 13. Qoh. 3, 1. 17. 8, 6; and NH.).

*חֵרֵף prob. *to stir up*, *incite*, 43, 17 (ܚܪܦ: *to reproach*, the sense of the root in Heb., yields a poor sense).

חָרַת *to cut in*, *engrave*, חָרוּת *engraven*, 45, 11 (Ex. 32, 16,—where, however, as an Aramaism is hardly probable, חָרוּת is probably an error of transcription for חָרוּשׁ, as Jer. 17, 1 [and חָרַשׁ, חָרָשׁ regularly]; cf. Targ. חְרִית Lev. 19, 28. Jer. 17, 1).

חֶשְׁבּוֹן *reckoning*, 42, 3. 42, 4ᵇ *marg.*; ? also 41, 21ᵇ *marg.* for חשבות (Qoh. 7, 25. 27. 9, 10; and NH.: cf. [חִשָּׁבוֹן], חִשְּׁבֹנוֹת Qoh. 7, 29. 2 Chr. 26, 15).

---

[1] With 𝔊 οἰκοδομίαν here, cf. περιοικοδομίαν in Ez. 39, 11 (the word being referred to the mouth of the valley, ויחסמו את הגיא: v. Cornill). Comp. also Deut. 8, 9, Targ. Jer. (*ap.* Levy) ובוריא חסימן נחשא, i.e. *built up firmly*.

חשבות 41, 21ᵇ *marg.*: either an error for חֶשְׁבּוֹן, or perhaps חִשָּׁבוּת, an Aramaizing inf. Pa. from חָשַׁב; cf. הַשְׁמָעוּת Ez. 24, 26, הִתְחַבְּרוּת Dan. 11, 23.

*טפש, fem. טְפֵשָׁה *fat* (fig.), *gross*, *unimpressionable*, *obdurate*, 42, 6 (Ps. 119, 70 טָפַשׁ, Targ. אִיטְפַּשׁ. In Targ. and NH. the root and its derivatives have the same meaning, as Is. 6, 10 for הַשְׁמֵן, 1 Sam. 25, 25 טפשותא for נְבָלָה).

*יִסּוּר *chastisement*, *suffering*, 40, 29ᵈ *marg.* (NH., Targ.: but the verb יִסֵּר is common in the O. T.). Cf. p. xxvii, No. LX.

יֵשׁ (as a *noun*) *substance*, *property*, 42, 3 (in this sense only Prov. 8, 21 לְהַנְחִיל אֹהֲבַי יֵשׁ, from which it is here probably a reminiscence).

יָשִׁישׁ *very aged*, 42, 8 (Job 12, 12. 15, 10. 29, 8, 32, 6; יָשֵׁשׁ 2 Chr. 36, 17).

הִתְכַּלְכֵּל *to maintain oneself*, *endure* (intrans.), 43, 3 (O. T. Pilpel כַּלְכֵּל Jer. 20, 9. Mal. 3, 2 *al.*; Sir. 45, 24. 49, 9).

*כִּנָּה *to call by an honourable name* or *title*, 44, 23 *marg.* 47, 6 (Is. 44, 5. 45, 4. Job 32, 21. 22).

*כְּתָב *writing*, 39, 32. 42, 7. 44, 5. 45, 11ᵈ (Ez. 13, 9. 1 Chr. 28, 19. 2 Chr. 2, 10. 35, 4. Dan. 10, 21; and often in Ezra, Est. Also in the Aram. of Ezra and Dan. Targ. כְּתָב, Syr. ܟܬܒܐ).

*לֹבֶן *whiteness*, 43, 18 (NH.: לבנה must, it seems, be read as לָבְנוֹ).

*הִלְוָה *to accompany*, 41, 12 (Qoh. 8, 15, in Qal: in old Heb. only Nif. נִלְוָה *to be joined to* . . .). Cf. p. xxvii, No. LXV.

לֶקַח *the act of taking*, 42, 7 (in O. T. only in the concrete sense of *teaching received*, *lore*, Prov. 1, 5 *al.*). Cf. under מתת.

מִגְעָל *loathing* (conj. for מענל), 40, 29ᵉ (cf. O.T. גָּעַל, with נֶפֶשׁ Lev. 26, 11. 15. 30. 43. Jer. 14, 19).

*מְחָה *to smite*; ממחיו 42, 5, apparently inf. Pa.= ܡܡܚܝܘ (cf. מְחִי *a blow*, Ez. 26, 9).

מַחֲלֹקֶת, pl. מַחְלְקוֹת, *division* in the sense of *act of dividing*, 41, 21ᵇ. 42, 3 (in O.T. only *division* = *thing divided*; cf., however, 1 Sam. 23, 28).

מֶחְקָרָה, pl. מֶחְקָרוֹת, *searchings out*, *care*, 44, 4 (in Ps. 95, 4 מֶחְקָר is *a place to be searched out*, *remotest part*).

מַטֶּה *act of stretching out*, 41, 19. [The readiness

with which the author forms (apparently new) *nomina verbi* by prefixing מ, deserves notice: comp. in the O.T. Num. 10, 2 לְמִקְרָא הָעֵדָה, וּלְמַסַּע אֶת־הַמַּחֲנוֹת, Deut. 10, 11 לְמַסַּע לִפְנֵי הָעָם, Jud. 7, 15 מִסְפַּר הַחֲלוֹם, Is. 53, 3 מַסְתֵּר פָּנִים, Ez. 17, 9 לְמַשְׂאוֹת אוֹתָהּ, 33, 31 וְיָבוֹאוּ אֵלֶיךָ כִּמְבוֹא־עָם, Est. 9, 19. 22 מִשְׁלוֹחַ מָנוֹת אִישׁ לְרֵעֵהוּ, 1 Chr. 6, 16 מִמְּנוֹחַ הָאָרוֹן, 2 Chr. 19, 7 אֵין עִם י״י . . . מַשּׂא פָנִים וּמִקַּח־שֹׁחַד.]

מַטְמֹנֶת *a treasure*, 42, 9 (cf. מַטְמוֹן Gen. 43, 23 *al.*).

מִין *kind*, 43, 25 (26 times in the Priests' Code; Deut. 14, 13. 14. 15. 18 [= Lev. 11, 14. 15. 16. 19]; Ez. 47, 10: NH. *kind*; *j.* Aram. *nation*).

מְכוֹנָה *fixed resting-place*, fig. for *a home*, 41, 1. 44, 6 (O. T. *stand, base*, 1 Ki. 7, 27 *al.*).

*מיני (i.e. מִנֵּי, as Ps. 45, 9) *strings*, 39, 15 (Syr. ܡܢܬܐ, pl. ܡ̈ܢܘܬܐ, *hair, string* (of a musical instrument): Ps. 150, 4 מִנִּים; 45, 9 מִנִּי for מִנִּים).

מִנּוֹ *from him*, 42, 20 *marg.*, for מִמֶּנּוּ.

מַעֲמָד *standing-place* (of water), *pond*, 43, 20 (in O. T., but not in this sense).

מַעֲרוֹם *naked place*, 42, 18 (2 Chr. 28, 15 [Baer]).

מַעֲרָף *a dropping*, 43, 22 (cf. עָרַף *to drop*, Deut. 32, 2. 33, 28).

מערין 43, 8 *marg.* ?

מִפְקָד *act of depositing*, 42, 7 *marg.* (cf. פָּקַד 2 Ki. 5, 24; and פִּקָּדוֹן). With מִפְקָד יָד comp. תְּשׂוּמֶת יָד Lev. 5, 21; and Deut. 15, 2. Neh. 10, 32.

מִקְנָה *act of buying*, 42, 4[c]. (In O.T. only in a concrete sense, *thing possessed*, usually = *cattle*.)

*מַרְדּוּת *discipline*, 42, 8 *marg.* (v. l. on מוּסָר. Perhaps 1 Sam. 20, 30. Talm.; Targ. מַרְדּוּ; Syr. ܡܪܕܘܬܐ).

מַתַּת (or מֹתַת ?) *the act of giving*, 41, 22[d] (prob.), 42, 7 (in O. T. מַתַּת is *a gift*). (In Rabb. מַשָּׂא וּמַתָּן *taking and giving* is a common expression for *commercial dealings, trade* [see p. xxiii, No. XXXIV; and in Aram., p. xxix[b]]; and מתת ולקח appears in 42, 7 to be used similarly.)

*נָאֶה *comely, becoming*, 41, 16 (NH.: in O. T. the form found is נָאוָה Ps. 33, 1 *al.*).

נָהַג *to comport oneself, behave*, 40, 23 (NH.: Qoh. 2, 3. In Old Hebrew always *to lead, guide*).

נִהְיוֹת *things to come*, 42, 19 (the Nif. נִהְיָה occurs frequently in O. T., e.g. 1 Ki. 12, 24; and the partcp. Prov. 13, 19 תַּאֲוָה נִהְיָה, Mic. 2, 4 (?); but not with this particular *nuance*).

*נְהָרָה *brightness, light*, 43, 1[b] *marg.* (Job 3, 4; cf. the verb twice, Is. 60, 5. Ps. 34, 6. Aram. נְהוֹר Dan. 2, 22 *Qrê*, and in Targ., Syr. ܢܘܗܪܐ; cf. the verb נְהַר, ܢܗܪ).

? נוֹהַּ *eminency, stateliness*, 43, 21 (Ez. 7, 11,—si vera l.: cf. Arab. ناه *elata fuit* res).

*נוּר *fire*, 43, 4[d] (Aram. נוּר, Dan. 3, 6 &c.; ܢܘܪܐ).

נוֹשֶׁבֶת 43, 4[c] appar. (the) *habitable* (land), (cf. Ex. 16, 35 ארץ נושבת; also ἡ οἰκουμένη, and ܡܬܝܒܠܐ).

*נָטַל עֵצָה *to take counsel*, 42, 8 (a NH. expression: נָטַל in Old Heb. is *to lift* or *take up*; but it is rare, and is not found in this idiom).

נין ונכד *offspring and progeny*, 41, 5. 47, 22[c] (Gen. 21, 23. Is. 14, 22. Job 18, 19).

*ניסוי (i.e. נִסּוּי) *probation*, 44, 20[d] (a NH. form of noun; Strack u. Siegfried, *Lehrb. der Neuhebr. Spr.* § 52[c]: comp. for Old Hebrew, König, *Lehrgeb.* ii. 1. § 74. 2).

הִנְעִים *to make sweet*, of the voice, 47, 9[b] *marg.* (so NH.: נָעַם in Qal often in O. T.).

*נְעִימָה *the sound of music*, 45, 9 (ܢܥܝܡܬܐ; NH. נְעִימָה).

*נִצַּח prob. *to make brilliant*, 43, 5. 13 (comp. نصح *splenduit, fulsit, inclaruit*, نصّح *celebrem, clarum fecit*, ناصح *splendens*, نصاحة *splendor, fulgor*. Usually in Aram. in the fig. senses of *to shine, be illustrious* or *distinguished* (Dan. 6, 4), *triumph, conquer*: in O. T. נִצֵּחַ *to preside*, 1 Chr. 23, 4. 2 Chr. 2, 1. 17. 34, 12. 13. Ezra 3, 8. 9; in music, 1 Chr. 15, 21, hence partcp. מְנַצֵּחַ, *leader* or *conductor*, Hab. 3, 19, and often in titles of Psalms).

*נָקַשׁ *to strike, knock*, 41, 2 (Aram. of Dan. 5, 6; Targ., Syr.).

*הִסְתַּיֵּד *to converse*, 42, 12 (ܐܶܣܬܰܘܰܕ = ὁμιλεῖν, διαλέγεσθαι, cf. 9, 4 𝔖; from ܣܘܕ *friendly* or *confidential discourse*).

*סִימָה *treasure*, 40, 18 *marg.*, 41, 12 *marg.*, 14 *marg.* (סִימָא, ܣܝܡܬܐ).

הִסְתּוֹלֵל (denom. from סֹלְלָה *a mound* thrown up against a city by besiegers) *to make oneself a mound*, fig. for *to advance against, beset*, 39, 24, almost (from the context) *to importune*, 40, 28 (Ex. 9, 17, of Pharaoh's advancing pretexts and excuses against the Israelites, in order to escape the necessity of letting them go).

הִסִּיק 43, 4 *marg.*, חִשִּׁיק 43, 23, *to kindle* (Ez. 39, 9.

Is. 44, 15; Nif. Ps. 78, 21. Targ. אַפֵּיק, Talm. הִפִּיק).

? הִסְעִיר lit. *to move as by a tempest, to agitate, perturb*, 47, 18 (סָעַר Is. 54, 11 *al.*: cf. for the fig. sense 2 Ki. 6, 11 וַיִּסָּעֵר לֵב מֶלֶךְ אֲרָם עַל הַדָּבָר הַזֶּה). Cf. 𝔖 *didst amaze.*

סָפַק *to suffice*, 39, 33 (? יספיק, as *v.* 16); * Hif. הִסְפִּיק *to prove oneself sufficient, be able*, 42, 17, *to supply*, 39, 16 (cf. שָׂפַק *to suffice*, 1 Ki. 20, 10; שֵׂפֶק *sufficiency*, Job 20, 22, and perhaps שֶׂפֶק, 36, 18. NH. הִסְפִּיק: with 39, 16 comp. *Mechilta* בשלח § 6, אם מספיק צרכינו נעבדנו 'if He *supplies our needs*, we will serve Him').

סִפְרָה *writing*, 44, 4[c] (Ps. 56, 9 = *book*).

סָרָב *given to contradiction*, 41, 2 (Ez. 2, 6: cf. ܣܪܒ *to talk emptily, contradict*; סָרֵיב *to refuse, be disobedient*).

*סָרַח *evil odour*, 42, 11[b] *marg.* (NH. סָרַח *to emit an evil odour*, Talm. סִירְחָא *evil odour*; cf. ܣܪܚ *to corrupt, deprave.* In O. T. סָרַח is *to extend, hang over*, סֶרַח Ex. 26, 12 *that which hangs over*; but נִסְרְחָה חָכְמָתָם Jer. 49, 7 means perhaps 'their wisdom *is corrupted*').

עֱזוּז *might*, 45, 18 (Is. 42, 25. Ps. 78, 4. 145, 6).

*עַלְעוֹל *storm*, 43, 18 *marg.*

עָמַד *to rise up*, 47, 1. 12 (for the classical קָם [47, 23[e]. 48, 1], as Qoh. 4, 15. Dan. 8, 22. 23. 11, 2. 3. 4. 7. 20. 21 *al.*; cf. Driver, *Introduction*, p. 475).

*עָנָה *to be occupied* (sq. בְּ), 42, 8 *marg.* (Syr. ܥܢܐ ܒ: cf. Qoh. 1, 13. 3, 10).

*עַנְוְתָנוּת *humility*, 45, 4 *marg.* (NH. *id.*; Targ. עִנְוְתָנוּ).

*עֵסֶק *business, occupation*, 40, 1 (NH.; Targ. עִיסַק. Cf. עֵשֶׂק, הִתְעַשְּׂקוּ, Gen. 26, 20).

*פָּחַז *to be licentious, wanton*, partcp. fem. פֹּחֲזָה 42, 10[c] *marg.* (cf. פֹּחֲזִים Jud. 9, 4. Zeph. 3, 4; פַּחֲזוּת Jer. 23, 32). In Aram. the root and derivatives have the same meaning, as Sir. 19, 2. 23, 4. 6. 16. 17 𝔖, and ܦܚܙܘܬܐ = ἀσέλγεια, 2 Cor. 12, 21; but Arab. فخر is *to act arrogantly*; and this (or an allied sense) is probably the meaning of the root in Jud. 9, 4 (Moore, 'reckless'). Zeph. 3, 4. Jer. 23, 32.

*פַּחַז *licentiousness, wantonness*, 41, 17 *marg.* (v. l. on וָנוּת. Cf. Gen. 49, 4; and see under פָּחַז).

פְּלָאוֹת *wonders*, 43, 25 (the *plur.* as Ps. 119, 129. Dan. 12, 6, and NH.: cf. פְּלָאִים Lam. 1, 9).

*פֶּקַע *crash, peal*, 46, 17 (Syr. ܦܩܥ).

*? הִפְרִיד *to put far away*, 42, 9 (read probably הִפְ[רִיד]; cf. 𝔖 in Walton's Polyglott (*ap.* Lagarde, p. VIII) ܡܪܚܩܢܐ. In O. T. *to set far apart, separate*, of *concrete* objects, Gen. 30, 40 *al.*: in Syr. spec. of *sleep*, both in the Peal, as Gen. 31, 40, and in the Pael and Afel, Sir. 31, 1. 2, and here in Walton's text).

הִתְפַּתָּה *to be deceived, seduced*, 42, 10[a] *marg.* (in O. T. the pass. פֻּתָּה is used, Prov. 25, 15. Ez. 14, 9. Jer. 20, 10, as in the text here).

צְדָקָה 40, 17. 24, perhaps, as in NH. (cf. Dan. 4, 24 [A. V. 27]), in the sense of *almsgiving* (comp. Delitzsch on Prov. 10, 2; Tob. 4, 7–11 (where the Aram. text has צדקתא). 12, 9; Mt. 6, 1; and Ryle and James, *The Psalms of Solomon*, on 9, 6. 20. 15, 15).

*הִצְהִיר *to shine*, 43, 3 (Talm., but rare).

צוּף *to overflow*, 47, 14 (either Qal וַתָּצֹף as 𝔊, *didst overflow with*, or Hif. וַתָּצֵף as 𝔖 [cf. 24, 26 𝔖], *didst cause to overflow*); 39, 22 הֵצִיפָהּ *caused it to overflow* (Qal, Lam. 3, 54: Hif., Deut. 11, 4 *to cause to overflow*, 2 Ki. 6, 6 *to cause to swim*).

*צוּר prob. *figure, form*, 43, 21 *marg.* (Ps. 49, 15 *Qrê*; cf. צוּרָה Ez. 43, 11, four times: Targ. צוּר, Syr. ܨܘܪܬܐ [fem.]).

*צינה (i.e. צִנָּה) *cold*, 43, 20 (Prov. 25, 13).

*צְמָחִים *growing things*, 40, 22. 43, 21 (NH.: in O. T. צֶמַח is used collectively, Gen. 19, 25 *al.*).

צָנוּעַ *humble, modest*, 42, 8[d] (Prov. 11, 2 and NH.; cf. הַצְנֵעַ לֶכֶת Mic. 6, 8).

*צָרַךְ *to need*, 42, 21[d] *marg.*

*צֹרֶךְ, צוֹרֶךְ *need*, 39, 16. 21. 30[c]. 33. 42, 23[b] (2 Chr. 2, 15).

*צָרִיךְ adj. *in need of, needing*, 42, 21[d]; perhaps 39, 33 *marg.*

*קִבֵּל *to receive*, 41, 1 (Prov. 19, 20. Job 2, 10. 1 Chr. 12, 18. 21, 11. 2 Chr. 29, 16. 22. Ezra 8, 30. Est. 4, 4. 9, 23. 27; and in the Aram. of Daniel).

*קִלֵּס *to celebrate, praise*, 47, 15 (O. T. *to mock*).

*? קְרוֹמִית, pl. קְרוֹמִיּוֹת, *stalk* (of reed), 40, 16 (conj.).

*הִקְרִים *to overlay with a skin or crust*, 43, 20 (קָרַם Ez. 37, 6. 8).

רַבָּה 43, 23. 25 apparently for תְּהוֹם רַבָּה (Am. 7, 4 *al.*) *the great* (deep).

*? רָגַשׁ *to be disquieted*, perhaps 40, 6 יִרְ[גַּ]שׁ (Ps.

2, 1: cf. רֶגֶשׁ *a bustling throng*, Ps. 55, 15. רִגְשָׁה Ps. 64, 3, and probably 68, 28 for רִגְמָה. Often in Targ. for Heb. הָמָה, as Ps. 42, 6).

*רטב רָטֹב *moist*, 43, 22 *marg*. (Job 8, 16; רָטַב Job 24, 8).

רצף *to lay side by side as in mosaic work, to tessellate, pave*, 43, 8d[1] (רָצוּף Cant. 3, 10; cf. רִצְפָּה Ez. 40, 17. 18. 42, 3. 2 Chr. 7, 3. Est. 1, 6, מַרְצֶפֶת 2 Ki. 16, 17. NH. רָצַף; Aram. רְצַף, ܪܨܦ).

*הִרְתִּיחַ *to heat*, 43, 3 (NH.: in O.T. *to boil*, Job 41, 23; so Pi. Ez. 24, 5, Pu. Job 30, 27).

שואה 42, 7 *marg.*, apparently (si vera l.) an anomalous fem. inf. שׂוֹאָה from נָשָׂא (cf. שׂוֹא Ps. 89, 10) *taking*; see s. v. מַתַּת.

הִשְׂרִיק *to emit a pale-red colour*, 43, 9 *marg*. (cf. שָׂרֹק *pale-red*, Zech. 1, 8; NH. סִירֵק *to colour pale-red*).

*שֶׁבַח *praise*, 44 *title* (NH.; Targ. שְׁבַח. שִׁבַּח *to laud* or *praise*, Ps. 63, 4. 117, 1. 145, 4. 147, 12. Qoh. 4, 2. 8, 15, and in the Aram. of Daniel; הִשְׁתַּבֵּחַ Ps. 106, 47 = 1 Chr. 16, 35).

*שְׁבִיב *flame*, 45, 19 (Job 18, 5: Aram. of Dan. 3, 22. 7, 9).

*הִשְׁגִּיחַ *to look at*, 40, 29 (Is. 14, 16. Ps. 33, 14. Cant. 2, 9; NH., Targ.).

שֶׁגֶר *the dropping* or *casting* (i.e. the *young*) of an animal, 40, 19c (Ex. 13, 12. Deut. 7, 13. 28, 4. 18. 51).

*? שִׁגְשֵׁג *to confuse, perturb*, perhaps 40, 6 [יִשְׂגְּשֵׁג] *is perturbed* (Aram.: cf. Luke 1, 12 ܐܫܬܓܫ for ἐταράχθη, John 12, 27 ܫܓܝܫܐ for τετάρακται).

*שׁוּתָּף *companion*, 41, 18c *marg.*, 42, 3 *marg.* (Aram. שׁוּתָּף, ܫܘܬܦܐ).

שָׁנָה *to change, alter* (intrans.), partcp. שׁוֹנִים מִן *different from*, 42, 24 (so Est. 1, 7. 3, 8); Pi. 40, 5d; Hithp. (of the moon) 43, 8 (שָׁנָה Lam. 4, 1. Mal. 3, 6, NH. and Aram.; שׁוֹנִים

=*dissidents*, Prov. 24, 21. The Pi. and Hithp. are found earlier, the former 1 Sam. 21, 14 *al.*, the latter 1 Ki. 14, 2).

*הִשְׁתַּעְּה *to narrate, tell*, 44, 8 (אִשְׁתְּעִי, ܐܫܬܥܝ).

שָׁעַע *to be smeared over*, Hif. inf. הָשַׁע *to smear over*, fig. *close up*, of the mouth, 41, 21a *marg.* (In O. T. of the eyes, Is. 6, 10. 29, 9. 32, 3 [l. תִּשְׁעֶינָה].)

*שָׁרַב *to be hot, parched* (or perhaps adj. *parched*), 43, 22 (שָׁרָב, ܫܪܒ).

הִתְוָה *to mark out*, 43, 13 (Ez. 9, 4 [1 Sam. 21, 14 read וַיָּתָף]).

*תּוֹעֶלֶה *profit*, 41, 14c (cf. NH. תּוֹעֶלֶת).

*תַּחְלִיף *successor*, 44, 17 (in a time of destruction Noah *became a successor*, i. e. humanity at large perished, but Noah was spared to carry on the succession, and keep the race alive[1]). 46, 12. 48, 8 (cf. ܚܠܝܦܐ *substitute, representative*; and Heb. הֶחֱלִיף *to cause to come in place of, make to succeed*, Is. 9, 9).

*[תַּחֲרוּת] *contention, strife*, 40, 5 *marg.* (NH.; Targ. תַּחֲרוּ: cf. תַּחֲרָה *to contend in rivalry*, Jer. 12, 5. 22, 15).

*תֵּמַהּ *a marvel*, pl. תְּמָהִים, constr. תִּמְהֵי מַעֲלָה 43, 25. 48, 14 (Aram. תִּמְהִין Dan. 3, 32. 33. 6, 28; תְּמִיהָה in *j*. Targ., oft. for Heb. מוֹפֵת. The *verb* תָּמַהּ is common in the O. T.).

*תיקן (i.e. תִּקֵּן) *to arrange*, 47, 9 (Qoh. 7, 13. 12, 9; תְּקַן intrans. *to be set right*, Qoh. 1, 15: Aram. תַּקֵּין, ܬܩܢ).

*תַּשְׁלוּמוֹת *recompences*, 48, 8 (cf. Talm. תַּשְׁלוּם, תַּשְׁלוּמִים; Targ. תַּשְׁלוּם, also fem. תּוּשְׁלָמָא).

תתה 42, 7 *marg.*, apparently (si vera l.) תֵּתָה, an anomalous (double) fem. form of תֵּת *giving*.

---

[1] If the reading be correct, the starry sky, lit up by the moon, will be compared poetically to a brightly variegated pavement. Comp. for the figure Shakespeare, ~~Romeo and Juliet~~, V. i, 'Look how the *floor of heaven* is *thick inlaid* with patines of bright gold.'

[1] Comp. Payne Smith, s. v. ܫܘܚܠܦܐ (which 𝔖 uses here for תחליף): 'Apud Sanct. Vit. 83 r. forte sit *prosapia, soboles*, quae locum patris capiat, vel *novus rerum ordo*, ܚܕܐ ܗܘܐ ܫܘܚܠܦܐ ܕܟܠܗ ܥܠܡܐ, de Noacho; voluit Deus quod e Noacho ܫܘܚܠܦܐ ܕܟܠܗ ܥܠܡܐ ܢܗܘܐ, Aphr. ܝܐ. 24.'

Add (perhaps) הִצְטַעֵר *to vex oneself, grieve*, 42, 10d (O.T. צָעַר *to be little*, esp. in position or esteem, Jer. 30, 19. Job 14, 21. Zech. 13, 7: hence in NH. and Aram. Pi. (Pa.) *to treat as little*, in an intensified sense *to vex, trouble* (Syr. *to slight, insult*), Hithp. (Ethp.) *to vex oneself*; cf. p. xxv, No. XLIII).

With כל מארץ 40, 11, כל מאפס 41, 10, comp. כל בשמים ובארץ 1 Chr. 29, 11, and כל בלבבו 2 Chr. 32, 31 (for the classical כל אשר..., e. g. 1 Sam. 9, 19). למען לא 45, 26, as Ez. 19, 9. 26, 20. Zech. 12, 7. Ps. 119, 11. 80. 125, 3.

NOTE.—The following orthographical peculiarities of the MS. (which, however, do not occur uniformly) deserve notice:—

a. Yod is used to express (α) *ĭ* before a following doubled letter, 39, 15 מיני, 39, 22 ריותה (i. e. רִוְּתָה), 42, 17 אימין (אִמֵּץ), 44, 20^{d} ניסוי, 47, 9 תיקן; and (β) *ē*, 40, 5^{d} שינת *sleep*, 40, 29 *marg.* מיעים (i. e. מֵעִים), 41, 1^{c} שֶׁלֵיו (as Job 21, 23. Jer. 49, 31), 6 *marg.* מבין (perhaps=מֵבֵן), 41, 21^{a} *marg.* מיהשע (מֵהֶשַׁע), 42, 12 תסתויד. Both these uses of י are common in NH. (Strack u. Siegfried, *Lehrb. der Neuhebr. Sprache*, § 15^{f}). דויד occurs 47, 2. 49, 4; דוד 44, 25. 47, 1. 48, 15. 16. 22.

b. Waw is used to express (α) *ŭ*, 41, 14^{b} מוסתר, 46, 13 (conj.) מושאל, and before a doubled letter 39, 19 *marg.* 41, 14^{b} *marg.* מסותר, 41, 2^{a} *marg.* חוקו, 3 חוקיך, 42, 10^{a} תפותה, 45, 24^{d} כתונה, 46, 15 קודש, 47, 3 דובים; (β) *o* (out of a primitive *ŭ*), 39, 30^{c} צורכם (Mass. צָרְכָּם), 43, 24 אוזננו (אָזְנֵנוּ), also צורך 39, 16 (with *marg.* צרך). 33. 42, 23^{b}, עול 40, 1, שורש 40, 15, עוז 40, 30. 45, 8, חוק 41, 2 *marg.* 42, 2. 43, 7. 12? 44, 5. 45, 17^{b} (but *v.*^{c} חק), רוגע 42, 14, אומר 42, 15^{c}, תואר 42, 25^{b} *marg.* 43, 1^{a} *marg.* 9. 18. 45, 7^{d} *marg.*, כוחו 43, 15 *marg.*, רוב 43, 32, דופי 44, 19 *marg.* (Mass. דָּפִי, in pause דֹּפִי), יופי 45, 12^{d}, כופר 46, 19^{c}, יושר 48, 16 (Strack u. Siegfried, §§ 15^{b}, 41^{a}, 89^{b}, 92^{b}: comp. above, p. xix ff., Nos. I. *a–d*, XV, XXXIX, etc.). In both *a* and *b*, it must naturally remain an open question whether this orthography is original, or whether it has been introduced by transcribers. Isolated examples of both uses occur in the O. T., though *a* (α) is exceedingly rare (1 Sam. 17, 35): see *e.g.* Ps. 19, 14 אֵיתָם, Job 6, 27 בְּרִיעֲכֶם; Jud. 18, 29 יוּלַּד, Jer. 31, 34 פוּלָּם, Ez. 20, 18 בְּחוּקֵּי; Dan. 11, 6 פּוֹחַ, 30 קוֹדֶשׁ: comp. also הובנים (*Qrê* הָבְנִים) Ez. 27, 15, אוניות (*Qrê* אֳנִיּוֹת) 2 Chr. 8, 18; and see further Ewald, *Lehrbuch*, § 15^{b}, with the notes; Olshausen, *Lehrbuch*, § 39 *e, f, h, k.* A non-etymological ו is also used somewhat more frequently than is usual in the O. T. to express the *ō* of a participle, as אוהב 41, 22, and elsewhere, and of an imperfect, as 40, 6 ישקום, 43, 28 נחקור.

c. There are many cases of the accidental transposition of letters (especially of ו), giving rise to a variation between text and margin: 39, 33 צורך and צרוך, 40, 3 לשוב and לובש, 41, 5 רעים and ערום, 14^{b} מוסתר and מסותרת, 20 משאול and משואל, 42, 11^{d} השבתך and הובישתך, 23^{b} צורך and צרוך, 43, 4 מצוק and מוצק, שולח and שלוח, 43, 12 אל and לא, 13 ברק and בקר, ותנצח and והונח, 17^{d} דרתו and רדתו, 18 ינהה and יהגה, 44, 23^{b} בברכה and בבכורה, 23^{g} מוצא and ומצא, 45, 7^{d} (prob.) תועפות and תעופה: cf. 39, 30 נבראו and נבחרו, 41, 12 חכמה and חמדה, 42, 5^{a} תמהות and תמורת, 45, 2 במרומים and במוראים. The same error is found sometimes in the O. T., *e.g.* Jer. 2, 25. 17, 23. 42, 20. The Massoretic compilation *Ochlah w'ochlah* (ed. Frensdorff) enumerates (No. 91) sixty-two instances (not all exegetically certain) of such transposition, which have been corrected in the *Qrê*. Whether in a given case, the text or the margin has the correct reading must be decided, here as in the O. T., upon exegetical grounds. In view of the frequency of the error in the present MS., emendations which assume it become the less questionable, viz. 39, 22 ברכתו for ברבות, 40, 29^{b} מנעל for מענל, 43, 10 יָשְׁנוּ for ישון, 44, 6 סמוכי for סומכי, 46, 13 מושאל for משואל, 47, 7^{b} עִירָם for ערים, 48, 7 השומע for השמיע (cf. below, *d*).

d. י and ו are several times confused: 40, 13 חול and חיל (twice), 18 יין ו and יותר, 21 חלול and חליל, 29^{c} מטעמו and מטעמי, 41, 2^{c} ינקש and ונוקש, 5 רעים and ערום, 12 *marg.* סומות for סימות, 16^{a} משפטי and משפטו, 19^{a} הנור and ונגיד, 42, 14 מטיב and מטוב, 17^{c} אימץ and אומץ, 43, 5 גדיל and גדול, 7 חמני and וממנו, 9 אורו and עדי, 17 יחול and יחיל. This error is one which is extremely common in the O. T., both as between the *Ktîb* and the *Qrê* (see *Ochlah w'ochlah*, Nos. 80, 81, 134–148), and also as between the Massoretic text and the versions, especially the LXX.

There are of course other errors of transcription in the MS.; but none recurring with sufficient frequency to call for special notice.

The Tetragrammaton is written regularly ייי.

To face p. xxxvii

MS. fol. 9 verso (see p. 40)

VERSIO VETUS LATINA.

[The verses are numbered to agree with the Greek text. Lagarde's numeration, where it differs, is added in parentheses.]

XXXIX.	(20)	15c	in canticis labiorum et citharis,		et sic dicitis in confessione:
	(21)	16	Opera domini universa bona valde.		
	(22)	17c	in verbo eius stetit aqua sicut congeries,		et in sermone oris illius sicut exceptorium aquarum.
	(23)	18	quoniam in praecepto ipsius placor fit,		et nón est minoratio in salute illius.
	(24)	19	opera omnis carnis coram illo,		et non est quicquam absconditum ab oculis eius.
	(25)	20	a saeculo usque in saeculum respicit,		
				20d	et nihil est mirabile in conspectu eius.
	(26)	21	non est dicere Quid est hoc, aut quid est illud?		omnia enim in tempore suo quaerentur.
	(27)	22	benedictio illius quasi fluvius inundavit,	(28)	et quo modo diluvium aridam inebriavit,
		23	sic ira ipsius gentes quę non exquisierunt eum hereditavit.	(29)	quo modo convertit aquas, et siccata est terra,
		24	et viae illius viis illorum directae sunt:		sic peccatoribus offensiones in ira eius.
	(30)	25	bona bonis creata sunt ab initio:		sic nequissimis bona et mala.
	(31)	26	initium necessariae rei vitae hominum		aqua, ignis et ferrum,
		26c	lac et panis similagineus et mel		et botrus uvae et oleum et vestimentum.
	(32)	27	haec omnia sanctis in bonis,		sic et impiis et peccatoribus in mala conversantur.
	(33)	28	sunt spiritus qui ad vindictam creati sunt,		et in furore suo confirmaverunt tormenta sua.
	(34)	28c	in tempore consummationis effundent virtutem,		et furorem eius qui fecit illos, placebunt.
	(35)	29	ignis, grando, fames et mors,		omnia haec ad vindictam creata sunt:
	(36)	30	bestiarum dentes et scorpii et serpentes		et romphea vindicans in exterminium impios.
				30d	et super terram in necessitatem praeparabuntur,
	(37)	31	in mandatis eius aepulabuntur,		et in temporibus suis non praeterient verbum.
	(38)	32	propterea ab initio confirmatus sum		et consiliatus sum, et cogitavi et scripta dimisi.
	(39)	33	omnia opera domini bona,		et omne opus ora sua subministravit.
	(40)	34	non est dicere Hoc illo nequius est:		omnia enim in tempore suo comprobabuntur.
	(41)	35	et nunc in omni corde et ore conlaudate		et benedicite nomen domini.
XL.		1	occupatio magna creata est omnibus hominibus,		et iugum gravem super filios Adam
		1c	a die exitus de ventre matris eorum		usque in diem sepulturae in matrem omnium.
		2	cogitationes eorum et timorem cordis,		adinventio exspectationis et dies finitionis,
		3	a sedentes super sedem gloriosam		usque ad humiliatum in terra et cinere,

4 ab eo qui utitur hyacinto et portat coronam usque ad eum qui operitur ligno crudo:
5 furor, zelus, tumultus, fluctuatio et timor mortis, iracundia perseverans et contentio,
(5) 5c et in tempore refectionis in cubile somnus noctis inmutat scientiam.
6 modicum tamquam nihil in requie, et ab eo in somnis quasi in die respectus.
(7) 6c cor turbatus est in visu cordis sui tamquam qui evaserit in die belli.
7 in tempore salutis suae exsurrexit, et admirans ad nullum timorem,
8 cum omni carne, ab homine usque ad pecus, et super peccatores septuplum.
9 ad haec mors, sanguinis, contentio et romphea, oppraessiones, famis et contritio et flagella.
10 super iniquos creata sunt haec omnia, et propter illos factus est catachismis.
11 omnia quae de terra sunt, in terram convertentur, et aquae omnes in mare convertentur.
12 et fides in saeculum stabit.
13 substantia iniustorum sicut fluvius siccabuntur, et sicut tonitruum magnum in pluvia personabunt.
14 in aperiendo manus suas lactabitur: sic praevaricatores in consummatione tabescent.
15 nepotes impiorum non multiplicab ramos, et radices inmundae super cacumen petrae sonant.
16 super omnem aquam viriditas, et ad horam fluminis omne faenum evelletur.
17 gratia sicut paradisus in benedictionibus, et misericordia in saeculo permanet.
18 fili, vita sibi sufficientis operarii condulcabitur, et in ea invenies thesaurum.
19 aedificatio civitatis confirmavit nomen,
19d et super haec mulier inmaculata computatur.
20 vinum et musica laetificant cor, et super utraque dilectio sapientiae.
21 tibiae et psalterium suabem faciunt melodiam, et super utraque lingua suavis.
22 gratiam et speciem desideravit oculus, et super haec verides sationes.
23 amicus et sodalis in tempore convenientes, et super utrosque mulier cum viro.
24 fratres in adiutorium in tempore tribulationis, et super eos misericordia liberavit.
25 aurum et argentum et constitutio peduum, et super utrumque consilium beneplacitum.
26 facultates et virtutes exaltant cor, et super haec timor domini.
(27) 26c non est in timore domini minoratio, et non est in eo quaerere adiutorium.
(28) 27 timor domini sicut paradisus benedictionis, et super omnem gloriam operuerunt illum.

de indigentia misera.

(29) 28 fili, in tempore vitae tuae ne indiges: melius est enim mori quam indigere.
(30) 29 vir respiciens in mensam alienam, non est vita eius in cogitatione victus:
29c alit enim animam suam cibis alienis.
(31) vir autem disciplinatus et eruditus custodiet se.
(32) 30 in ore inprudentis condulcabitur inopia, et in ventre eius ignis ardebit.

de memoria et iudicium mortis.

XLI. 1 o mors, quam amara est memoria tua. homini iusto et pacem habenti in substantiis suis,
(2) 1c viro quieto et cuius viae directae sunt in omnibus, et adhuc valenti accipere cibum.

(3) 1	o mors, bonum est iudicium tuum		homini indigenti et qui minoratur viribus,
(4) 2c	defecto aetate et cui de omnibus cura est		et incredibili qui perdit sapientiam.
(5) 3	noli metuere iudicium mortis.		memento . . . . . e te fuerunt et quae superventura sunt tibi:
4	hoc iudicium a domino omni carni.	(6)	et quid superveniet in beneplacito altissimi?
4c	sive decem sive centum sive mille anni.	(7)	non est enim in inferno accusatio vitae.
(8) 5	fili abominationum. fiunt fili peccatorum,		et qui conversantur secus domos impiorum.
(9) 6	filiorum peccatorum periet hereditas,		et cum semine illorum assiduitas obprobrii.
(10) 7	de patre impio quaeruntur filii,		quoniam propter illum sunt in opprobrio.
(11) 8	vae vobis, viri impii,		qui dereliquistis legem domini altissimi.
(12) 9	et si nati fueritis, in maledictione nascemini,		
		9b	et si mortui fueritis, in maledictione erit mors vestra.
(13) 10	omnia quae de terra sunt, in terram convertentur:		sic impii a maledicto in perditionem,
(14) 11	luctus hominum in corpore ipsorum:		nomen autem impiorum delebitur.
(15) 12	curam habe de bono nomine: hoc enim magis permanebit tibi		quam mille thesauri magni pretiosi.
(16) 13	bonae vitae numerus dierum.		bonum autem nomen permanebit in aevo.
(17) 14	disciplinam in pace conservate, filii:		
14b	sapientia enim abscondita et thesaurus invisus,		quae utilitas in utrisque?
(18) 15	melior est homo qui abscondit stultitiam suam,		quam homo qui abscondit sapientiam suam.
		(19) 16	verum tamen reveremini in his quae procedunt de ore meo.
(20) 16b	non est enim bonum omnem in reverentiam observare,		et non omnia omnibus bene placent in fide.

ab omnibus vitiis declinandum.

(21) 17	erubescite patrem et matrem de fornicatione,		et a praesidente et a potente de mendacio,
(22) 18	a principe et iudice de delicto,		a synagoga et plebe de iniquitate,
(23) 18c	a socio et amico de iniustitia	19	et de loco in quo habitas, (24) de furto,
19b	de veritate dei et testamento,		de discubitu in panibus
19d	et ab obfuscatione dati et accepti,	(25) 20	a salutantibus de silentio,
20b	a respectu mulieris fornicariae,	21	ab aversione vultus cognati.
		(26)	ne avertas facie . m a proximo tuo,
21b	et ab auferendo partem et non restituendo.	(27) 21c	ne respicias mulierem alieni viri,
22	et ne scruteris ancillam eius,		neque steteris ad lectum eius.
(28) 22c	a . b amicis de sermonibus improperii,		et cum dederis, ne improperis.
XLII. 1	non duplices sermonem auditus		de revelatione sermonis absconditi,
1c	et eris vere sine confusione,		et invenies gratiam in conspectu omnium hominum:
1e	ne pro his omnibus confundaris,		ne accipias personam ut delinquas.
2	de lege altissimi et testamento,		de iudicio iustificare impium,
3	de verbo sociorum et viatorum		et de datione hereditatis amicorum,
4	de aequalitate staterae et ponderum,		et de adquisitione multorum et paucorum,
5	de corruptione emtionis et negotiatorum		et de multa disciplina filiorum

			et servo pessimo latus sanguinare.
	6	super mulierem nequam bonum est signum.	(7) ubi manus multae sunt, clude,
	7	et quodcumque trades, numera et appende,	datum vero et acceptum omne describe.
	8	de disciplina insensati et fatui	et de senioribus qui iudicantur ab adulescentibus,
	8°	et eris eruditus in omnibus,	et probabilis in conspectu omnium virorum.
	9	filia patris abscondita est vigilia,	et sollicitudo eius auferet somnium,
	9°	ne forte in adulescentia sua adultera efficiatur,	et commorata cum viro odibilis fiat.
	10	ne quando polluatur in virginitate sua,	et in paternis suis gravida inveniatur:
	10°	ne forte cum viro commorata transgrediatur,	aut certe sterelis efficiatur.
	11	super filiam luxuriosam confirma custodiam,	ne quando faciat te in opprobrium venire inimicis
	11°	a detractione in civitate et abiectione plebis,	et confundat te in multitudinem populi.
	12	omni homini noli intendere in specie,	et in medio mulierum noli commorari.
	13	de vestimentis enim procedit tinea,	et a muliere iniquitas viro.
	14	melior iniquitas viri quam benefaciens mulier,	et mulier confundens in opprobrium,
	15	memor ero igitur operum domini,	et quae vidi, adnuntiabo.
	15°	in osermonibus domini opera eius.	
	16	sol inluminans per omnia respexit,	et gloria domini plenum est opus eius.
	17	nonne dominus fecit sanctos	enarrare omnia mirabilia sua
	17°	quae confirmavit dominus omnipotens	stabilis in gloria sua?
	18	abyssum et cor hominum investigavit,	et in astutia illorum excogitavit.
	(19) 18°	cognovit enim dominus omnem scientiam,	et inspexit in signum aevi,
	19	annuntians quae prae . terierunt et quae superventura sunt,	revelans vestigia occultorum.
	20	et non praeterit illum omnis cogitatus,	et non abscondit se ab eo ullus sermo.
	21	magnalia sapientiae suae decoravit	qui est ante saeculum et usque in saeculum,
	21°	neque adiectum est (22) neque minuetur,	et non eget alicuius consilio.
	(23) 22	quam desiderabilia omnia opera eius,	et tamquam scintillam quam est considerare.
	(24) 23	omnia haec . . . ent et manent in saeculum,	et in omni necessitate omnia obaudiunt ei.
	(25) 24	omnia duplicia, unum contra unum,	et non fecit quicquam deesse.
	(26) 25	uniuscuiusque confirmavit bona,	et quis satiabitur videns gloriam eius?
XLIII.	1	altitudinis firmamentum pulchritudo est,	species caeli in visione gloriae.
	2	sol in aspectu annuntians in exitu,	vas ammirabile, opus excelsi.
	3	in meridiano exurit terram,	et in conspectu ardoris eius quis poterit sustinere?
	4	fornacem custodiens in operibus . rdoris.	(4) tripliciter sol exurens montes.
	4°	radios igneos exuflans	et refulgens radiis suis obcaecat oculos.
	5	magnus dominus qui fecit illum,	et in sermonibus eius festinavit.
	6	iter (6) luna in omnibus in tempore suo,	ostensio temporis et signum aevi.
	7	a luna signum diei festi,	luminare quod minuitur in consummatione.
	8	mensis secundum nomen eius est,	crescens ammirabiliter in consummationem.
	(9) 8°	vas castrorum in excelsis,	in firmamento caeli resplendens gloriosum.
	(10) 9	species caeli gloria stellarum	mundum inluminans in excelsis dominus.

	(11) 10	in verbis sancti stabunt ad iudicium,	et non deficient in vigiliis suis.
	(12) 11	vide arcum, et benedic qui fecit illum:	valde speciosus est in splendore suo.
	(13) 12	giravit caelum in circuitu gloriae suae:	manus excelsi aperuerunt illum.
	(14) 13	imperio suo adcelebravit nivem,	et adcelerat coruscationes emittere iudicii sui.
	(15) 14	propterea aperti sunt thesauri,	et evolaverunt nebulae sicut aves.
	(16) 15	in magnitudine sua posuit nubes,	et confracti sunt lapides grandinis.
	(17) 16	in conspectu eius commovebuntur montes,	et in voluntate eius aspiravit notus.
	(18) 17	vox tonitrui eius verberavit terram,	tempestas aquilonis et congregatio spiritus.
	(19) 17[c]	sicut avis deponens ad sedendum adspargit nivem,	et sicut lucusta demergens descensus eius.
	(20) 18	pulchritudinem candoris eius ammirabitur oculus,	et super imbrem eius expavescit cor.
	(21) 19	gelum sicut salem effundet super terram,	et dum zelaverit, fiet tamquam cacumina tribuli.
	(22) 20	frigidus ventus aquilo flavit,	et gelavit cristallus ab aqua:
	20[c]	super omnem congregationem aquarum requiescit,	et sicut lorica induit se aquis.
	(23) 21	devoravit montes et exuret desertum,	et extinguet viridem sicut ignem.
	(24) 22	medicina omnium in festinationem nebulae,	et ros obvians ab ardore venienti humilem efficiet eum.
	(25) 23	in sermone eius siluit ventus, cogitatione sua placabit abyssum	et plantavit illum dominus ihs.
	(26) 24	qui navigat mare, enarrat pericula eius,	et audiente . . . ribus non ammirabimur.
	(27) 25	illic praeclara et mira et mirabilia opera,	varia genera bestiarum et omnium peccorum et creatura beluarum.
	(28) 26	propter ipsum consummatus est itineris finis,	et in sermone eius composita sunt omnia.
	(29) 27	multa dicimus et deficiemus verbis,	consummatio autem sermonum ipse est in omnibus.
	(30) 28	gloriantes ad quid vale[bi]mus?	ipse enim omnipotens super omnia opera sua.
	(31) 29	terribilis dominus et magnus vehementer,	et mirabilis potentia ipsius.
	(32) 30	glorificantes dominum,	quantumcumque potueritis, supervalebit adhuc, et ammirabilis magnificentia eius.
	(33)	be . edicentes dominum, exaltate illum quantum potestis:	maior est enim omni laude.
	(34) 30[c]	exaltantes eum replebimini virtute:	ne laboretis, non enim pervenietis.
	(35) 31	quis vidit eum, et enarrabit?	et quis magnificavit eum sicut est ab initio?
	(36) 32	multa abscondita sunt maiora his:	pauca enim vidimus operum eius.
	(37) 33	omnia autem dominus fecit,	et pie agentibus dedit sapientiam.
XLIV.	1	laudemus viros gloriosos,	et parentes nostros in generatione sua.
	2	multam gloriam fecit dominus	magnificentia sua a saeculo.
	3	dominantes in potestatibus suis,	homines magni virtute
	3[c]	et prudentia sua praediti,	nuntiantes dignitatem prophetarum.
	4	et inperantes in praesenti[s] populorum	et virtute prudentiae populi
	(5) 4[c]	sanctissima verba, et in pueritia sua	
	5	requirentes modos musicos	et narrantes carmina scribturarum.
	6	homines divites in virtute, pulchritudinis studium habentis,	pacificantes in domibus suis.

7 omnes isti in generationibus gentis suae gloriam adepti sunt, et in diebus suis habentur in laudibus.
8 qui de illis nati sunt, relinquerunt nomen narrandi laudes eorum.
9 et sunt quorum non est . . memoria: perierunt quasi qui non fuerunt,
9c et nati sunt quasi non nati, filii ipsorum cum illis.
10 sed illi viri misericordiae sunt quorum pietates non defuerunt,
11 et cum semine ipsorum perseverat bona hereditas. (12) nepotum illorum
11c & 12 semen in testamento stetit, (13) et filiorum ipsorum propter illos
13 usque in aeternum manet semen eorum, et gloria eorum non derelinquetur.
14 corpora ipsorum in pace sepulta sunt, et nomen eorum vivet in generationes et generationes.
15 sapientiam ipsorum narrent populi, et laudem eorum nuntiet ecclesia.
16 Enoch placuit deo, et translatus est in paradiso, ut det gentibus paenitentiam.
17 Noe inventus est perfectus iustus, et in tempore iracundiae factus est reconciliatio,
(18) 17c ideo redimissum est reliquum terrae, cum factum est diluvium.
(19) 18 testamenta saeculi posita sunt apud illum, ne deleri possit diluvio omnis caro.
(20) 19 Abraham magnus pater multitudinis gentium, et non est inventus similis illi in gloria,
20 qui conservavit legem excelsi, et fuit in testamento cum illo.
(21) 20c in cane eius stare fecit testamentum, et in temtatione inventus est fidelis.
(22) 21 ideo iure iurando dedit illi gloriam in gente sua,
21c crescere illum quasi terrae harenam, (23) et ut stellas exaltare semen eius,
21e et hereditare illos a mari usque ad mare et a flumine usque ad terminos terrae.
(24) 22 et in Isaac eodem fecit modo propter Habraham patrem ipsius.
(25) 22c benedictionem omnium gentium dedit illi. 23 et testamentum confirmavit super capud Iacob.
(26) 23b agnovit eum in benedictionibus suis, et dedit illi hereditatem,
23d et divisit ei partem, in tribus duodecim,
(27) 23f et conservavit illis homines misericordiae, invenientes gratiam in oculis omnis carnis.

XLV. 1 dilectus a deo et hominibus Moses, cuius memoria in benedictione est.
2 similem illum fecit in gloria sanctorum, et magnificavit eum in timore inimicorum,
3 et in verbis suis monstra placavit. (3) glorificavit illum in conspectu regum,
3c et iussit illi coram populo suo, et ostendit illi gloriam suam.
4 in fide et lenitate ipsius sanctum fecit illum, et elegit illum de omni carne.
5 audivit enim eum et vocem ipsius, induxit illum in nubem.
(6) 5c et dedit illi coram praecepta, legem vitae et disciplinae,
5e docere Iacob testamentum, et iudicia sua Israhel.
(7) 6 excelsum fecit Aaron fratrem eius, et similem sibi de tribu Levi. (8) 7 statuit ei testamentum aeternum,
7b et dedit illi sacerdotium gentis, et beabit illum in gloria,
(9) 7d et circumcinxit illum zona gloriae:
8 induit illum stolam gloriae, et coronavit illum in vasis virtutis.
(10) 8c circumpediles et femoralia et humeralem posuit ei, 9 et cinxit illum tintinnabulis
9b aureis plurimis in gyro, (11) dare sonitum in incessu suo,

9^{d} audiuum facere sonitum in templo	in memoria filii gentis suae.
(12) 10 stola sancta auro et hyacintho	et purpura opus textile viri sapientes
10^{c} iudicio et veritate praediti.	(13) 11 torto cocco opus artificis
11^{b} figuratis	in ligatura auri et opere lapidarii
11^{d} insculptilis in memoriam	secundum numerum tribum Isrl.
(14) 12 coronam auream supra mitram eius	expraessam signo sanctitatis,
12^{c} gloriam honoris et opus virtutis,	desideria oculorum ornata.
(15) 13 sic pulchra ante ipsum non fuerunt alia .	usque ad originem. (16) non indutus est illa alienigena aliquis,
13^{c} sed tantum filii ipsius soli	et nepotes eius per omne tempus.
(17) 14 sacrificia ipsius consummata sunt igni	cotidie.
(18) 15 complevit Moses manum eius,	et unxit illum oleo sancto,
(19) 15^{c} factus est illi in testamentum aeternum	et semini eius sicut dies caeli,
15^{e} fungi sacerdotio et habere laudem	et glorificare populum suum in nomine suo.
(20) 16 ipsum elegit ab omni viventem	afferre sacrificium deo,
16^{c} incensum et bonum odorem in memoriam	placare pro populo suo.
(21) 17 dedit illi in praeceptis suis	potestatem in testamentis iudiciorum
17^{c} docere Iacob testimonia	et in legem suam lucem dare Israhel.
(22) 18 quia contra illum steterunt alieni,	et propter invidiam circumdederunt illum in deserto
18^{c} homines qui erant cum Dathan et Abiron	et congregatio Core in iracundiam.
(23) 19 vidit dominus deus et non placuit illi,	et consumti sunt in inpetu iracundiae.
(24) 19^{c} fecit illis monstra,	et consumsit eos in flamma ignis.
(25) 20 et addidit Aaron gloriam	et dedit illi hereditatem,
20^{c} et primitias fructuum terrae divisit illi.	(26) panem ipsis in primis parabit in satietate:
21 nam sacrificia domini edent	quae dedit ipsi et semini eius.
(27) 22 ceterum in terra gentes non hereditabit,	et pars non est illi in gente:
	22^{c} ipse enim pars eius est et hereditas.
(28) 23 Finees filius Eleazari	terti . . in gloria
23^{c} in imitando ipsum in timore domini	(29) et stare in reverentia gentis,
23^{e} in bonitate et alacritate animae suae	placuit deo Israhel.
(30) 24 ideo statuit ad illum testamentum pacis,	principem sanctorum et gentis suae,
24^{c} ut sit illi et semini eius	sacerdotii dignitas in aeternum.
(31) 25 et testamentum David regis	filio Iesse de tribu Iuda,
	25^{d} hereditas ipsi et semini eius,
26 ut daret sapientiam in cor nostrum,	iudicare gentem suam in iustitia,
26^{c} ne abolerentur bona ipsorum,	et gloriam in gentem eorum aeternam fecit.
XLVI. 1 fortis in bello Iesu Nave	successor Mosi in prophetis,
1^{c} qui fuit magnus secundum nomen suum,	(2) maximus in salutem electorum dei,
1^{e} expugnare insurgentes hostes,	ut consequeretur hereditatem Israhel.
(3) 2 quam gloriam adeptus est in tollendo manus suas	et iactando contra civitates romfeas?
(4) 3 quis ante illum sic restitit?	nam hostes ipse dominus perduxit.
(5) 4 aut non iracundia eius impetus est sol,	et una dies facta est quasi duo?
(6) 5 invocabit altissimum potentem	in oppugnando inimicos undique,
5^{c} et audivit illum magnus et sanctus deus	in saxis grandinis virtutis valde fortis.

(7) 6 impetum fecit contra gentem hostilem,	et in descensum perdidit contrarios,
(8) 6^{c} ut cognoscant gentes potentiam eius,	quia contra dominum pugnare non est facile.
6^{e} et secutus est a tergo potentes.	(9) 7 et in diebus Mosi misericordiam fecit,
7^{b} ipse et Caleb filius Ieffonne,	stare contra hostem
7^{d} et prohibere gentem a peccatis	et perfringere murmur malitiae.
(10) 8 et ipsi duo constituti a periculo liberati sunt,	a numero sescentorum milium peditum
8^{c} inducere illos in hereditatem,	in terram quae manat lac et mel.
(11) 9 et dedit dominus ipsi Caleb fortitudinem,	et usque ad senectutem perman^e^it illi virtus,
9^{c} ut ascenderet in excelsum terrae locum,	et semen ipsius obtinuit hereditatem,
(12) 10 ut viderent omnes filii Isr̄l	quia bonum est obsequi sancto deo.
(13) 11 et iudices singuli suo nomine	quorum non est corruptum cor,
11^{c} qui non aversi sunt a domino nostro,	(14) ut sit memoria illorum in benedictionem,
	(15) et nomen eorum permanet in aeternum:
12 et ossa eorum pullulent de loco suo.	permanens ad filios illorum sanctorum virorum gloria.
(16) 13 dilectus a deo suo Samuhel	
13^{e} propheta domini, renovabit imperium	et unxit principes in gente sua.
(17) 14 et lege domini iudicavit congregationem,	et vidit dominus Iacob,
15 et fide sua probatus est propheta.	(18) et cognitus est in verbis suis fidelis, quia vidit deum lucis.
(19) 16 et invocavit deum potentem	in oppugnando hostes circumstantes undique
16^{c} in oblatione viri inmaculati..	(20) 17 et intonuit e caelo dominus,
17^{b} et in sonitu magno auditam fecit vocem suam.	(21) 18 et contrivit principes Tyriorum, et omnes duces Filisthim.
(22) 19 et ante tempus vitae suae et saeculi	testimonium praebuit et in conspectu domini et Christi:
19^{c} pecunias et usque ad calciamenta ab omni carne non accepit,	et non accusabit illum homo.
(23) 20 et post hoc dormivit et notum fecit regi,	et ostendit illi finem vitae suae,
20^{c} et exaltavit vocem suam de terra	in prophetiam delere impietatem gentis.
XLVII. 1 post hoc surrexit Natham	prophetam in diebus David,
2 et quasi adeps separatus est a carne,	sic David a filiis Israhel.
3 cum leonibus lusit quasi cum agnis,	et in ursis similiter fecit sicut cum agnis ovium
4 in iuventute sua. (4) numquid non occidit gigantem,	et abstulit obprobrium de gente?
(5) 4^{c} in tollendo manum in saxo fundae	et deiecit exultationem Goliae.
(6) 5 nam invocavit deum potentem	et dedit in dexteram eius
5^{c} tollere hominem fortem in bello	et exaltare cornum gentis suae.
(7) 6 sic in decem milibus glorificavit eum,	et laudavit eum in benedictionibus domini
6^{c} in offerendo illi coronam gloriae.	(8) 7 contrivit enim inimicos undique,
7^{b} et extirpavit Filistim contrarios	usque in in hodiernum diem: contrivit cornum ipsorum usque in aeternum
(9) 8 in omni opere. dedit confessionem	sancto et excelso in verbo gloriae.

(10) 8^c de omni corde suo laudavit dominum,	et dilexit deum qui fecit illum,
	et dedit illi contra inimicos potentiam.
(11) 9 stare fecit cantores contra altare,	et in sono eorum dulces fecit modos.
(12) 10 et dedit in celebrationibus decus,	et ornavit tempora usque ad consummationem vitae,
10^c ut laudarent nomen sanctum domini	et amplificarent mane dei sanctitatem.
(13) 11 $\overline{\text{xps}}$ purgavit peccata ipsius	et exaltavit in aeternum cornum eius,
11^c et dedit illi testamentum regum	et sedem gloriae in Isrl.
(14) 12 post ipsum surrexit	filius sensatus, et propter illum deiecit omnem potentiam inimicorum.
(15) 13 Salomon imperavit in diebus pacis,	cui subiecit deus omnes hostes,
13^c ut conderet domum in nomine suo	et pararet sanctitatem in sempiternum.
14 quem ad modum eruditus est in iuventute sua	(16) et inpletus est quasi flumen sapientia
15 et terram retexit anima tua.	(17) et replesti in comparationibus enigmata:
16 ad insulas longe divulgatum est nomen tuum,	et dilectus in pace tua.
(18) 17 in cantilenis et proverbiis et comparationibus	et interpraetationibus miratae sunt terrae.
(19) 18 et in nomine domini	cui est cognomen deus Israhel
(20) 18^c collegisti quasi o . . . . um aurum,	et ut plumbum complesti argentum.
(21) 19 et inclinasti femora tua mulieribus:	potestatem habuisti in tuo corpore.
(22) 20 dedisti maculam in gloria tua,	et profanasti semen tuum
20^c inducere iracundiam ad liberos tuos,	et incitaris stultitiam tuam,
(23) 21 ut faceres imperium bipertitum,	et ex Efraim imperare imperium durum.
(24) 22 deus autem non relinquit misericordiam suam,	et non corrumpit neque delebit opera sua,
22^c neque perdet ab stirpe nepotes electi sui,	et semen eius qui diligit dominum, non corrumpit.
(25) 22^e dedit autem reliquum Iacob	et David de ipsa stirpe.
(26) 23 et finem habuit Salomon cum patribus suis.	(27) et relinquit post se de semine suo
23^c gentis stultitiam (28) et minutum prudentiam	Roboam, qui avertit gentem consilio suo.
	(29) 23^f et hieroboam filium Nabath qui peccare fecit Isrl.
23^g et dedit Efraim viam peccandi,	24 et plurima redundaverunt peccata ipsorum (30) valde,
24^b averterunt illos de terra sua.	(31) 25 et quaesivit omnem nequitiam usque dum perveniret ad illos defensio,
	et ab omnibus peccatis liberavit eos.
XLVIII. 1 et surrexit Helias propheta quasi ignis,	et verbum ipsius quasi fax ardebat.
2 qui induxit in illos famem,	et inritantes illum invidia sua pauci facti sunt:
non poterant enim sustinere praecepta domini.	
3 verbo domini continuit caelum,	et deiecit a se ignem terrae.
4 sic amplificatus est Helias in mirabilibus suis.	et quis potest similiter gloriari tibi?

5	qui sustulisti mortuum ab inferis		de sorte mortis in verbo domini dei.
6	qui deiecisti reges ad perniciem et confregisti facile potentiam ipsorum,	6b	et gloriosos de lecto suo.
7	qui audis in Sion iudicium		et in Coreb iudicia defensionis
8	qui ungis reges ad paenitentiam		et prophetas facis successores post te.
9	qui receptus es in turbidine ignis,		in curru equorum igneorum.
10	qui inscriptus es in indiciis temporum		lenire iracundiam domini,
10c	conciliare cor patris ad filium		et restituere tribus Iacob.
11	beati sunt qui te viderunt et in amicitia tua decorati sunt.	(12)	nam nos vita vivimus tantum,
	post mortem autem non erit tale nomen nostrum.		
(13) 12	Helias quidem in turbidine tectus est,		et in Helisaeo completus est spiritus eius:
12c	in diebus suis non pertimuit principem,		et potentiam nemo vincit illum.
(14) 13	nec superavit illum verbum aliquod,		et mortuum prophetavit corpus eius.
(15) 14	in vita sua fecit monstra,		et in morte mirabilia opera eius.
(16) 15	in omnibus istis non pęnituit populus,		et non recesserunt a peccatis suis,
15c	usque dum eiecti sunt de terra sua,		et dispersi sunt in omnem terram.
(17) 15e	et relicta est gens perpauca,		et princeps in domo David.
(18) 16	quidam ipsorum fecerunt quod placeret deo,		alii autem multa commisserunt peccata.
(19) 17	Ezechias munivit civitatem suam,		et induxit in medium ipsius aquam,
17c	et fodiit ferro rupem,		et aedificavit ad aquam puteum.
(20) 18	in diebus ipsius ascendit Sinnacerim,		et misit Rapsacen, et sustulit manum suam contra illos,
18c	et extulit manum suam in Sion,		et superbus factus est potentia sua.
(21) 19	tunc mota sunt corda et manus ipsorum,		et doluerunt quasi parturientes mulieres.
(22) 20	et invocaverunt dominum misericordem:		expandentes manus, extulerunt ad caelum,
20c	et sanctus dominus deus audivit cito vocem ipsorum.	(23)	non est commemoratus peccatorum illorum,
	neque dedit illos inimicis suis,	20d	sed purgabit illos in manu Esaię sancti prophetae.
(24) 21	subiecit castra Assyriorum,		et contrivit illos angelus dei.
(25) 22	nam fecit Ezechias quod placuit deo,		et fortiter ibit in via David patris sui,
22c	quam mandavit illi Esaias propheta,		magnus et fidelis in conspectu dei.
(26) 23	in diebus ipsius retro redit sol		et addidit regi vitam.
(27) 24	spiritu magno vidit ultima,		et consolatus est lugentes in Sion
25	usque in sempiternum. (28) ostendit futura		et abscondita ante quam evenirent.
XLIX. 1	memoriam Iosiae in compositionem odoris		factam, opus pigmentarii.
(2) 1c	in omni ore quasi mel indulcabitur eius memoria,		et ut musica in convivio vini.
(3) 2	ipse est directus divinitus in paenitentia gentis,		et tulit abominationes impietatis.
(4) 3	et gubernavit ad dominum cor ipsius,		et in diebus peccatorum corroboravit pietatem.
(5) 4	praeter David et Ezechiam et Iosiam		omnes peccatum commiserunt:
(6) 4c	nam reliquerunt legem potentem		reges Iuda, et contemserunt timorem dei.

(7) 5	dederunt enim regnum suum aliis,	et gloriam suam alienae genti.
(8) 6	incenderunt electam sanctitatis civitatem,	et desertas fecerunt vias ipsius
6c	in manu Hieremiae. (9) 7 nam male tractaverunt illum	qui a ventre matris consecratus est propheta
7c	evertere et eruere et perdere	et iterum aedificare et renobare.
(10) 8	Ezechiel qui vidit conspectum gloriae	quam ostendit illi in curru Cerubin.
(11) 9	nam commemoratus est inimicorum in imbri	bene facere illis qui ostenderunt rectas vias.
(12) 10	et duodecim prophetarum	ossa pullulent de loco suo:
10c	nam conroboraverunt Iacob	et redimerunt se in fide virtutis.
(13) 11	quo modo amplicemus Zorobabel?	nam et ipse quasi signum in dextera manu in Israhel.
(14) 12	et Hiesum filius Iosedec	qui in diebus suis aedificaverunt domum.

(Cambridge, recto.)

XXXIX.	15c [בש]ירות נֵבֶל ובלי מִיּנִי[1]	וכן תאמר בתרועה:	
	16 . . . אל כֻּלם טובים	וכֻל צורך בעתו ° יספיק:	לכל צרך ב׳ יספיקו:
	17c . . . . . . יעריך כ. [2]	ומוצא פיו אוצרו:	
	18 תחֿתֿ[יו][3] רצונו יצליח	ואין מעצור[4] לתשועתו:	
	19 מעשה כל בשר נגדו	ואי[ן] נסֿתר מנגד עיניו:	מבוהר
	20 מעולם ועד עולם יביט	[הי]ש[5] מספר לתשועתו:	
	20c אין קטן ומעט עמו	ואין נפלא וחזק ממנו:	
	21 אין לאמר זה למה זה	כי הכל לצרכו ° נבחֿר:	בעתו יגבר
	21c אין ל[אמר] זה רע מזה	כי הכל בעתו יגבר:	
	22 ברֿכות כיאר הציפה	וכנהר תבל ריותה:	
. . . [6]	23 כי זעמו גוים יוריש	ויהפך למלח משקה:	
[א]רחותיו: ישרים[7]	24 [ארחו]ת ° תמים יישרו	כן לזרים יסתֿוללו:	
	25 . . . ל[ט]וב חלק מראש	כן לרעים טוב וריֿע:	רע
	26 . . . . לחֿיי אדם מים	ואש וברזל ומלח:	
	26c . . . . חלב ודבש	דם ענב יצהר ובגד:	
	27 כל א[לה] ל[ט]ובים ייטיבו	כן לרעים לרעֿה נהפכו:	לורא
נביאו	28 יש ר[וחות] . . . . . . [נו]צרֿו	. . . . . . [הר]ים יעתיק[ו:]	
	28c	. . . .	

[1] There is no sign of a final ם or of an erasure. [2] The כ is fairly distinct: after it there is a blot which *may* conceal a ד (cf. 𝔊) or a ר; there is no sign of a third letter. [3] This word appears to have been altered by a second hand: the ח is clear, but the rest is not certain. [4] 1 Sam. 14, 6. [5] Job 25, 3. [6] There is a marginal note here, but illegible. [7] Perhaps לישרים.

XXXIX.	15c ܫܒܚܘ ܒܬܫܒܘܚܬܗ ܒܡܙܡܘܪܐ.	ܘܒܬܘܕܝܬܐ ܘܒܩܠܐ ܢܒܠܐ. ܘܗܟܢܐ ܐܡܪܘ.
	16 ܟܠܗܘܢ ܥܒܕܘܗܝ ܕܐܠܗܐ ܛܒܝܢ ܛܒܐ.	ܘܟܠܗܘܢ ܒܙܒܢܗܘܢ ܐܬܒܪܝܘ.
	21 ܘܠܝܬ ܕܢܐܡܪ ܗܢܐ ܠܡܢܐ ܗܢܐ.	ܡܛܠ ܕܟܠܗܘܢ، ܒܙܒܢܗܘܢ ܡܬܒܥܝܢ.
	21c ܘܠܝܬ ܕܢܐܡܪ ܕܗܢܐ ܒܝܫ ܗܢܐ ܛܒ.	ܡܛܠ ܕܟܠܗܘܢ، ܒܨܒܝܢܗ ܡܫܬܡܠܝܢ. ܒܡܠܬܗ ܩܡܘ ܡܝܐ ܘܒܡܠܬܗ ܗܘ ܦܬܚ ܠܗ.
	18 ܒܦܘܩܕܢܗ ܨܒܝܢܗ ܡܬܥܒܕ.	ܘܠܝܬ ܕܡܟܠܐ ܠܦܘܪܩܢܗ.
	19 ܥܒܕܝܗܘܢ ܕܟܠ ܒܢܝ ܒܣܪܐ ܠܩܘܒܠܗ.	ܘܠܝܬ ܕܛܫܐ ܡܢ ܩܕܡܘܗܝ.
	20c ܠܝܬ ܕܒܨܝܪ ܘܙܥܘܪ ܩܕܡܘܗܝ.	ܘܠܝܬ ܕܪܚܝܩ ܘܩܫܐ ܠܡܥܒܕܗ.
	22 ܒܘܪܟܬܗ ܐܝܟ ܢܗܪܐ ܪܘܐ.	ܘܐܝܟ ܢܗܪܐ ܠܬܒܝܠ ܡܫܩܝܐ.
	23 ܘܗܟܢܐ ܪܘܓܙܗ ܠܥܡܡܐ ܢܐܪܬ.	ܘܗܦܟ ܐܪܥܐ ܕܡܫܩܝܐ ܠܡܠܚܐ.
	24 ܐܘܪܚܬܗ ܕܙܕܝܩܐ ܬܪܝܨܢ ܩܕܡ ܐܠܗܐ.	ܘܐܦ ܠܥܘܠܐ ܗܟܢ ܡܬܬܩܠܢ.
	25 ܛܒܬܐ ܡܢ ܒܪܫܝܬ ܠܛܒܐ ܐܬܒܪܝ.	ܘܐܦ ܠܚܛܝܐ ܛܒܐ ܘܐܦ ܒܝܫܐ.
	26 ܪܫܐ ܕܟܠܗܘܢ ܚܫܚܬܐ ܕܡܬܒܥܝܢ ܠܚܝܐ ܕܒܢܝܢܫܐ ܡܝܐ	ܘܢܘܪܐ ܘܦܪܙܠܐ ܘܡܠܚܐ.
	26c ܘܚܠܒܐ ܘܕܒܫܐ. ܘܚܛܐ ܘܣܡܝܕܐ.	ܘܚܡܪܐ ܘܡܫܚܐ· ܘܠܒܘܫܐ ܘܟܠܗܘܢ.
	27 ܟܠܗܘܢ ܗܠܝܢ ܠܛܒܐ ܡܬܒܪܝܢ.	ܘܟܠܗܝܢ ܠܚܛܝܐ ܠܒܝܫܬܐ ܡܬܗܦܟܢ.
	28 ܐܝܬ ܪܘܚܐ ܕܠܕܝܢܐ ܐܬܒܪܝ.	ܘܒܪܘܓܙܗ ܛܘܪܐ ܥܩܪ.
	28c ܘܒܥܕܢ ܚܘܪܒܐ ܚܝܠܗܘܢ ܡܫܬܦܟ.	ܘܪܘܚܐ ܕܥܒܕ ܕܐܬܐ ܐܬܒܪܝ ܡܒܛܠܝܢ.

(Cambridge, recto.)

XXXIX. 15c [With s]ongs of the harp and of stringed instruments, — and thus with a shout shalt thou say:

16 All [the works of] God are good, — and he supplieth[1] every need in its season.

17c . . . . . appraise[2] . . . . . — and the utterance of his mouth is his treasure.

18 In [his] place[3] he maketh his pleasure to prosper, — and there is no restraint to his salvation.

19 The works of all flesh are before him, — and there is nothing hid from before his eyes.

20 He beholdeth from everlasting to everlasting: — [is there] limit to his salvation[4]?

20c There is nothing small or light with him, — and there is nothing too wonderful or hard for him.

21 None may say, Wherefore is this? — for all things are chosen for their uses[5].

21c None may [say], This is worse than that, — for all things prevail in their season.

22 He maketh his blessing[6] to overflow as the Nile, — and it saturateth the land like a river.

23 For[7] his wrath dispossesseth nations, — and he turneth a watered land into salt.

24 [The path]s of the perfect man[8] are plain, — so to strangers do they oppose themselves.

25 [Good things] he allotted to the [g]ood from the beginning, — so to the evil good and evil[9];

26 [The chief things] for the life of man are water, — and fire, and iron, and salt,

26c [Flour of wheat], milk, and honey, — the blood of the grape, fresh oil, and clothing.

27 All th[ese] bring good to the [g]ood, — so for the evil they are turned to evil[10];

28 There be w[inds which are fo]rmed[11] [for vengeance], — . . . [they] remove mountains.

28c . . . . — . . . .

[1] Marg. they supply. [2] So text, but the sense is obscure. [3] So the text appears to read, but? [4] ? understanding (לתבונתו), as Schechter (Ps. 147, 5). [5] Marg. prevail in their season. [6] Reading ברכתו for ברכות. [7] The margin is illegible: ? בזעמו by his wrath he. [8] Marg. His paths to the straightforward (supposing a ל to have been lost before ישרים), with a play on יישרו (are straight); cf. ver. 27. [9] So marg. [10] Marg. to loathsomeness (Num. 11, 20). [11] Marg. are created.

XXXIX. 15c ἐν ᾠδαῖς χειλέων καὶ ἐν κινύραις — καὶ οὕτως ἐρεῖτε ἐν ἐξομολογήσει

16 Τὰ ἔργα Κυρίου πάντα ὅτι καλὰ σφόδρα, — καὶ πᾶν πρόσταγμα ἐν καιρῷ αὐτοῦ ἔσται·

17 οὐκ ἔστιν εἰπεῖν Τί τοῦτο; εἰς τί τοῦτο; — πάντα γὰρ ἐν καιρῷ αὐτοῦ ζητηθήσεται.

17c ἐν λόγῳ αὐτοῦ ἔστη ὡς θιμωνιὰ ὕδωρ, — καὶ ἐν ῥήματι στόματος αὐτοῦ ἀποδοχεῖα ὑδάτων.

18 ἐν προστάγματι αὐτοῦ πᾶσα ἡ εὐδοκία, — καὶ οὐκ ἔστιν ὃς ἐλαττώσει τὸ σωτήριον αὐτοῦ.

19 ἔργα πάσης σαρκὸς ἐνώπιον αὐτοῦ, — καὶ οὐκ ἔστιν κρυβῆναι ἀπὸ τῶν ὀφθαλμῶν αὐτοῦ·

20 ἀπὸ τοῦ αἰῶνος εἰς τὸν αἰῶνα ἐπέβλεψεν,

20d καὶ οὐθέν ἐστιν θαυμάσιον ἐναντίον αὐτοῦ.

21 οὐκ ἔστιν εἰπεῖν Τί τοῦτο; εἰς τί τοῦτο; — πάντα γὰρ εἰς χρείας αὐτῶν ἔκτισται.

22 ἡ εὐλογία αὐτοῦ ὡς ποταμὸς ἐπεκάλυψεν, — καὶ ὡς κατακλυσμὸς ξηρὰν ἐμέθυσεν·

23 οὕτως ὀργὴν αὐτοῦ ἔθνη κληρονομήσει, — ὡς μετέστρεψεν ὕδατα εἰς ἅλμην.

24 αἱ ὁδοὶ αὐτοῦ τοῖς ὁσίοις εὐθεῖαι, — οὕτως τοῖς ἀνόμοις προσκόμματα·

25 ἀγαθὰ τοῖς ἀγαθοῖς ἔκτισται ἀπ' ἀρχῆς, — οὕτως τοῖς ἁμαρτωλοῖς κακά.

26 ἀρχὴ πάσης χρείας εἰς ζωὴν ἀνθρώπου, — ὕδωρ, πῦρ καὶ σίδηρος καὶ ἅλα καὶ σεμίδαλις,

26c πυρὸς καὶ μέλι καὶ γάλα, — αἷμα σταφυλῆς καὶ ἔλαιον καὶ ἱμάτιον·

27 ταῦτα πάντα τοῖς εὐσεβέσιν εἰς ἀγαθά, — οὕτως τοῖς ἁμαρτωλοῖς τραπήσεται εἰς κακά.

28 ἔστιν πνεύματα ἃ εἰς ἐκδίκησιν ἔκτισται, — καὶ ἐν θυμῷ αὐτῶν ἐστερέωσαν μάστιγας αὐτῶν·

28c καὶ ἐν καιρῷ συντελείας ἰσχὺν ἐκχεοῦσιν, — καὶ τὸν θυμὸν τοῦ ποιήσαντος αὐτοὺς κοπάσουσιν.

(Cambridge, verso.)

Margin	Verse	First half	Second half	Margin
	29	אש וברד רע ודבר	גם אלה למשפט נ[וצרו:]	להרים
	30	חית שן עקרב ופתן	וחרב נקמות להחרים . . .	חר[ב ע קמת סם
גם נבחרו	30c	כל אלה לצורכם נבראו	והמה באוצר ולעת יפקדו:	באוצרו לעת
	31	בצותו אותם ישישו	ובחקם לא ימרו פיו:	פיהו
	32	על כן מראש התיצבתי	והתבוננתי ובכתב הנחתי:	
הכל	33	מעשה אל כלם טובים	לכל צורך בעתו יספוק:	צורך[1]
אין מזה	34	אל לאמר זה רע מה זה	כי הכל בעתו יגביר:	יגבר
. פה	35	עתה בכל לב הרנינו	וברכו את שם הק[דוש:][2]	קדשו
עליון	XL. 1	עסק גדול חלק אל	ועול כבד על בני אדם:	
	1c	מיום צאתו מרחם אמו	עד יום שובו אל אם כל חי:	ארץ כ ח
. . .[3]	3	מיושב כסא לגבה	עד לשוב עפר ואפר:	לובש לבש
	4	מעוטה צניף וציץ	ועד עוטה שמלת . . .	עד עושה
	5	אך קנאה דאגה ופחד	אימת מות תחרה וריב:	מ הת וריב
	5c	ועת נוחו על משכבו	שינת לילה [ת]שנה . . .	ה ושנו
קה	6	מעט לריק כרגע ישקוט	ומבין בהל[ות] . . . ש:	
	6c	מעט טע מחזות[4] נפשו	כשריד ר . . . . . רודף:	
	7	. ר עורך מ . . . . קץ[5]	ומראו[5] . . . מנוח:	
	8	. . . .	. . . .	

[1] Perhaps צריך. [2] *Or* [ורים]הק. [3] Marginal note illegible. [4] The first three words of this line are written almost as one. [5] Only the tops of the letters are visible. צרך seems to have been retouched. Perhaps 7[a] was עד יעור משנתו ויקץ until he is aroused from his sleep and awaketh.

29	ܢܘܪܐ ܘܒܪܕܐ ܘܟܦܢܐ ܘܡܘܬܐ.	ܟܠܗܝܢ ܗܠܝܢ ܠܕܝܢܐ ܐܬܒܪܝ.
30	ܚܝܘܬܐ ܫܢܐ. ܘܥܩܪܒܐ ܘܚܘܘܬܐ	ܣܝܦܐ ܕܦܘܪܥܢܐ ܠܡܘܒܕܘ ܠܪܫܝܥܐ.
31	ܘܡܠܬܐ ܕܦܩܕ ܠܗܘܢ. ܚܕܝܢ.	ܘܟܠ ܦܘܩܕܢܘܗܝ. ܠܐ ܡܥܒܪܝܢ ܡܠܬܗ.
32	ܡܛܠ ܕܡܢ ܒܪܫܝܬ ܐܬܒܪܝܘ.	ܐܬܒܩܝܬ ܒܚܘܫܒܐ ܘܒܟܬܒܐ ܐܘܕܥܬ ܟܠܗܘܢ ܗܠܝܢ.
33	ܘܟܠܗܘܢ ܥܒܕܘܗܝ ܛܒܝܢ.	ܘܟܠ ܨܒܘ ܒܥܕܢܗ ܐܬܒܪܝܬ.
34	ܘܠܝܬ ܕܢܐܡܪ ܗܢܐ ܒܝܫ ܡܢ ܗܢܐ.	ܡܛܠ ܕܟܠ ܒܙܒܢܗ. ܡܫܬܟܚ ܒܕܘܟܬܗ. ܘܒܟܠ ܐܒܢܘܗܝ. ܡܫܬܒܚܝܢ.
35	ܡܛܠ ܒܟܠܗ ܠܒܟܘܢ ܫܒܚܘ ܠܐܠܗܐ!	ܘܒܪܟܘ ܠܫܡܗ.
XL. 1	ܙܘܥܐ ܪܘܪܒܐ ܒܪܐ ܐܠܗܐ.	ܘܢܝܪܐ ܝܩܝܪܐ ܥܠ ܒܢܝ ܐܢܫܐ.
1c	ܡܢ ܝܘܡܐ ܕܢܦܩܘ ܡܢ ܟܪܣܐ ܕܐܡܗܘܢ:	ܘܥܕܡܐ ܕܗܦܟܝܢ ܠܐܪܥܐ ܕܚܝܐ.
2	ܠܡܚܫܒܬܗܘܢ ܘܠܪܢܝܐ ܕܠܒܗܘܢ	ܘܣܒܪܐ ܕܡܣܟܝܢܗܘܢ. ܥܕܡܐ ܠܝܘܡܐ ܕܡܘܬܗܘܢ.
3	ܡܢ ܝܬܒܝ ܟܘܪܣܘܬܐ ܕܡܠܟܐ	ܘܥܕܡܐ ܠܝܬܒܝ ܥܦܪܐ ܘܩܛܡܐ.
4	ܡܢ ܠܒܫܝ ܬܓܐ ܘܥܕܡܐ	ܠܐܝܠܝܢ ܕܠܒܝܫܝܢ ܠܒܘܫܐ ܕܡܣܟܢܘܬܐ.
5	ܚܣܡܐ ܘܚܪܝܢܐ ܘܙܝܥܐ.	ܘܕܚܠܬܐ ܘܕܚܠܬ ܡܘܬܐ. ܘܚܪܝܢܐ ܘܚܣܡܐ.
5c	ܘܒܥܕܢܐ ܕܡܬܢܝܚ ܥܠ ܡܫܟܒܗܘܢ.	ܫܢܬܐ ܕܠܠܝܐ ܫܢܝܐ ܠܗܘܢ.
6c	ܘܡܬܒܥܬܝܢ ܒܚܠܡܐ ܕܠܠܝܐ.	ܐܝܟ ܥܒܕܐ ܕܥܪܩ ܡܢ ܩܕܡ ܪܕܘܦܐ.
7	ܐܝܟ ܕܚܠܡܐ ܚܠܡܘ. ܡܬܬܥܝܪ	ܘܚܙܐ ܕܠܝܬ ܠܗ ܡܕܡ.
8	ܥܡ ܟܠܗܘܢ ܒܢܝ ܒܣܪܐ ܕܥܡܗܘܢ ܒܥܝܪܐ.	ܘܥܠ ܪܫܝܥܐ ܫܒܥ ܥܠܝܗܘܢ.

(Cambridge, verso.)

29 Fire and hail, evil[1] and pestilence, these also are [formed] for judgement.
30 Beast of tooth, scorpion and cobra, and a sword of vengeance[2] to ban[3] [the wicked].
30c All these are created[4] for their uses, and they are in his treasure-house[5], against the time when they are required.
31 When he commandeth them they rejoice, and in their prescribed tasks they rebel not against his [word.
32 Therefore from the beginning I took my stand, and I considered, and set it down in writing:
33 All the works of God are good; he sufficeth for[6] every need[7] in its season.
34 None[8] may say, This is evil, What is this[8]? for he maketh all things to prevail[9] in their season.
35 Now with all (your) heart[10] sing aloud, and bless the name of the H[oly One[11]].
XL. 1 Great occupation hath God[12] allotted, and a heavy yoke is upon the sons of men;
1c From the day of his coming forth from his mother's womb, until the day of his returning to the mother[13] of all living;
3 From him that sitteth loftily on a throne, even unto him that is clothed[8] in dust and ashes.
4 From him that weareth a diadem and (priestly) plate[14], even unto him that weareth[16] a mantle [of poverty]:
5 Anger[15], jealousy, anxiety, and fear, the terror of death, strife[8], and contention[8]:
5c And in the time when he resteth upon his bed, the sleep of night changeth [his thought[8]];
6 A little . . . . for a moment he is quiet, and from the midst of terror[s he is perturbed[17]?];
6c . . . . . . from the vision of his soul, (he is) as a fugitive [hurrying on before] the pursuer.
7 . . . . [aw]aketh . . . visions (?) . . . rest.
8 . . . . [18]

[1] Read probably רעב famine, as 𝔊 𝔖. [2] Marg. an avenging sword. [3] Marg. to lift up (?). [4] Marg. These also are chosen. [5] So marg. [6] Read probably יפיק supplieth, as 39, 16. [7] Marg. *perhaps*, needy person. [8] Marg. This is worse than that. [9] Marg. all things prevail. [10] Marg. mouth. [11] *Or* the H[oly] name. Marg. His Holy name. [12] Marg. the Most High. [13] Marg. land, as 𝔖. [14] Exod. 28, 36. [15] Marg. maketh. [16] אף for אך. [17] Reading ישֻׁשׁ; or ? ירגש is disquieted. [18] Marg. (probably referring to this line), even to (?) all . . . . . yea, and with . . .

29 πῦρ καὶ χάλαζα καὶ λιμὸς καὶ θάνατος, πάντα ταῦτα εἰς ἐκδίκησιν ἔκτισται·
30 θηρίων ὀδόντες καὶ σκορπίοι καὶ ἔχεις καὶ ῥομφαία ἐκδικοῦσα εἰς ὄλεθρον ἀσεβεῖς,
30d καὶ ἐπὶ τῆς γῆς εἰς χρείας ἑτοιμασθήσονται,
31 ἐν τῇ ἐντολῇ αὐτοῦ εὐφρανθήσονται, καὶ ἐν τοῖς καιροῖς αὐτῶν οὐ παραβήσονται λόγον.
32 διὰ τοῦτο ἐξ ἀρχῆς ἐστηρίχθην καὶ διενοήθην καὶ ἐν γραφῇ ἀφῆκα.
33 τὰ ἔργα Κυρίου πάντα ἀγαθά, καὶ πᾶσαν χρείαν ἐν ὥρᾳ αὐτῆς χορηγήσει·
34 καὶ οὐκ ἔστιν εἰπεῖν Τοῦτο τούτου πονηρότερον, πάντα γὰρ ἐν καιρῷ εὐδοκιμηθήσεται.
35 καὶ νῦν ἐν πάσῃ καρδίᾳ καὶ στόματι ὑμνήσατε, καὶ εὐλογήσατε τὸ ὄνομα Κυρίου.
XL. 1 Ἀσχολία μεγάλη ἔκτισται παντὶ ἀνθρώπῳ, καὶ ζυγὸς βαρὺς ἐπὶ υἱοὺς Ἀδάμ,
1c ἀφ' ἡμέρας ἐξόδου ἐκ γαστρὸς μητρὸς αὐτῶν ἕως ἡμέρας ἐπὶ ταφῇ εἰς μητέρα πάντων·
2 τοὺς διαλογισμοὺς αὐτῶν καὶ φόβον καρδίας, ἐπίνοια προσδοκίας, ἡμέρα τελευτῆς.
3 ἀπὸ καθημένου ἐπὶ θρόνου ἐν δόξῃ καὶ ἕως τεταπεινωμένου ἐν γῇ καὶ σποδῷ,
4 ἀπὸ φοροῦντος ὑάκινθον καὶ στέφανον καὶ ἕως περιβαλλομένου ὠμόλινον·
5 θυμὸς καὶ ζῆλος καὶ ταραχὴ καὶ σάλος καὶ φόβος θανάτου καὶ μηνίαμα καὶ ἔρις.
5c καὶ ἐν καιρῷ ἀναπαύσεως ἐπὶ κοίτης ὕπνος νυκτὸς ἀλλοιοῖ γνῶσιν αὐτοῦ·
6 ὀλίγον ὡς οὐδὲν ἐν ἀναπαύσει, καὶ ἀπ' ἐκείνου ἐν ὕπνοις ὡς ἐν ἡμέρᾳ σκοπιᾶς·
6c τεθορυβημένος ἐν ὁράσει καρδίας αὐτοῦ, ὡς ἐκπεφευγὼς ἀπὸ προσώπου πολέμου·
7 ἐν καιρῷ σωτηρίας αὐτοῦ ἐξηγέρθη, καὶ ἀποθαυμάζων εἰς οὐδένα φόβον.
8 μετὰ πάσης σαρκὸς ἀπὸ ἀνθρώπου ἕως κτήνους, καὶ ἐπὶ ἁμαρτωλῶν ἑπταπλάσια πρὸς ταῦτα·

(Oxford, fol. 1 recto.)

	9 [דב]ר ודם חרחר וחרב[1]	שד ושבר רעה ומו[ת:]		
	10 על רשע נבראה רעה	ובעבור המוש כלה:	ובעבורו ת׳ רעה:	בגשמם
	11 כל מארץ אל ארץ ישוב	ואשר ממרום אל מרום:	וימ׳	
חל מחיל	13 מחול אל חול כנחל איתן	ומאפיק אדיר בחזיז קולות[2]:	וכאפיק	
עם שאתו	14 עם עם שאתו כפים יגילו	כי פתאם לנצח יתם:		
	15 נוצר מחמס לא ינקה	כי שורש חנף על שן סלע[3]:		
	16 כקרדמות על גפת נחל	מפני כל מטר נדעכו[4]:	לפני נדעכו:	
	17 וחסד לעולם לא ימוט	וצדקה לעד תכון:		
יותר שכל	18 חיי יין ושכר ימתקו	ומשניהם מוצא אוצר:	כימה	
	19 ילד ועיר יעמידו שם	ומשניהם מוצא חכמה:		
	19c שגר[5] ונטע יפריחו שם	ומשניהם אשה נחשקת:		
	20 [יי]ן ושכר יעליצו לב	ומשניהם אהבת דודים:		
חליל	21 [ח]ל[ו]ל ונבל יעריבו שיר	ומשניהם לשון ברה:		
	22 . . . . . . [יח]מידו עין	ומשניהם צמחי שדה:	שדי	
	23 . . . . [ע]ת ינהגו	ומשניהם אשה משכלת:		
	24 אח . . . . ת צרה	ומשניהם צדק מצלת:	צדקה	
	25 זהב וכס[ף] . . . . . [רג]ל	ומש[ניהם]		
	26 חיל וכח יגב[יהו] לב	ומשניה[ם י]ראת אלהים:		

נצר חמס לא יכה בו · ושורש חנף על שן צור:

כל ימי עני רעים · בן סירא אומר אף בלילות
בשפל גגים גגו · במרום הרים כרמו:
ממטר גגים לגגו מעפר כרמו לכרמים:
מי כאביר כו אין טא ביתשמתי אצל
בוד אלא נאקל [כי] נגפת

[1] Deut. 28, 22 (חֶרֶב). [2] Job 38, 25. [3] Job 39, 28. [4] Job 6, 17. [5] Exod. 13, 12, &c.

9
10
11 ܟܠ ܡܕܡ ܕܡܢ ܐܪܥܐ ܗܘ ܠܐܪܥܐ ܗܦܟ. ܘܕܡܢ ܪܘܡܐ ܠܪܘܡܐ.
12 ܟܠ ܡܢ ܕܢܣܒ ܫܘܚܕܐ ܢܬܚܒܠ. ܘܡܗܝܡܢ ܒܥܠܡܐ ܗܘ ܢܩܘܡ ܠܥܠܡܝܢ.
13 ܢܟܣܐ ܕܥܘܠܐ ܐܝܟ ܢܚܠܐ ܢܬܝܒܫܘܢ. ܘܐܝܟ ܢܗܘܪܐ ܕܡܛܪܐ ܡܢ ܥܢܢܐ ܕܩܠܐ.
14 ܡܢ ܩܕܡ ܟܐܦܐ ܢܬܓܠܘܢ.
15 ܘܣܘܟܐ ܠܐܝܠܢܐ ܕܥܘܠܐ ܠܐ ܢܗܘܐ. ܥܒܕܘܗܝ ܐܝܟ ܫܪܫܐ ܕܥܠ ܫܢܐ ܕܫܘܥܐ
16 ܘܐܝܟ ܣܟܠܬܐ ܕܥܠ ܟܐܦܐ ܕܢܚܠܐ. ܕܡܢ ܟܠ ܡܛܪ ܢܚܫܠ.
17 ܘܛܝܒܘܬܐ ܕܟܐܢܐ ܠܥܠܡ ܡܫܬܡܠܝܐ. ܘܙܕܩܬܐ ܠܥܠܡ ܡܫܬܡܠܝܐ.
18b ܘܡܫܬܥܒܕܝܢ ܠܗܘܢ ܐܝܟ ܥܒܕܐ ܘܡܫܡܫܢ ܡܫܡܫܢܐ.
19 ܒܢܝܐ ܘܡܕܝܢܬܐ ܢܩܝܡܘܢ ܫܡܐ. ܘܡܢ ܬܪܝܗܘܢ ܡܢ ܕܡܫܟܚ ܚܟܡܬܐ.
19c ܚܟܡܬܐ ܘܡܪܕܘܬܐ ܡܩܝܡܢ ܫܡܐ. ܘܡܢ ܬܪܝܗܘܢ ܐܢܬܬܐ ܡܫܟܠܬܐ.
20 ܚܡܪܐ ܥܬܝܩܐ ܡܚܕܐ ܠܒܐ. ܘܛܒ ܡܢܗ ܚܘܒܐ ܕܪܚܡܐ.
21 ܙܡܪܐ ܘܩܝܬܪܐ ܡܒܣܡܝܢ ܙܡܪܐ. ܘܡܢ ܬܪܝܗܘܢ ܠܫܢܐ ܕܟܝܐ.
22 ܫܘܦܪܐ ܘܚܘܙܝܐ ܪܓܬܐ ܕܥܝܢܐ. ܘܡܢ ܬܪܝܗܘܢ ܨܡܚܐ ܕܚܩܠܐ.
23 ܪܚܡܐ ܘܚܒܪܐ ܒܥܕܢܐ ܡܬܕܒܪܝܢ. ܘܡܢ ܬܪܝܗܘܢ ܐܢܬܬܐ ܡܫܟܠܬܐ.
24 ܐܚܐ ܘܡܥܕܪܢܐ ܒܥܕܢܐ ܕܐܘܠܨܢܐ. ܘܡܢ ܬܪܝܗܘܢ ܙܕܩܬܐ ܦܪܩܐ.
25 ܕܗܒܐ ܘܣܐܡܐ ܡܩܝܡܝܢ ܪܓܠܐ. ܘܡܢ ܬܪܝܗܘܢ ܡܠܟܐ ܛܒܐ.
26 ܚܝܠܐ ܘܥܘܫܢܐ ܡܪܝܡܝܢ ܠܒܐ. ܘܡܢ ܬܪܝܗܘܢ ܕܚܠܬܗ ܕܐܠܗܐ.

(Oxford, fol. 1 recto.)

9 [Pestile]nce and bloodshed, fever and drought, devastation and destruction, evil and death.
10 Against the wicked, evil is created, and because of him[1] ruin[2] departeth [not?[3]].
11 All things that are from the earth return to the earth, and that which is[4] from the height (returneth) to the height.
13 Riches born of (?) riches[1] are like an ever-flowing [stream, and as[1] a mighty water-course in the flashing of [thunder:
14 With his lifting up of (his) hands[5] men rejoice, for suddenly he perisheth for ever.
15 The branch of violence[1] shall not be unpunished, for the root of the godless is on the point of a crag.
16 Like axes[6] (?) upon the bank of a stream, before[1] all rain[7] they are extinguished.
17 But kindness shall never be moved, and righteousness (*or* almsgiving) shall be established [for ever.
18 A life of wine[8] and strong drink is sweet, but he that findeth a treasure is above them both.
19 A child and a city establish a name, but he that findeth wisdom is above them both.
19^c Offspring (of cattle) and planting make a name to flourish, but a woman beloved is above them both.
20 Wine and strong drink cause the heart to exult, but the love of lovers is above them both.
21 Pipe and harp make sweet the song, but a sincere tongue is above them both.
22 [Grace and beauty] delight the eye, but the growing things of the field are above them both.
23 [A friend and a partner] behave [as occasion requires], but a prudent wife is above them both.
24 A brother [and a helper are for a ti]me of adversity, but righteousness (*or* almsgiving) delivereth above [them both.
25 Gold and silver [make the foot stand sure]: but [good counsel[9]] is above them both.
26 Riches and strength lift up the heart, but the fear of God is above them both.

[1] So marg. [2] Marg. evil. [3] Cf. Prov. 17, 13. [4] Marg. and there is that (?). [5] So marg.; but the sense is obscure, and the text doubtless corrupt. [6] ? (reed-)stalks (קרומיות ?). [7] ? all grass (𝔊 𝔖); cf. Job 8, 12. [8] Marg. the life of him that excels in prudence. At 40, 22 the margin has: 'All the days of the poor are evil. Ben Sira says, At night also. His roof is the lowest of roofs, and his vineyard is in the height of the mountains: the rain of other roofs falls on his roof, and the earth of his vineyard falls on other vineyards.' (Then in Persian:) می مانید کو این نا بینوسختی اصل بود ایلا ناقول [می] گوفت 'It is probable that this was not in the original copy, but it is used as a proverb.' (See the list of proverbs, p. xxviii). [9] So 𝔊(B^{ab} ℵ A C) 𝔖.

9 θάνατος καὶ αἷμα καὶ ἔρις καὶ ῥομφαία,
10 ἐπὶ τοὺς ἀνόμους ἐκτίσθη ταῦτα πάντα, καὶ δι' αὐτοὺς ἐγένετο ὁ κατακλυσμός.
11 πάντα ὅσα ἀπὸ γῆς εἰς γῆν ἀναστρέφει, καὶ ἀπὸ ὑδάτων εἰς θάλασσαν ἀνακάμπτει.
12 πᾶν δῶρον καὶ ἀδικία ἐξαλειφθήσεται, καὶ πίστις εἰς τὸν αἰῶνα στήσεται.
13 χρήματα ἀδίκων ὡς ποταμὸς ξηρανθήσεται, καὶ ὡς βροντὴ μεγάλη ἐν ὑετῷ ἐξηχήσει·
14 ἐν τῷ ἀνοῖξαι αὐτὸν χεῖρας εὐφρανθήσεται, οὕτως οἱ παραβαίνοντες εἰς συντέλειαν ἐκλείψουσιν.
15 ἔκγονα ἀσεβῶν οὐ πληθυνεῖ κλάδους, καὶ ῥίζαι ἀκάθαρτοι ἐπ' ἀκροτόμου πέτρας·
16 ἄχει ἐπὶ παντὸς ὕδατος καὶ χείλους ποταμοῦ πρὸ παντὸς χόρτου ἐκτιλήσεται.
17 χάρις ὡς παράδεισος ἐν εὐλογίαις, καὶ ἐλεημοσύνη εἰς τὸν αἰῶνα διαμενεῖ.
18 ζωὴ αὐτάρκους ἐργάτου γλυκανθήσεται, καὶ ὑπὲρ ἀμφότερα ὁ εὑρίσκων θησαυρόν.
19 τέκνα καὶ οἰκοδομὴ πόλεως στηρίζουσιν ὄνομα,
19^d καὶ ὑπὲρ ἀμφότερα γυνὴ ἄμωμος λογίζεται.
20 οἶνος καὶ μουσικὰ εὐφραίνουσιν καρδίαν, καὶ ὑπὲρ ἀμφότερα ἀγάπησις σοφίας.
21 αὐλὸς καὶ ψαλτήριον ἡδύνουσιν μέλη, καὶ ὑπὲρ ἀμφότερα γλῶσσα ἡδεῖα.
22 χάριν καὶ κάλλος ἐπιθυμήσει ὁ ὀφθαλμός σου, καὶ ὑπὲρ ἀμφότερα χλόην σπόρου.
23 φίλος καὶ ἑταῖρος εἰς καιρὸν ἀπαντῶντες, καὶ ὑπὲρ ἀμφότερα γυνὴ μετὰ ἀνδρός.
24 ἀδελφοὶ καὶ βοήθεια εἰς καιρὸν θλίψεως, καὶ ὑπὲρ ἀμφότερα ἐλεημοσύνη ῥύσεται.
25 χρυσίον καὶ ἀργύριον ἐπιστήσουσιν πόδα, καὶ ὑπὲρ ἀμφότερα γυνὴ εὐδοκιμεῖται.
26 χρήματα καὶ ἰσχὺς ἀνυψώσουσιν καρδίαν, καὶ ὑπὲρ ἀμφότερα φόβος Κυρίου·

(fol. 1 verso.)

	26c אין [ב]יראת ײ מחסור	ואין לבקש עמה [מטמ]ון[1]:	
	27 יראת אלהים כעדן ברכה	וכן כל כבוד חפתה[2]:	
בני	28 מני חיי מתן אל תחי	טוב נאסף ממסתולל:	
	29 איש משגיח על שלחן זר	אין חייו למנות חיים:	
מיגל נפשו מבימי ובר	29c מעגל נפש ממטעמו	לאיש יודע סוד מעים:	יסור מיעים
כו נפשות המהיק	30 לאיש עז[3] נפש תמתיק שאלה	ובקרבו תבער כמו אש:	כאש בוערה
הוי	XLI. 1 חיים למות מה [מ]ר זכרך	לאיש שוק[ט] על מכונתו:	
	1c איש שליו ומצליח בכל	ועוד ב[ו ח]יל לקבל תענוג:	
חוק	2 האח למות כי טוב חקיך	לאיש אונים[4] וחסר עצמה:	
חוק חוקי ונוקש	2c איש כושל ינקש בכל	סרב ואבד תקוה:	
	3 אל תפחד ממות חוקיך	זכר כי ראשנים ואחרנ[ים] עמך:	
	4 זה חלק כל בשר מאל[5]	ומה תמאס בתורת עלי[ו]:	
כי בן נמאס דבת שרים	4c לאלף שנים מאה ועשר	איש תוכחות בש[או]ל:	אין חיים:
	5 נין נמאס דבר רעים[6]	ונכד[7] אויל . . . . ע:	
מבין זול	6 מבן עול ממשלת רע	. . זרע[ו]	
	7 אב רשע יקו[ב י]לד	כי [בג]לל[ו] . . .	
	8 . . . ל	. . . . [על]יון:	
הפרו	9 אם ת . . . . . . ידי אסון	. . . [ת]ולידו לאנחה:	

איש כושל ונוקש בכל אפס המראה ואבד תקוה:
איש נוקש ומושל בכל אפס המראה ואבד תקוה:
אב רשע יקוב ילד כי בגללו היו בוז:

[1] Prov. 2, 4. [2] Is. 4, 5. [3] Is. 56, 11. [4] Is. 40, 26. [5] Job 20, 29. [6] רוים is written above רעים. [7] Gen. 21, 23. Job 18, 19. Is. 14, 22. [8] So MS. (ס).

26c ܠܝܬ ܒܕܚܠܬܗ ܕܐܠܗܐ ܚܘܣܪܢܐ. ܘܠܝܬ ܠܡܒܥܐ ܥܡܗ ܣܘܥܪܢܐ.
ܘܕܚܠܬܗ ܕܐܠܗܐ ܥܠ ܟܠ ܡܕܡ ܐܬܝܬܪܬ. ܐܣܘܪܗ ܒܪ̈ܬܐ ܘܠܐ ܡܫܬܪܐ. ܡܛܠ ܕܠܝܬ ܐܣܘܪܗ.
27 ܕܚܠܬܗ ܕܐܠܗܐ ܒܓܢܬܐ ܡܒܪܟܬܐ. ܘܛܒܐ ܡܢ ܟܠ ܐܢܫ ܗܘ ܡܫܬܡܠܝܐ.
28 ܒܪܝ ܚܝܐ ܕܫܐܠܬܐ ܚܝܝ. ܠܐ ܬܚܝܘܗܝ. ܘܠܐ ܬܗܘܐ ܠܟ ܠܡܫܠܡܘ. ܐܠܐ ܗܘܝ ܠܟ ܠܡܢܝܚܘ.
29 ܓܒܪܐ ܕܚܐܪ ܥܠ ܦܬܘܪܐ ܕܐܚܪܢܐ. ܠܐ ܐܝܬ ܕܡܬܚܫܒ ܐܝܟ ܕܚܝܐ ܗܘ.
29c ܛܒܐ ܢܦܫܗ ܦܡܗ ܕܐܟܠ ܡܓܠܐ. ܘܠܓܒܪܐ ܪܕܐ ܗܕܝܢ ܥܠܠ ܐܝܟ ܕܩܕܚܐ.
30 ܒܦܘܡܗ ܕܚܨܝܦܐ ܡܒܣܡ ܫܐܠܬܗ. ܘܐܝܟ ܢܘܪܐ ܝܩܕܐ ܒܓܘܗ.
XLI. 1 ܗܐ ܡܘܬܐ ܡܐ ܒܣܡ ܐܢܬ. ܠܓܒܪܐ ܕܫܠܝܐ ܘܫܬܐ ܥܠ ܢܩܫܘܗܝ.
1c ܓܒܪܐ ܕܫܠܝܢ ܘܡܨܠܚ ܒܟܠ ܚܝܘܗܝ. ܘܠܘܬ ܐܝܬ ܒܗ ܚܝܠܐ ܠܡܩܒܠܘ ܦܘܢܩܐ.
2 ܐܘ ܡܘܬܐ ܡܐ ܛܒ ܐܢܬ. ܠܓܒܪܐ ܕܐܟܝܪ ܘܚܣܝܪ ܢܦܫ.
2c ܓܒܪܐ ܟܦܝܦܐ ܘܡܬܬܩܠ ܒܟܠ ܚܝܝ. ܘܚܣܝܪ ܡܣܒܪܢܘܬܐ ܘܠܝܬ ܒܗ ܚܝܠܐ ܠܡܬܚܘܣ.
3 ܠܐ ܬܕܚܠ ܡܢ ܡܘܬܐ ܡܛܠ ܕܗܘܝܘ ܡܢܬܟ. ܐܬܕܟܪ ܕܩܕܡܝܐ ܘܐܚܪܝܐ ܥܡܟ ܐܢܘܢ.
4 ܡܛܠ ܕܗܕܐ ܗܝ ܚܘܠܩܐ ܕܟܠܗܘܢ ܒܢܝܢܫܐ ܡܢ ܐܠܗܐ.

5 ܐܝܟܐ ܡܫܡܥܬܐ ܠܡܠܬܐ ܕܚܛܝܐ. ܘܡܬܚܠܦܐ ܕܗܘ ܒܢ̈ܝ ܠܥܠܡܐ ܕܚܛܝܐ.
6 ܡܢ ܒܪܐ ܚܛܝܐ ܬܐܒܕ ܡܠܟܘܬܐ. ܘܥܡ ܙܪܥܗ ܢܬܡܪ ܚܘܣܪܢܐ.
7 ܠܐܒܐ ܚܛܝܐ ܒܢܘܗܝ ܩܒܠܝ ܒܛܠܘܗܝ. ܕܡܛܠܬܗ ܗܘܘ ܒܙܚܐ ܒܥܠܡܐ.
8 ܘܝ ܠܟܘܢ ܐܢܫܐ ܚܛܝܐ. ܕܫܒܩܬܘܢ ܢܡܘܣܗ ܕܥܠܝܐ ܒܪܢܫܐ ܕܡܬܩܪܐ.

(fol. 1 verso.)

26c In the fear of the Lord there is no want, and it needeth not to seek for [treasure] with it.
27 The fear of God is as an Eden of blessing, and so[1] all glory is its canopy.
28 My son[2], live not a life that subsists on giving: better is he that is taken away (in death) than he that is importunate.
29 A man that looketh at the table of a stranger, his life is not to be numbered as a life:
29c His dainties[3] are a loathing[4] of the soul; to a man that hath understanding (they are as) pain[5] of the bowels.
30 Begging is sweet to the greedy man, but in his inward parts it burneth as fire[6].
XLI. 1 Ah[6] Death! how [bit]ter is the remembrance of thee to a man that liveth qui[etly] in his place;
1c To a man that is at ease and prospereth in all things, and that hath yet strength to receive pleasure.
2 Aha Death! for acceptable (*lit.* good) is thy sentence unto him that hath no[6] might, and lacketh strength;
2c (To) the man that stumbleth and striketh against all things, who loveth contradiction and hath lost hope[7].
3 Be not afraid of death, (which is) thy sentence, remember that they which went before and they which come after (will be) with thee.
4 This is the portion of all flesh from God, and why dost thou refuse the law of the Most High?
4c Whether it be for a thousand years, or an hundred, or ten, there are no[2] corrections[8] in Sh[eo]l.
5 A reprobate progeny is a byword[2] of the evil[9], and the offspring of the foolish is [... of the wic]ked.
6 From an unrighteous son[10] cometh a rule of evil, [and with his] seed [abideth want[11]].
7 An ungodly father a [chi]l[d] doth curse, because [on his] acc[ount he suffereth reproach].
8 [Woe] to [you, ye wicked, because ye have forsaken the law of the Most] High.
9 If [ye increase[12], it shall be into] the hands of bodily mishap; [and if ye] beget, it shall be for sighing.

[1] ? over (as 𝔊 𝔖 and Is. 4, 5). [2] So marg. [3] Marg. bestowed dainties. [4] Reading מְגֹאָל for מגעל. [5] Marg. as burning fire. [6] אֵין for איש (Is. 40, 26). [7] Marg. (To) the man that stumbleth and striketh against all things; who hath no sight and hath lost hope. (To) the man that striketh and stumbleth (l. כושל for כישל) against all things; who hath no sight and hath lost hope. [8] Marg. corrections for life. [9] Marg. of cities. [10] Marg. from among the uncircumcised (*or* from an uncircumcised son). [11] So 𝔖 (חֹסֶר): 𝔊 reproach (חֶסֶד). [12] Marg. are fruitful.

26c οὐκ ἔστιν φόβῳ Κυρίου ἐλάττωσις, καὶ οὐκ ἔστιν ἐπιζητῆσαι ἐν αὐτῷ βοήθειαν·
27 φόβος Κυρίου ὡς παράδεισος εὐλογίας, καὶ ὑπὲρ πᾶσαν δόξαν ἐκάλυψαν αὐτόν.
28 τέκνον, ζωὴν ἐπαιτήσεως μὴ βιώσῃς· κρεῖσσον ἀποθανεῖν ἢ ἐπαιτεῖν.
29 ἀνὴρ βλέπων εἰς τράπεζαν ἀλλοτρίαν, οὐκ ἔστιν αὐτοῦ ὁ βίος ἐν λογισμῷ ζωῆς, [τρίοις·
29c ἀλισγήσει τὴν ψυχὴν αὐτοῦ ἐν ἐδέσμασιν ἀλλο- ἀνὴρ δὲ ἐπιστήμων καὶ πεπαιδευμένος φυλάξεται.
30 ἐν στόματι ἀναιδοῦς γλυκανθήσεται ἐπαίτησις, καὶ ἐν κοιλίᾳ αὐτοῦ πῦρ καήσεται.
XLI. 1 Ὦ θάνατε, ὡς πικρόν σου τὸ μνημόσυνόν ἐστιν ἀνθρώπῳ εἰρηνεύοντι ἐν τοῖς ὑπάρχουσιν αὐτοῦ,
1c ἀνδρὶ ἀπερισπάστῳ καὶ εὐοδουμένῳ ἐν πᾶσιν καὶ ἔτι ἰσχύοντι ἐπιδέξασθαι τροφήν.
2 ὦ θάνατε, καλόν σου τὸ κρίμα ἐστὶν ἀνθρώπῳ ἐπιδεομένῳ καὶ ἐλασσουμένῳ ἰσχύι,
2c ἐσχατογήρῳ καὶ περισπωμένῳ περὶ πάντων, καὶ ἀπειθοῦντι καὶ ἀπολωλεκότι ὑπομονήν.
3 μὴ εὐλαβοῦ κρίμα θανάτου, μνήσθητι προτέρων σου καὶ ἐσχάτων·
4 τοῦτο τὸ κρίμα παρὰ Κυρίου πάσῃ σαρκί, καὶ τί ἀπαναίνῃ ἐν εὐδοκίᾳ Ὑψίστου;
4c εἴτε δέκα εἴτε ἑκατὸν εἴτε χίλια ἔτη, οὐκ ἔστιν ἐν ᾅδου ἐλεγμὸς ζωῆς.
5 τέκνα βδελυκτὰ γίνεται τέκνα ἁμαρτωλῶν, καὶ συναναστρεφόμενα παροικίαις ἀσεβῶν·
6 τέκνων ἁμαρτωλῶν ἀπολεῖται κληρονομία, καὶ μετὰ τοῦ σπέρματος αὐτῶν ἐνδελεχιεῖ ὄνειδος.
7 πατρὶ ἀσεβεῖ μέμψεται τέκνα, ὅτι δι' αὐτὸν ὀνειδισθήσονται.
8 οὐαὶ ὑμῖν ἄνδρες ἀσεβεῖς, οἵτινες ἐγκατελίπετε νόμον θεοῦ Ὑψίστου·
9 καὶ ἐὰν γεννηθῆτε, εἰς κατάραν γεννηθήσεσθε,

(fol. 2 recto.)

	[א]ם תכשלו לשמחת עולם	9^b ואם תמותו לקללה:	לקללהה
כל מאונם א׳ אונם	10 כל מאפס אל אפס ישוב	כן חנף מתהו אל תהו:	בן
בני	11 הבל אדם בגויתו	אך שם חסד לא יכרת:	
	12 פחד על שם כי הוא ילוך[1]	מאלפי אוצרות חכמה:	חמדה
טוב חי מספר ימים	13 טובת חי ימי מספר	וטובת שם ימי אין מספר:	וטוב
וסימה מסותרת	14^b חכמה טמונה ואוצר מוסתר	מה תועלה בשתיהם:	תעלה
	15 טוב א[י]ש מצפן אולתו	מאיש מצפין חכמתו:	מאות
	מוסר בשת שמ	מוסר בשת:	
	14^a מוסר בשת שמעו בנים	16 והכלמו על משפטי:	משפטו
	16^b לא כל בשת נאה לשמר	ולא כל הכלם נבחר:	
על סתו	17 בוש מאב ואם אל זנות	מנשיא יושב אל כחש:	ושר על
	18 מארון וגברת על שקר	מעדה ועם על פשע:	
משותף מסקום	18^c . . . . זרע על מעל	19 וממקום תגור על זר:	ונגיד על זר:
	19^b . . . . [א]לה ובריתֿ	ממטה אציל אל לחם:	
	19^d מ . . . . . . [ש]אלה	21 מחשב אפי רעך:	מהשיב פי
	21^b מהש[בות מ]חלקות מנה	20 מ[ש]אול שלום מהחריש:	משואל
אשה	20^b[2] מהביט	21^c[3] ומהי . ק[4] . . . ל	[נע]רה:
ובר חסר	22^c מאוהב על [דב]רי חרפה	ומאחרי מתת אל תנאץ:	שאלה

[1] Eccles. 8, 15. [2] Or ? 21^c. [3] Or ? 22^a.

[4] Of the doubtful letters here the ה may be a ח, the י may be a ו, and the ק any final letter.

9 [illegible]

[illegible]

10^b [illegible]

11^b [illegible]

12 [illegible]

[illegible]

19^b [illegible]

20 [illegible]

[illegible]

(fol. 2 recto.)

If ye stumble, it shall be for perpetual joy;
9b and if ye die, it shall be for a curse.
10 All things[1] from nothing turn to nothing[1] again,
so[2] the godless (go) from emptiness to emptiness.
11 The vanity of man[3] is in his body,
but a godly name shall not be cut off.
12 Fear for (thy) name, for that will accompany thee,
more than thousands of precious[4] treasures.
13 The goodness of life[5] hath days that may be numbered,
but goodness of name hath days without number.
14b Buried wisdom and a hidden treasure,
what profit is in them both?
15 Better is a man that hideth his foolishness,
than a man[6] that hideth his wisdom.

The discipline of shame.

14a Hearken, O children, to the discipline of shame,
16 and be abashed according to my[7] judgement.
16b Not every kind of shame is it fitting to retain,
nor is every kind of abashment approved.
17 Be ashamed before father and mother, of whoredom[8];
before a prince sitting (in judgement)[9], of a lie;
18 Before master and mistress, of deceit;
before the congregation and the people, of transgression; [a stranger[12];
18c [Before a partner] and a friend, of trespass[10];
19 and before the place where thou sojournest[11], of
19b [Of breaking an o]ath and a covenant,
of stretching out the elbow at meat;
19d Of refusing to grant a request[4];
21 of reckoning the face[13] of thy friend;
21b Of reckoning the dividing of a portion[4];
20 before him that saluteth[4], of silence[14];
20b Of gazing on a woman[4] [that is a harlot ?];
21c and of . . . . .
22c Before a friend, of reproachful [word[4]]s;
and after giving[15], spurn not.

[1] Marg. from their trouble turn to their trouble (?), *or* from trouble turn to trouble (?). [2] Marg. the son of the godless (*or* a godless son). [3] Marg. of the sons of men. [4] So marg. [5] Reading חיים for חי. [6] Marg. a lord. [7] Marg. its judgement. [8] Marg. of wantonness. [9] Marg. before a prince and a governor. [10] Lev. 5, 21. [11] Marg. the place and a prince. [12] Marg. of pride. [13] Perhaps משוב of turning away the face (𝔊): marg. from closing up the mouth of. [14] Marg. will ye be silent? [15] Marg. a request.

9b καὶ ἐὰν ἀποθάνητε, εἰς κατάραν μερισθήσεσθε.
10 πάντα ὅσα ἐκ γῆς εἰς γῆν ἀπελεύσεται,
οὕτως ἀσεβεῖς ἀπὸ κατάρας εἰς ἀπωλίαν.
11 πένθος ἀνθρώπων ἐν σώμασιν αὐτῶν,
ὄνομα δὲ ἁμαρτωλῶν οὐκ ἀγαθὸν ἐξαλειφθήσεται.
12 φρόντισον περὶ ὀνόματος, αὐτὸ γάρ σοι διαμενεῖ
ἢ χίλιοι μεγάλοι θησαυροὶ χρυσίου·
13 ἀγαθῆς ζωῆς ἀριθμὸς ἡμερῶν,
καὶ ἀγαθὸν ὄνομα εἰς αἰῶνα διαμενεῖ.
14 παιδείαν ἐν εἰρήνῃ συντηρήσατε, τέκνα·
14b σοφία δὲ κεκρυμμένη καὶ θησαυρὸς ἀφανής,
τίς ὠφελία ἐν ἀμφοτέροις;
15 κρείσσων ἄνθρωπος ἀποκρύπτων τὴν μωρίαν αὐτοῦ
ἢ ἄνθρωπος ἀποκρύπτων τὴν σοφίαν αὐτοῦ.
16 τοιγαροῦν ἐντράπητε ἐπὶ τῷ ῥήματί μου·
16b οὐ γάρ ἐστιν πᾶσαν αἰσχύνην διαφυλάξαι καλόν,
καὶ οὐ πάντα πᾶσιν ἐν πίστει εὐδοκιμεῖται.
17 αἰσχύνεσθε ἀπὸ πατρὸς καὶ μητρὸς περὶ πορνείας,
καὶ ἀπὸ ἡγουμένου καὶ δυνάστου περὶ ψεύδους,
18 ἀπὸ κριτοῦ καὶ ἄρχοντος περὶ πλημμελίας,
ἀπὸ συναγωγῆς καὶ λαοῦ περὶ ἀνομίας,
18c ἀπὸ κοινωνοῦ καὶ φίλου περὶ ἀδικίας,
19 καὶ ἀπὸ τόπου οὗ παροικεῖς περὶ κλοπῆς,
19b καὶ ἀπὸ ἀληθείας θεοῦ καὶ διαθήκης,
καὶ ἀπὸ πήξεως ἀγκῶνος ἐπ' ἄρτους,
19d ἀπὸ σκορακισμοῦ λήμψεως καὶ δόσεως,
20 καὶ ἀπὸ ἀσπαζομένων περὶ σιωπῆς,
20b ἀπὸ ὁράσεως γυναικὸς ἑταίρας,
21 καὶ ἀπὸ ἀποστροφῆς προσώπου συγγενοῦς,
21b ἀπὸ ἀφαιρέσεως μερίδος καὶ δόσεως,
καὶ ἀπὸ κατανοήσεως γυναικὸς ὑπάνδρου,
22 ἀπὸ περιεργείας παιδίσκης αὐτοῦ,
καὶ μὴ ἐπιστῇς ἐπὶ τὴν κοίτην αὐτῆς·
22c ἀπὸ φίλων περὶ λόγων ὀνειδισμοῦ,
καὶ μετὰ τὸ δοῦναι μὴ ὀνείδιζε·

(fol. 2 verso.)

	XLII. 1 משנות דבר תשמע	ומחסוף כל °סוד עצה	°על אור׳
	1c והיית בוש באמת	ומצא חן בעיני כל חי׃	
אל	1e אך עֿל אלה אל תבוש	ואל תשא פנים וחטא׃	
אל	2 עֿל תורת עליון וחוק	ועל מצֿדיק להצדיק רשע׃	משפט
שותף	3 על חשבון חוֹבר ואדון[1]	ועל מחלקות נחלה וישֿ[2]׃	וישר
	4a ועל שחק מאזנים[3] ופלס	5a ועל תמהותֿ איפהֿ ואבן׃	תמורת אפה ואפה
השבון	4b על מֿקנה בין רב למעט	5c ועל ממֿחיו עבר בנד׃	מוכר
מפשה	6 על אשה רעֿה חותם׃ חכם	ומקום ידים רפות תפתח׃	
מפקד יד החשב	7 עֿל מקום תפקר° ידי[4] ֿתספר	ומתת וֿלקח הכל בכתב׃	ושואה ותתה
מרדות	8 על מֿוסר פותה וכסיל	ושב וֿישיש ונוטל[5] עֿצה °בזנות׃	ושב כושל ושנה בוטח
	8c והיית זהיר באמת	ואיש צנוע לפני כל חי׃	
מטמון	9 בת לאב מטמנת שקר	ראֿגה תפ[ריר] . . . . ׃	ודאגתה
	9c בנעוריה פן תנור	ובבתוליה פן	
תחפתה	10 בבתוליה פן תפֿותה	ובבית . . ל ֿ. ל	סה׳׃
א׳ פתוה	10c בבית אביה פן ֿ. . . .	ובבית א[יש]ה . . . . נֿר[7]׃	
	11 . . . . ל . . . . ל . . הֿקמת	. . . . שם סרֿה׃	סרח׃
	11c דבת עיר וקללת עם	והושֿבתך [בע]דת שער׃	והובישתך

Vertical marginal notes: ע׳ אשה ו׳ חותם ם׳ ד׳ ו׳ חכמת / בבית אביה פ[ן] ת[ה]יה בב׳ לי הכבה / בבתוליה פ׳ תחפתה ובב׳ אישׁ ם׳ ה[ש]ה / בב׳ פ׳ ג׳ החזק משמר פ׳ תה ש׳ א׳ / רבה פ׳ ולא תחבטה / בבית ששׂ

[1] ואורח is written above וארוך. [2] Prov. 8, 21. [3] Is. 40, 15. [4] Cf. Lev. 5, 21. [5] Between ver. 8[b] and 8[d] (under ונוטל) ושואל. [6] The ב is very doubtful, only the lower left-hand corner being left. The two letters may possibly belong to the text. [7] Of the נ, only the foot is left, which may be part of a ת, צ, ע, or possibly כ. ? פן הבטר lest she be vexed, *or* be unhappy.

XLII. 9	ܒܪܬܐ ܥܠ ܐܒܘܗ̇ ܡܣܝܐ ܫܢܬܗ.	ܘܒܪܘܒܝܗ̇ ܡܣܝܒܐ ܡܛܠܗ̇.
9c	ܒܛܠܝܘܬܗ̇ ܕܠܐ ܬܬܓܠܐ.	ܘܡܢ ܒܥܠܗ̇ ܕܠܐ ܬܫܬܒܩ.
10	ܒܒܬܘܠܘܬܗ̇ ܕܠܐ ܬܬܛܢܦ.	ܘܥܠ ܒܥܠܗ̇ ܕܒܥܠܐ ܠܐ ܬܚܛܐ ܒܥܒܕܘܗ̇. ܘܐܢ ܠܐ ܒܥܠܗ̇ ܒܢܝܐ ܐܚܪܢܐ +
11	ܥܠ ܒܪܬܐ ܐܚܝܕ ܡܛܪܬܐ.	ܕܠܐ ܬܥܒܕ ܠܟ ܫܡܐ ܒܝܫܐ.
11c	ܘܡܫܡܥܬܐ ܘܢܛܘܪܐ ܒܥܡܐ.	ܘܬܒܗܬܟ ܒܬܪܥܐ ܠܟܢܘܫܬܐ ܕܥܡܐ.

(fol. 2 verso.)

XLII. 1 Of repeating a word that thou hearest, and of laying bare any secret counsel[1]:
1c So shalt thou be truly shamefast, and finding favour in the sight of all living.
1e But of these things be not ashamed, and accept not persons unto sin[2]:
2 Of the law of the Most High and the statute, and of judgement[3] to do justice to the wicked,
3 Of reckoning with a partner and a master[4], and of the division of an inheritance and a property,
4a Of the small dust of the scales[5] and balance, 5a and of exchange by ephah and stone (weight),
4b Of buying[6] between much and little, 5c and of smiting[7] a deceitful [servant].
6 Upon an evil[8] woman set[9] a seal, but a place of weak hands thou mayest open[10].
7 In the place where thou committest[9] a deposit, [count[11], and let giving and receiving all be in writing.
8 (Be not ashamed) of the correction of the simple and the fool, or of him that is grey-headed and very aged, and that (yet) taketh counsel for[12] whoredom.
8c So shalt thou be well-advised in truth, and lowly before all living.

9 A daughter is to a father a deceptive treasure, and the care of her[8] [putteth away his sleep]:
9c In her youth lest she commit adultery, and in her virginity lest [she be defiled],
10 In her virginity lest she be seduced, and in the house of [her lord lest she bear not ?],
10c In the house of her father lest [she play the harlot ?], and in the house of her hu[sband lest] . . . . .
11 [My son, keep a strict watch over thy daughter, lest she make thee[3]] a name of evil odour[3],
11c A byword in the city and a cursing of the people, and shame[3] thee [in the con]gregation of the gate.

[1] Marg. laying counsel bare to the light. [2] Reading [illegible] (for [illegible]), as 𝔊. [3] So marg. [4] Marg. (fellow-) traveller. [5] Is. 40, 15. [6] Marg. reckoning. [7] Marg. the correction of. On vers. 9c–11c, the marg. has: In the house of her father le[st she play the harlot, and] in the house of her lord lest she be forgotten; in her virginity lest she be seduced, and in the house of her husband lest she go astray. My son, keep a strict watch over thy daughter, lest she make thee a derision (Exod. 32, 25: 𝔊 ἐπίχαρμα) to thine enemies; a byword in the city and a cursing of the people, and thou be shamed in the congregation of the gate. [8] Marg. obdurate. [9] Reading [illegible] for תפח. [10] So text: *perhaps*, and where there are many (רבות) hands, open [not]. Cf. 𝔊. [11] Marg. reckon. [12] Marg. and stumbleth, and is (yet) occupied in: *also between the lines*, asketh *for* taketh.

XLII. 1 ἀπὸ δευτερώσεως καὶ λόγου ἀκοῆς, καὶ ἀπὸ ἀποκαλύψεων λόγων κρυφίων·
1c καὶ ἔσῃ αἰσχυντηρὸς ἀληθινῶς, καὶ εὑρίσκων χάριν ἔναντι παντὸς ἀνθρώπου.
1e μὴ περὶ τούτων αἰσχυνθῇς, καὶ μὴ λάβῃς πρόσωπον τοῦ ἁμαρτάνειν·
2 περὶ νόμου Ὑψίστου καὶ διαθήκης, καὶ περὶ κρίματος δικαιῶσαι τὸν ἀσεβῆ,
3 περὶ λόγου κοινωνοῦ καὶ ὁδοιπόρων, περὶ δόσεως κληρονομίας ἑταίρων,
4 περὶ ἀκριβείας ζυγοῦ καὶ σταθμίων, περὶ κτήσεως πολλῶν καὶ ὀλίγων,
5 περὶ ἀδιαφόρου πράσεως καὶ ἐμπόρων, καὶ περὶ παιδείας τέκνων πολλῆς,
5c καὶ οἰκέτῃ πονηρῷ πλευρὰν αἱμάξαι·
6 ἐπὶ γυναικὶ πονηρᾷ καλὸν σφραγίς, καὶ ὅπου χεῖρες πολλαὶ κλεῖσον·
7 ὃ ἐὰν παραδιδῷς, ἐν ἀριθμῷ καὶ σταθμῷ, καὶ δόσις καὶ λῆμψις παντὶ ἐν γραφῇ·
8 περὶ παιδείας ἀνοήτου καὶ μωροῦ καὶ ἐσχατογήρως κρινομένου πρὸς νέους,
8c καὶ ἔσῃ πεπαιδευμένος ἀληθινῶς καὶ δεδοκιμασμένος ἔναντι παντὸς ζῶντος.

9 θυγάτηρ πατρὶ ἀπόκρυφος ἀγρυπνία, καὶ ἡ μέριμνα αὐτῆς ἀφιστᾷ ὕπνον·
9c ἐν νεότητι αὐτῆς μή ποτε παρακμάσῃ, καὶ συνῳκηκυῖα μή ποτε μισηθῇ·
10 ἐν παρθενείᾳ μή ποτε βεβηλωθῇ καὶ ἐν τοῖς πατρικοῖς αὐτῆς ἔγκυος γένηται·
10c μετὰ ἀνδρὸς οὖσα μή ποτε παραβῇ, καὶ συνῳκηκυῖα μή ποτε στειρώσῃ.
11 ἐπὶ θυγατρὶ ἀδιατρέπτῳ στερέωσον φυλακήν, μή ποτε ποιήσῃ σε ἐπίχαρμα ἐχθροῖς,
11c λαλιὰν ἐν πόλει καὶ ἔκκλητον λαοῦ, καὶ καταισχυνεῖ σε ἐν πλήθει πολλῶν.

(fol. 3 recto.)

11e [ס]קום תער אל יהי אשנב — ובית מביט מבוא סביב:
12 לכל זְכר אל תתן תאר — ובית נשים אל תסתוֹיד: — הוכר — תסהיד
13 כי מבגד יצא עש — ומאשה רעת אשה:
14 מטוב רוע איש מטיב אשה — ובית מחרפת תביע אשה:

[illegible]

15 אזכר נא מעשי אל — חה חזיתי ואספרה:[1]
15c באומר אלהים רצֹ[ו]נו — ופועל רצונו לקְחו: — מעשיו — לקח:
16 שמש זו[רח]ת על כל נגלתה — וכבוד ייי על כל מעשיו:
17 לא הספיקו קדושי אל — לספר נפלאות ייי: — גבורותיו
17c אִמץ אלהים צבאיו — להִתחזק לפני כבודו: — אומין — להחזיק
18 תהום ולב חקר — ובכל מערומיהם יתבונן:
19 מחוה חליפות נֹהיות — ומגלה הקר נסתרות: — ונהיות
20 ל[א נ]עדר ממנו כל שכל — ולא חלפו כל דבר: — חלף ממנו כ דבר:
21 גְ[בורֹת הכמ]תו תכן — אחד הוא מעולם: — גבורות — מהעולם
21c ל[א] . . . . [נ]לא נאצל — ולא צריך לכל מבין: — צרך
23a הוא ח . . . . . ל . . — 25a זה על [ז]ה חלף טובו: — יקים — לכל צורך הכל נשמע
25b וימי ישב[ע] ל[הביט תואר] — XLIII. 1a ? . ?[2] . . . . ל . . . .
XLIII. 1b ועצם שמי[ם[3] מ]רביט הדרו — XLII. 23b ולכל צורך הכל ישמע:

[1] Job 15, 17. [2] Only the tail of the ן remains: before it there is a blot. [3] Exod. 24, 10.

11e ܐܬܪ ܕܕܡܟܐ ܠܐ ܬܬܦܬܚ ܟܘܐ. — ܘܒܒܝܬܐ ܠܐ ܬܗܘܐ ܚܙܝܐ.
12 ܠܟܠ ܓܒܪ ܠܐ ܬܬܠ ܥܠ ܕܠܟܝ. — ܘܒܝܬ ܢܫܐ ܠܐ ܬܬܒ ܒܩܘܒܠܐ.
13 ܡܛܠ ܕܐܝܟܢܐ ܕܒܠܒܘܫܐ ܢܦܠ ܣܣܐ. — ܗܟܢܐ ܓܒܪܐ ܕܐܚܝܬܐ ܡܢ ܒܥܠܬܗ ܕܚܒܪܬܗ ❖

15 ܐܬܕܟܪ ܗܫܐ ܠܥܒܕܘܗܝ ܕܐܠܗܐ. — ܘܡܢ ܡܐ ܕܚܙܝܬ ܐܢܐ ܐܫܬܥܐ.
15c ܒܡܠܬܗ ܐܠܗܐ ܥܒܕܘܗܝ. — ܘܥܒܕܝܢ ܒܢܝܗ̇ ܨܒܝܢܗ ܒܥܒܕܝ.
16 ܐܝܟ ܫܡܫܐ ܕܕܢܚ ܥܠ ܟܠ. ܐܬܓܠܝܬ — ܫܘܒܚܗ ܕܡܪܝܐ ܥܠ ܟܠܗܘܢ ܥܒܕܘܗܝ.
17 ܠܐ ܣܦܩܘ ܩܕܝܫܘܗܝ ܕܡܪܝܐ. — ܠܡܫܬܥܝܘ ܓܒܪܘܬܗ ܕܦܪܝܫܘܬܗ.
17c ܓܒܪܘܬܐ ܝܗܒ ܠܩܕܝܫܘܗܝ. — ܠܡܩܡ ܩܕܡ ܐܝܩܪܗ.
18 ܬܗܘܡܐ ܘܠܒܐ ܗܘ ܒܨܐ. — ܘܒܟܠܗܘܢ ܬܪܥܝܬܗܘܢ ܕܒܢܝܢܫܐ ܐܝܟ ܡܕܡ ܓܠܝܢ ܩܕܡܘܗܝ
18c ܡܛܠ ܕܠܐ ܒܨܐ — ܡܢ ܩܕܡ ܐܠܗܐ ܩܕܝܡ.
19 ܘܡܚܘܐ ܡܕܡܘܗܝ ܥܠ ܕܐܬܝܢ ܒܥܠܡܐ. ܕܗܘܝ ܘܕܥܬܝܕܝܢ. — ܘܡܚܘܐ ܡܕܡܘܗܝ ܟܠܗܘܢ ܟܣܝܬܐ.
20 ܘܠܐ ܚܣܝܪ ܡܢ ܡܕܡܘܗܝ ܟܠ ܣܘܟܠܐ. — ܘܠܐ ܥܒܪ ܡܢ ܡܕܡܘܗܝ ܟܠ ܕܐܦ ܡܠܬܐ.
21 ܘܓܒܪܘܬܐ ܡܕܡܘܗܝ ܡܬܩܢܐ ܠܥܠܡ. — ܘܡܬܝܬܪܐ ܡܬܚܫܒ ܡܠܗܘܢ.
22 ܘܟܠܗܘܢ ܥܒܕܘܗܝ ܠܥܠܡܝܢ ܒܩܘܝܡܐ ܡܫܪܐ. — ܘܟܠܗܘܢ ܕܦܠܚܘܢ ܒܗ ܟܠܗܘܢ ܫܡܥܝܢ. ܘܡܫܬܡܥܝܢ ܠܗ ܒܦܘܠܚܢܗܘܢ.
23 ܘܚܝ ܘܡܩܝܡ ܠܥܠܡ. — ܘܠܐ ܓܙܪ ܚܕ ܡܢܗܘܢ ܠܚܠܦܗ.
24 ܘܟܠܗܘܢ ܬܪܝܢ ܚܕ ܠܘܩܒܠ ܚܕ — ܘܥܒܕ ܢܦܫܗ ܠܒܢܝܐ ܐܦܝܗܘܢ.
25 ܐܠܐ ܗܘܐ ܒܗ ܗܘܐ ܦܓܥܝܢ.

(fol. 3 recto.)

11c In the place where she lodgeth let there be no lattice, nor a chamber looking upon the entrance round about.

12 Let her not show her beauty to any male, and[1] in the house of[1] women let her not converse.

13 For from a garment cometh forth a moth, and from a woman a woman's wickedness.

14 [2]Better is the wickedness of a man than the goodness of a woman[2], and the house of her that causeth shame[2] poureth forth reproach[2].

15 I will remember now the works of God, and that which I have seen I will recount.

15c By the word of God is his pleasure[3], and him that doeth his pleasure he hath accepted.

16 The rising sun is revealed over all things, so the glory of the Lord is over all his works.

17 The saints of God do not suffice to recount the wonders of the Lord[4].

17c God hath given strength unto[5] his hosts, that they may endure firmly before his glory.

18 He searcheth out the deep and the heart, and understandeth all their nakednesses;

19 Declaring things that are past and[2] that are to come, and revealing the remotest[6] of hidden things.

20 No knowledge is lacking to him, and no matter escapeth him.

21 [The might[7] of his wisdom] he hath regulated, he is one from everlasting.

21c Nothing [hath been added (unto him), or] diminished (from him), and he hath no need[2] of any instructor[8].

23a He [establisheth[2] all things for ever], 25a one thing upon another for the sake of its good.

25b [2]And who can [be fi]lled with [beholding (his) beauty[2]?] XLIII. 1a . . . .

XLIII. 1b And the body of heaven beholding[2] his majesty[9], XLII. 23b and all things are obedient to every use.

[1] *Or perhaps*, among. [2] So marg. [3] Marg. by the word of God are his works. [4] Marg. of his mighty acts. [5] Marg. the strength of God is. [6] *Lit.* the search, Job 11, 7. 38, 16. [7] Marg. mighty acts. [8] Is. 40, 14. [9] The marginal note at the top of the next page (referring to verse 25a seq.) is as follows: One thing upon another for the sake of good: and who can be filled with beholding beauty? The beauty of the height spread out ([illegible]) upon (?) clearness (Exod. 24, 10), and the body of heaven (*ibid.*) beholding the light.

12 παντὶ ἀνθρώπῳ μὴ ἔμβλεπε ἐν κάλλει, καὶ ἐν μέσῳ γυναικῶν μὴ συνέδρευε·

13 ἀπὸ γὰρ ἱματίων ἐκπορεύεται σής, καὶ ἀπὸ γυναικὸς πονηρία γυναικός.

14 κρείσσων πονηρία ἀνδρὸς ἢ ἀγαθοποιὸς γυνή, καὶ γυνὴ καταισχύνουσα εἰς ὀνειδισμόν.

15 μνησθήσομαι δὲ τὰ ἔργα Κυρίου, καὶ ἃ ἑόρακα ἐκδιηγήσομαι·

15c ἐν λόγοις Κυρίου τὰ ἔργα αὐτοῦ.

16 ἥλιος φωτίζων κατὰ πᾶν ἐπέβλεψεν, καὶ τῆς δόξης αὐτοῦ πλῆρες τὸ ἔργον αὐτοῦ.

17 οὐκ ἐνεποίησεν τοῖς ἁγίοις Κύριος ἐκδιηγήσασθαι πάντα τὰ θαυμάσια αὐτοῦ,

17c ἃ ἐστερέωσεν Κύριος ὁ παντοκράτωρ, στηριχθῆναι ἐν δόξῃ αὐτοῦ τὸ πᾶν.

18 ἄβυσσον καὶ καρδίαν ἐξίχνευσεν, καὶ ἐν πανουργεύμασιν αὐτῶν διενοήθην·

18c ἔγνω γὰρ ὁ κύριος πᾶσαν εἴδησιν καὶ ἐνέβλεψεν εἰς σημεῖον αἰῶνος,

19 ἀπαγγέλλων τὰ παρεληλυθότα καὶ ἐπεσόμενα, καὶ ἀποκαλύπτων ἴχνη ἀποκρύφων·

20 οὐ παρῆλθεν αὐτὸν πᾶν διανόημα, οὐκ ἐκρύβη ἀπ' αὐτοῦ οὐδὲ εἷς λόγος.

21 τὰ μεγαλεῖα τῆς σοφίας αὐτοῦ ἐκόσμησεν· καὶ ἕως ἔστιν πρὸ τοῦ αἰῶνος καὶ εἰς τὸν αἰῶνα,

21c οὔτε προσετέθη οὔτε ἠλαττώθη, καὶ οὐ προσεδεήθη οὐδενὸς συμβούλου.

22 ὡς πάντα τὰ ἔργα αὐτοῦ ἐπιθυμητά, καὶ ὡς σπινθῆρός ἐστιν θεωρῆσαι.

23 πάντα ταῦτα ζῇ καὶ μένει εἰς τὸν αἰῶνα ἐν πάσαις χρείαις, καὶ πάντα ὑπακούει·

24 πάντα δισσά ἓν κατέναντι τοῦ ἑνός, καὶ οὐκ ἐποίησεν οὐδὲν ἐκλιπόν·

25 ἓν τοῦ ἑνὸς ἐστερέωσεν τὰ ἀγαθά, καὶ τίς πλησθήσεται ὁρῶν δόξαν αὐτοῦ;

XLIII. 1 γαυρίαμα ὕψους στερέωμα καθαριότητος, εἶδος οὐρανοῦ ἐν ὁράματι δόξης.

(fol. 3 verso.)

	24 בלם שונים זה מזה	ולא עשה מהם שו[א:]		
XLIII.	2 שמש מביע °בצרתו חמה	מה נורא מעשי ײ׳:		מופיע בצאתו
	3 בהצהירו ירתיח תבל	לפני חרבו מי יתכלכל:		
	4 כור נפוח מהם מצוק	שולח שמש ידליק הרים:	שולח ש׳ יסיק	מוצק
	4ᶜ לשאון מאור תגמר נושבת	ומנורה תכוה עין:		לשון
	5 כי גדול ײ׳ °עושהו	ודבריו ינצח אביריו:	ינצח	כי גדול עליון עשה
	6 וגם ירח ירח עתות שבות	[מ]משלת קץ ואות עולם:		עת עת עד עת
	7 בם °מועד חמני חוק	והפין ע . ה בתקופתו:		בו מו׳ ומכתו
	8 חדש בחדשו הוא מתחדש	מה נורא בהשתנותו:	בתשובתו:	כשמו והוא
	8ᶜ כלי צבא נבלי מרום	מרצף רקיע מזהירתו:	מסיך ושדי	
	9 תואר שמים והדר כוכב	ואורו מזהיר במרומי[2] אל:	מזריק נ׳ אל:	
	10 בדבר אל יעמד חק	ולא ישח באשמורותם:	ישון	
	11 ראה קשת וברך עושיה	כי מאד נאדרה [בכב]וד:	נהורה	עושה
	12 חוק °הקיפה °בכבורה	ויד אל נטתה בג̅ . .	לא	הוד הקיפה בגבורו
	13 גבורתו תתוה ברק	ותנצח °זיקות	[ותנ]צח זיקים	
	14 למען ברא אוצ[ר]	ויעף ש̅		למענו
	. . . .	ל		
	17 °קול רעמו יחול ארצו	ולעפו[ת צ]פון סופה וסערה:		

Marginal note (beside verses 24–5):[1]
זה על זה חלף כוב
ומי ישבית לדבים הואר
הואר כרום רקע על בהר
ועצם שמים כניב מהרה:

Marginal note (beside verses 13–17):
קול רעמו יחיל ארצו
ובכחו יזיים הרים:
אימתו התרף היםן
עלעול סופה וסערה:

[illegible]

[1] See xlii. 25 and xliii. 1; and for the translation, p. 15, note 9.

[2] Job 25, 2.

XLIII. 2 ܒܦܩ ܫܡܫܐ ܒܡܕܢܚܐ ܘܒܫܡܫܗ. ܡܐܢܐ ܕܬܕܡܘܪܬܐ ܥܒܕܗ ܕܡܪܝܡܐ.

3 ܒܦܠܓܘܬܗ ܕܛܗܪܐ ܡܫܚܢ ܠܗ ܠܐܪܥܐ. ܘܩܕܡ ܚܘܡܗ ܡܢܘ ܢܩܘܡ ܒܩܘܡ.

4 ܐܝܟ ܟܘܪܐ ܕܢܦܚ ܒܚܡܝܐ ܘܡܫܚܢ. ܚܕ ܠܬܠܬܐ ܒܠܗܘܒܘܗܝ ܫܡܫܐ ܡܫܚܢ ܛܘܪܐ.

4ᶜ ܒܠܫܢܗ ܐܝܟ ܠܗܒܐ ܕܢܘܪܐ. ܘܡܢܗܪ ܠܥܝܢܘܗܝ ܘܡܥܘܪ ܥܝܢܐ.

5 ܪܒ ܗܘ ܡܪܝܐ ܕܥܒܕܗ. ܘܒܡܠܬܗ ܢܨܝܚܐ ܡܕܒܪ ܡܗܠܟܬܗ.

6 ܘܣܗܪܐ ܡܩܝܡ ܠܙܒܢܘܗܝ. ܠܫܘܠܛܢܐ ܕܩܝܛܐ ܘܐܬܐ ܕܡܢ ܥܠܡ.

7 ܡܢܗ ܣܗܪܐ ܚܙܝ ܐܬܘܬܐ ܕܥܐܕܐ. ܢܗܘܪܐ ܢܚܣܪ ܠܐܚܪܢܐ.

8 ܚܕܬܐ ܐܝܟ ܫܡܗ ܐܝܬܘܗܝ. ܘܡܬܪܘܪܒܐ ܡܪܡܪܡܐ ܒܡܘܠܕܗ.

8ᶜ ܡܐܢܐ ܕܡܫܪܝܬܐ ܕܪܘܡܐ. ܕܡܢܗܪ ܒܪܩܝܥܐ ܕܫܡܝܐ.

9 ܝܩܪܐ ܕܫܡܝܐ ܘܫܘܒܗܪܐ ܕܟܘܟܒܐ.

10 ܒܡܠܘܗܝ ܕܩܕܝܫܐ ܢܩܘܡܘܢ ܐܝܟ ܕܝܢܗܘܢ. ܘܒܢܛܘܪܬܗܘܢ ܠܐ ܢܫܬܠܝܘܢ.

(fol. 3 verso.)

24 All of them are different, one from another, and he hath made none of them [in vain].

XLIII. 2 The sun, when he goeth forth[1], poureth out warmth: how terrible are the works of the Lord!

3 By his shining he heateth the world; before his drought who can maintain himself?

4 A fierce[2] furnace is established[3] by them (?), the sun being sent[1] forth setteth the mountains in a blaze.

4^c A tongue[1] of light consumeth the inhabited (country), and with its fire the eye is scorched:

5 For great[1] is the Lord that made him[4], and (with) his words he maketh brilliant (?) his mighty [ones.

6 Moreover moon by moon the seasons[5] return, (for) a limited rule, but an everlasting sign:

7 By her[1] are the appointed feast and the prescribed times[6], and in her circuit [she doeth] (her) business:

8 With every (new) month she is renewed[7], how terrible is she in her changing[8]!

8^c An instrument of the host of the (rain-)vessels[9] on high, paving[10] the firmament with her shining:

9 The beauty of heaven, and the glory of a star, and her light shining in[11] the heights of God.

10 By the word of God a statute is established, and they sleep[12] not in their watches.

11 Behold the (rain)bow, and bless him that made it, for exceeding majestic is it [in glo]ry:

12 It compasseth with its glory the vault (of heaven)[13], and the hand of God[14] hath stretched it out in [its pride].

13 His might marketh out the lightning, and maketh brilliant the flashes [in judgement][15].

14 On that account[1] he hath created a treasure-house, and hath made [the clouds?] to fly forth . . . .

. . . .

17 The voice of his thunder maketh[1] his land to be in anguish, the hot winds of the north, the tempest, and the whirlwind[16].

[1] So marg. [2] *Lit.* blown upon. [3] So marg. (cf. Job 11, 15). [4] Marg. for great is the Most High who made him. [5] Marg. moon by moon, season by season. *Or* until the season. [6] Marg. by her is the appointed feast, and from her is the prescribed ordinance. [7] Marg. (the new month) is like its name, for it (is renewed). [8] Marg. in her returning. [9] *Lit.* (water-)skins; cf. Job 38, 37: but perhaps it is due to dittography from כלי. [10] Marg. terrifying (?). [11] Marg. and a red-gleaming ornament in (בּ for כּ) the heights of God. [12] Reading יָשְׁנוּ for ישון of the margin. [13] חוג for חוק (Job 22, 14). [14] Marg. and no hand hath. [15] Marg. his rebuke (גערתו for גבורתו) marketh out the morning (בֹּקֶר for ברק), and casteth off the living substance (תומה יקום error for ותוצא ויקץ) in [judgement]. [16] Marg. the voice of his thunder maketh his land to be in anguish, and by his strength he maketh the mountains indignant (?): his terror inciteth the south wind, the storm, the tempest, and the whirlwind.

2 ἥλιος ἐν ὀπτασίᾳ διαγγέλλων ἐν ἐξόδῳ, σκεῦος θαυμαστόν, ἔργον Ὑψίστου·

3 ἐν μεσημβρίᾳ αὐτοῦ ἀναξηραίνει χώραν, καὶ ἐναντίον καύματος αὐτοῦ τίς ὑποστήσεται;

4 κάμινον φυλάσσων ἐν ἔργοις καύματος, τριπλασίως ἥλιος ἐκκαίων ὄρη·

4^c ἀτμίδας πυρώδεις ἐμφυσῶν, καὶ ἐκλάμπων ἀκτῖνας ἀμαυροῖ ὀφθαλμούς.

5 μέγας Κύριος ὁ ποιήσας αὐτόν, καὶ ἐν λόγοις αὐτοῦ κατέσπευσεν πορείαν·

6 καὶ ἡ σελήνη ἐν πᾶσιν εἰς καιρὸν αὐτῆς, ἀνάδειξιν χρόνων καὶ σημεῖον αἰῶνος·

7 ἀπὸ σελήνης σημεῖον ἑορτῆς, φωστὴρ μειούμενος ἐπὶ συντελείας·

8 μὴν κατὰ τὸ ὄνομα αὐτῆς ἐστιν, αὐξανομένη θαυμαστῶς ἐν ἀλλοιώσει.

8^c σκεῦος παρεμβολῶν ἐν ὕψει, ἐν στερεώματι οὐρανοῦ ἐκλάμπων·

9 κάλλος οὐρανοῦ, δόξα ἄστρων, κόσμος φωτίζων, ἐν ὑψίστοις Κύριος·

10 ἐν λόγοις ἁγίοις στήσονται κατὰ κρίμα, καὶ οὐ μὴ ἐκλυθῶσιν ἐν φυλακαῖς αὐτῶν.

11 ἴδε τόξον, καὶ εὐλόγησον τὸν ποιήσαντα αὐτό, σφόδρα ὡραῖον ἐν τῷ αὐγάσματι αὐτοῦ·

12 ἐγύρωσεν οὐρανὸν ἐν κυκλώσει δόξης, χεῖρες Ὑψίστου ἐτάνυσαν αὐτό.

13 προστάγματι αὐτοῦ κατέπαυσεν χιόνα, καὶ ταχύνει ἀστραπὰς κρίματος αὐτοῦ·

14 διὰ τοῦτο ἠνεῴχθησαν θησαυροί, καὶ ἐξέπτησαν νεφέλαι ὡς πετεινά·

15 ἐν μεγαλείῳ αὐτοῦ ἴσχυσεν νεφέλας, καὶ διεθρύβησαν λίθοι χαλάζης.

16 καὶ ἐν ὀπτασίαις αὐτοῦ σαλευθήσεται ὄρη, ἐν θελήματι πνεύσεται νότος.

17 φωνὴ βροντῆς αὐτοῦ ὠνείδισεν γῆν, καὶ καταιγὶς βορέου καὶ συστροφὴ πνεύματος.

(fol. 4 recto.)

כר׳	17c [בר̊]שף יניף שלנו	וכארבה ישבון דר̊תו :	׳רר׳
יהגה	18 תואר לבנה ינ̊הה עינים	וממטרו יהמה לבב :	
ישסך	19 וגם כפור במלח ישכ̊ון	ויציין כספיר ציצים :	
	20 צינת רוח צפון ישיב	וברקב יקפיא מקו̊רו :	מקוה
	20c על כל מעמד מים יקרים	וכשרין ילבש מקוה :	
	21 יבול בחרב[1] ישיק	ונו̊ה[2] צמחים כלהבה :	וצור
טל פורע	22 מרפא כל מערף ענן טל	פורע לדשן שר̊ב :	רבב
משובהו	23 מחשבתו . . שיק רבה	וים בתהום אי̊ים :	אוצר
	24 יורדי הים יספרו קצהו	לשמע אזננו נשתומם :	-
מעשיו	25 שם פלאות תמהי מעש̊הו	מין כל חי וגבורות רבה :	
למענהו[3] למען	26 למענ̊ו יצלח מלאך	ובדבריו יפעל רצון :	
	27 עוד באלה לא נוסף	וקץ דבר הוא הכל :	
נגלה	28 נ[גד̊]לה עוד כי לא נחקור	והוא גדול מכל מעשיו :	
	29 נ[ורא] . . [מ]אד̇ מאד	ונפלאות דבר̊יו :	גבורתו
	30 מ[גד]ל[י] . . הרימו קול בכל תובלו כי יש עוד : 30c מרוממים תחליפו כח[4] ואל תלאו כי לא ת[חקרו :]		מרוממיו החליפו כח ואל הלאו כי לא תמצ[או]
	32 רוב נ . . . . ן [מ]אלה	מעט ראיתי ממעשיו :	
	33 את הכל	ז̇ל	

[1] Above כחרב is written הרים (see Job 40, 20). [2] Ezek. 7, 11. [3] Prov. 16, 4. [4] Is. 40, 31.

(fol. 4 recto.)

17c Like[1] darting flashes he sheddeth abroad his snow, and like locusts (when) they settle is the falling down[3] thereof;
18 The beauty of its whiteness dazzleth[2] the eyes, and the heart is disquieted[3] at the raining of it.
19 The hoar-frost also he poureth out[4] like salt, and maketh it to bloom with flowers like sapphire.
20 The cold of the north wind he causeth to blow, and congealeth his spring[5] like rottenness (?).
20c Over every standing water he spreadeth a crust, and a pond putteth on as it were a breastplate.
21 It burneth up the produce like drought[6], and the stateliness[7] of growing things as a flame.
22 The dropping of a cloud healeth all things, (even) dew[1] releasing (?) the parched[8] young grass[9].
23 His counsel[10] burneth up (?) the great (deep), and he planteth[11] islands[12] in the ocean.
24 They that go down to the sea tell of its bounds, when we hear it with our ears, we are astonished.
25 Therein are wonders, the marvels of his work, variety of all things living, and the mighty things of the great (deep).
26 By reason of him[13] [his] messenger[14] prospereth, and by his words he performeth (his) pleasure.
27 More like this we will not add, and the conclusion of the matter is, He is all.
28 Let us still be magnifying him[15], for we shall not search him out, and he is great beyond all his works.
29 [The Lord is] exceeding [terrible], and wonderful are his mighty acts[16].
30 [Ye that magnify the Lord], lift up your voice all that ye can, for there is yet more;
30c ye that exalt him[1], renew your strength, and be not weary, for ye will not [search (him) out].
32 Many [hidden things hath he established (?) more than] these; a little only have I seen of his works.
33 All things [hath the Lord made], and to [the godly hath he given wisdom].

[1] So marg. [2] יגור for יהה. Or ? יְהַהֶה *dimmeth*. [3] *Or* marvels, reading יתמה, as 𝔊. [4] So marg.: text, settleth. [5] Marg. the pond. [6] *Above the line*, of the mountains. [7] Marg. form (Ps. 49, 15). [8] Marg. moist. [9] Reading דשא. [10] Marg. from his quietness (?). [11] Reading ויטע, as 𝔊. [12] Marg. a treasure. [13] Marg. for his own purpose (Prov. 16, 4). [14] ? יצליח מלאכה he maketh (his) business to prosper. [15] Marg. rejoicing. [16] So marg. (יו-): text, his words.

17c ὡς πετεινὰ καθιπτάμενα πάσσει χιόνα καὶ ὡς ἀκρὶς καταλύουσα ἡ κατάβασις αὐτῆς·
18 κάλλος λευκότητος αὐτῆς ἐκθαυμάσει ὀφθαλμός, καὶ ἐπὶ τοῦ ὑετοῦ αὐτῆς ἐκστήσεται καρδία.
19 καὶ πάχνην ὡς ἅλα ἐπὶ γῆς χέει, καὶ παγεῖσα γίνεται σκολόπων ἄκρα.
20 ψυχρὸς ἄνεμος βορέης πνεύσει, καὶ παγήσεται κρύσταλλος ἀφ' ὕδατος·
20c ἐπὶ πᾶσαν συναγωγὴν ὕδατος καταλύσει, καὶ ὡς θώρακα ἐνδύσεται τὸ ὕδωρ.
21 καταφάγεται ὄρη καὶ ἔρημον ἐκκαύσει, καὶ ἀποσβέσει χλόην ὡς πῦρ.
22 ἴασις πάντων κατὰ σπουδὴν ὁμίχλη, δρόσος ἀπαντῶσα ἀπὸ καύσωνος ἱλαρώσει.
23 λογισμῷ αὐτοῦ ἐκόπασεν ἄβυσσον, καὶ ἐφύτευσεν αὐτὴν Ἰησοῦς.
24 οἱ πλέοντες τὴν θάλασσαν διηγοῦνται τὸν κίνδυνον αὐτῆς, καὶ ἀκοαῖς ὠτίων ἡμῶν θαυμάζομεν·
25 καὶ ἐκεῖ τὰ παράδοξα καὶ θαυμάσια ἔργα, ποικιλία παντὸς ζῴου, κτίσις κητῶν.
26 δι' αὐτὸν εὐωδία τέλος αὐτοῦ, καὶ ἐν λόγῳ αὐτοῦ σύγκειται πάντα.
27 πολλὰ ἐροῦμεν καὶ οὐ μὴ ἀφικώμεθα, καὶ συντέλεια λόγων Τὸ πᾶν ἐστιν αὐτός.
28 δοξάζοντες ποῦ ἰσχύσωμεν; αὐτὸς γὰρ ὁ μέγας παρὰ πάντα τὰ ἔργα αὐτοῦ.
29 φοβερὸς Κύριος καὶ σφόδρα μέγας, καὶ θαυμαστὴ ἡ δυναστεία αὐτοῦ.
30 δοξάζοντες Κύριον ὑψώσατε καθ' ὅσον ἂν δύνησθε, ὑπερέξει γὰρ καὶ ἔτι.
30c καὶ ὑψοῦντες αὐτὸν πληθύνατε ἐν ἰσχύϊ· μὴ κοπιᾶτε, οὐ γὰρ μὴ ἀφίκησθε.
31 τίς ἑόρακεν αὐτὸν καὶ ἐκδιηγήσεται; καὶ τίς μεγαλυνεῖ αὐτὸν καθώς ἐστιν;
32 πολλὰ ἀπόκρυφά ἐστιν μείζονα τούτων, ὀλίγα γὰρ ἑωράκαμεν τῶν ἔργων αὐτοῦ.
33 πάντα γὰρ ἐποίησεν ὁ κύριος, καὶ τοῖς εὐσεβέσιν ἔδωκεν σοφίαν.

(fol. 4 verso.)

שבח אבות עולם:

אח	XLIV. 1 אהללה נא אנשי חסד	אבותינו בדורותם:	
	2 רב כבוד חלק° עליון	וגדלו מימות עולם:	להם
דורי	3 דו̊רי ארץ במלכותם	ואנשי שם בגבו̊רתם:	בגבורם
יו'	3c היו̊עצים בתבונתם	וחוזי כל בנבואתם:	
	4 שרי גוים במזמתם	ורוזנים במחקרותם:	
גמ"'	4c חכמי שיח בס̊פרתם	ומושלים במשמרותם:	
קי	5 חוקרי מזמור על חו̊ק	נושאי משל בכתב:	
	6 אנשי חיל וסומכי כח	ושוקטים על מכונתם:	
נכבדו	7 כל אלה בדורם°	ומי̊מיהם[1] תפארתם:	ובימיהם
	8 יש מהם הניחו שם	להשתע̊̊נות בנחלתם:	להשתעות להשענת
	9 ויש מהם אשר אין לו זכר	וישבתו כאשר שבתו:	
	9c כאשר לא היו היו[2]	ובניהם מאחריהם:	
	10 ואולם אלה אנשי חסד	וחקותם לא̄ [תשב]ת:	
	11 עם זרעם נאמן טובם	ונחלתם לב̄[ני בנים:]	
	13 עד עולם יעמד זכרם	וצדקתם ל[א] . . .	
	14 . . . . [בש]ל[ום]	. . . . . . ל[דור] ודור:	

16 חנוך [נמ]צא תמים והתהלך עם ייי ו[י]לקח אות דעת לדור ודור:

[1] Job 38, 12, &c.   [2] Job 10, 19. Obad. 16.

XLIV. 1 ܘܐܦ ܐܢܐ ܐܫܒܚ ܠܓܒܪܐ ܕܛܝܒܘܬܐ.	ܠܐܒܗܝܢ ܕܗܘܘ ܒܕܪܝܗܘܢ܂
2 ܣܓܝ ܐܝܩܪܐ ܕܦܠܓ ܠܗܘܢ.	ܘܪܒܘ ܒܪܒܘܬܗܘܢ. ܥܠ ܕܪ̈ܐ ܕܥܠܡܐ.
	3d ܘܚܙܘ ܒܢܒܝܘܬܗܘܢ
4 ܐܠܘܦܐ ܘܡܠܟܐ ܒܡܠܟܘܬܗܘܢ.	
4c ܣܦܪܐ ܚܟܝܡܐ ܒܡܫܡܠܝܘܬܗܘܢ.	ܘܡܠܝܟܐ ܚܟܝܡܐ ܒܡܫܟܢܝܗܘܢ.
5 ܥܠ ܐܝܟ ܡܠܘܐ ܘܡܢ̈ܐ.	ܘܐܡܪܝ ܡܬܠܐ ܒܟܬܒܐ
6 ܓܒܪ̈ܐ ܕܚܝܠܐ. ܘܡܣܡܟܝܢ ܚܝܠܐ.	ܘܝܬܒܝܢ ܥܠ ܫܘܠܛܢܗܘܢ.
7 ܟܠܗܘܢ ܗܠܝܢ ܒܕܪܝܗܘܢ ܗܘܘ ܠܗܘܢ ܐܝܩܪܐ.	ܘܡܫܘܡܕܢܘܬܗܘܢ ܠܡܚܪܬܗܘܢ
8 ܐܝܬ ܡܢܗܘܢ ܕܫܒܩܘ ܫܡܐ	ܒܡܫܠܡܢܘܬܐ ܥܠ ܝܪܬܘܬܗܘܢ.
9 ܘܐܝܬ ܡܢܗܘܢ ܕܠܝܬ ܠܗܘܢ ܕܘܟܪܢܐ.	ܘܫܒܩܘ ܐܝܟ ܡܐ ܕܫܒܩܘ.
10 ܒܪܡ ܗܠܝܢ ܐܢܫܐ ܕܛܝܒܘܬܐ ܘܙܕܝܩܘܬܐ.	ܛܒܘܬܗܘܢ ܠܐ ܬܛܥܐ.
11 ܘܥܡ ܙܪܥܗܘܢ ܩܝܡ ܛܘܒܗܘܢ.	ܘܝܪܬܘܬܗܘܢ ܠܒܢܝ ܒܢܝܗܘܢ.
ܘܒܩܝܡܗܘܢ. 12 ܩܡ ܙܪܥܗܘܢ.	ܘܒܢܝ ܒܢܝܗܘܢ ܒܒܪܬܐ ܛܒܐ.
13 ܘܥܕܡܐ ܠܥܠܡ ܩܝܡ ܕܘܟܪܢܗܘܢ.	ܘܐܝܩܪܗܘܢ ܠܐ ܢܬܛܥܐ.
14 ܦܓܪܝܗܘܢ ܒܫܠܡܐ ܐܬܩܒܪܘ.	ܘܫܡܗܘܢ ܚܝ ܠܕܪ ܕܪܝܢ.
15 ܘܬܫܒܘܚܬܗܘܢ ܢܫܬܥܐ ܥܕܬܐ܀	

(fol. 4 verso.)

Praise of the Patriarchs.

XLIV. 1 Let me now praise godly men, our fathers in their generations.
2 Great glory the Most High allotted (to them[1]), and they were great from days of old:
3 Rulers[2] of the earth in their royalty, and men of renown in their might;
3c Who gave counsel[3] by their understanding, and saw all things in their prophecy;
4 Princes of nations in their prudence, and potentates in their care[4];
4c Wise of meditation in their writing, and governing in their watchfulness;
5 Who sought out music according to rule[5], and took up the proverb in writing;
6 Men of worth, and supported[6] with strength, and that lived quietly upon their places.
7 All these in their generation (were honoured[1]), and from their birth[7] was their glory.
8 There be of them that have left a name, that men might tell of it in their inheritance:
9 And there be of them which have no memorial, and have ceased as they have ceased;
9c They were as though they had not been, and their children after them.
10 Nevertheless these were godly men, and their hope [shall not peri]sh;
11 With their seed their goodness remaineth sure, and their inheritance unto chil[dren's children];
13 Their memory standeth fast for ever, and their righteousness [shall not be forgotten];
14 [Their bodies were buried in p]eac[e, but their name liveth] unto all generations[8].
16 Enoch [was f]ound perfect, and walked with the Lord, and was taken, being an example (*lit.* sign) of knowledge to all generations.

[1] Marg. adds this. [2] So marg. [3] Marg. Counsellors. [4] *Lit.* searchings out. [5] Marg. measure. [6] Reading וסמוכי. [7] Marg. in their days. [8] Marg. adds here: 15 The congregation heareth their wisdom, and the assembly recounteth their praise.

Πατέρων ὕμνος.

XLIV. 1 Αἰνέσωμεν δὴ ἄνδρας ἐνδόξους καὶ τοὺς πατέρας ἡμῶν τῇ γενέσει.
2 πολλὴν δόξαν ἔκτισεν ὁ κύριος, τὴν μεγαλωσύνην αὐτοῦ ἀπ' αἰῶνος.
3 κυριεύοντες ἐν ταῖς βασιλείαις αὐτῶν, καὶ ἄνδρες ὀνομαστοὶ ἐν δυνάμει·
3c βουλεύσονται ἐν συνέσει αὐτῶν, ἀπηγγελκότες ἐν προφητείαις·
4 ἡγούμενοι λαοῦ ἐν διαβουλίοις καὶ συνέσει γραμματείας λαοῦ,
4c σοφοὶ λόγοι ἐν παιδείᾳ αὐτῶν·
5 ἐκζητοῦντες μέλη μουσικῶν, διηγούμενοι ἔπη ἐν γραφῇ·
6 ἄνδρες πλούσιοι κεχορηγημένοι ἰσχύι, εἰρηνεύοντες ἐν παροικίαις αὐτῶν·
7 πάντες οὗτοι ἐν γενεαῖς ἐδοξάσθησαν, καὶ ἐν ταῖς ἡμέραις αὐτῶν καύχημα.
8 εἰσὶν αὐτῶν οἳ κατέλιπον ὄνομα τοῦ ἐκδιηγήσασθαι ἐπαίνους,
9 καὶ εἰσὶν ὧν οὐκ ἔστιν μνημόσυνον καὶ ἀπώλοντο ὡς οὐχ ὑπάρξαντες,
9c καὶ ἐγένοντο ὡς οὐ γεγονότες, καὶ τὰ τέκνα αὐτῶν μετ' αὐτούς.
10 ἀλλ' ἢ οὗτοι ἄνδρες ἐλέους, ὧν αἱ δικαιοσύναι οὐκ ἐπελήσθησαν·
11 μετὰ τοῦ σπέρματος αὐτῶν διαμενεῖ ἀγαθὴ κληρονομία ἔκγονα αὐτῶν·
11c ἐν ταῖς διαθήκαις 12 ἔστη σπέρμα αὐτῶν, καὶ τὰ τέκνα αὐτῶν δι' αὐτούς,
13 ἕως αἰῶνος μενεῖ σπέρμα αὐτῶν, καὶ ἡ δόξα αὐτῶν οὐκ ἐξαλειφθήσεται·
14 τὸ σῶμα αὐτῶν ἐν εἰρήνῃ ἐτάφη, καὶ τὸ ὄνομα αὐτῶν ζῇ εἰς γενεάς·
15 σοφίαν αὐτῶν διηγήσονται λαοί, καὶ τὸν ἔπαινον ἐξαγγέλλει ἐκκλησία.
16 Ἐνὼχ εὐηρέστησεν Κυρίῳ καὶ μετετέθη, ὑπόδειγμα μετανοίας ταῖς γενεαῖς.

(fol. 5 recto.)

17 [נ]ח צדיק נמצא תמים[1] — לעת כלה היה תחליף: ב׳

17c בעבורו היה שארית — ובבריתו חדל מבול:

18 באות עולם[2] נכרת עמו — לבלתי השחית כל בשר: נרת

19 אברהם אב המון גוים — לא נתן בכבודו מום: רופי

20 אשר שמר מצות עליון — ובא בברית עמו:

20c בבשרו כרת לו חק — ובניסוי נמצא נאמן:

21 על כן בש[בו]עה הקים לו — לברך בזרעו גוים:

21e להנחילם [מי]ם ועד ים — ומנהר ועד אפסי ארץ:

22 וגם ליצחק הקים בן — בעבור אברהם אביו: כן

22c ברית כל ראשון נתנו — 23 וברכה נחה על ראש ישראל:

23b ויכוננהו בברכה — ויתן לו נחלתו: ויכנהו בבכורה

23d ויציבהו לשבטים — לחלק שנים עשר:

23f [ויוצ]א ממנו איש — מוצא חן בעיני כל חי: ומצא

XLV. 1 א[הוב א]להים ואנשים — משה זכרו לטובה:

2 . . . . . . [א]להים — ויאמצהו במרומים: גמוראים ויכ׳ חי

3 בר[בריו] . . . . . חר[3] — ויחזקהו לפני מלך: ברברו

3c ויצוהו [א]ל[4] . . . — ויר[אהו] . . . . .

4 באמונתו ובענותו — בחר בו מכל . . . ובענותונותו

[1] Gen. 6, 9. [2] Gen. 9, 12, &c. [3] Of the letter before ח only the top remains. It seems most to resemble that of an א or ם. [4] Exod. 6, 13.

17 ܢܘܚ ܙܕܝܩܐ ܐܫܬܟܚ ܒܕܪܗ ܫܠܝܡ. — ܒܥܕܢܐ ܕܛܘܦܢܐ ܗܘܐ ܚܠܦܐ ܠܥܠܡܐ.

17c ܘܡܛܠܬܗ ܗܘܐ ܫܘܪܒܐ. — ܘܩܝܡ ܠܗ ܐܠܗܐ ܕܠܐ ܢܗܘܐ ܬܘܒ ܛܘܦܢܐ.

18 ܒܩܝ̈ܡܬܐ ܩܝܡ ܠܗ ܠܥܠܡ. — ܕܠܐ ܢܚܒܠ ܟܠ ܒܣܪ.

19 ܐܒܪܗܡ ܐܒܐ ܕܟܢܘܫܬܐ ܕܥܡܡܐ. — ܘܠܐ ܐܣܝܡ ܡܘܡܐ ܒܐܝܩܪܗ

20 ܕܢܛܪ ܦܘܩܕܢܘܗܝ ܕܥܠܝܐ — ܘܥܠ ܒܩܝܡܐ ܥܡܗ.

20c ܘܒܒܣܪܗ ܐܩܝܡ ܠܗ ܩܝܡܐ. — ܘܒܢܣܝܘܢܗ ܐܫܬܟܚ ܡܗܝܡܢ.

21 ܡܛܠ ܗܢܐ ܒܡܘܡܬܐ ܩܝܡ ܠܗ ܐܠܗܐ. — ܕܢܬܒܪܟܘܢ ܒܙܪܥܗ ܟܠܗܘܢ ܥܡܡܐ ܕܐܪܥܐ.

21c ܘܠܡܣܓܝܘ ܙܪܥܗ ܐܝܟ ܚܠܐ ܕܝܡܐ. — ܘܠܡܣܓܝܘ ܙܪܥܗ ܛܒ ܡܢ ܟܠܗܘܢ ܥܡܡܐ.

21e ܠܡܘܪܬܘ ܐܢܘܢ ܡܢ ܝܡܐ ܠܝܡܐ. — ܘܡܢ ܦܪܬ ܥܕܡܐ ܠܣܘܦܝܗ ܕܐܪܥܐ.

22 ܘܐܦ ܠܐܝܣܚܩ ܩܝܡ — ܡܛܠ ܐܒܪܗܡ ܐܒܘܗܝ.

22c ܘܒܘܪܟܬܐ ܕܟܠ ܩܕܡܝܐ — 23 ܡܬܢܝܚܐ ܥܠ ܪܫܗ ܕܐܝܣܪܝܠ.

23b ܕܐܬܝܗܒ ܥܠ ܪܫܗ ܐܝܣܪܝܠ. — ܘܝܗܒ ܠܗ ܝܘܪܬܢܐ

23d ܘܐܩܝܡܗ ܐܒܐ ܠܫܒܛܐ. — ܘܦܠܓܗ ܘܐܬܦܠܓܘ ܠܬܪܥܣܪ ܫܒܛܝܢ.

23f ܘܢܦܩ ܡܢܗ ܓܒܪܐ ܙܕܝܩܐ. — ܡܫܟܚ ܪܚܡܐ ܒܥܝܢܝ̈ ܟܠܗܘܢ ܚܝ̈ܐ.

XLV. 1 ܘܐܬܪܚܡ ܩܕܡ ܐܠܗܐ ܘܐܦ ܒܥܝܢܝ̈ ܒܢܝ̈ ܐܢܫܐ. — ܡܘܫܐ ܕܕܘܟܪܢܗ ܠܛܘܒܬܐ

2 ܘܐܟܢܗ ܒܡܘܙܓܐ — ܘܐܫܘܗ ܠܡܠܐ̈ܟܐ.

3b ܘܐܩܝܡܗ ܩܕܡ ܡܠܟܐ

3c ܘܦܩܕܗ ܥܠ ܥܡܐ. — ܘܚܘܝܗ ܐܝܩܪܗ ܘܐܫܡܥܗ ܩܠܗ.

4 ܒܗܝܡܢܘܬܗ ܘܒܡܟܝܟܘܬܗ. — ܘܓܒܝܗ ܡܢ ܟܠܗܘܢ ܒܢܝ̈ ܐܢܫܐ.

(fol. 5 recto.)

17 Noah the righteous was found perfect, in a season of destruction he became the successor[1];
17c For his sake was there a remnant, and through the covenant with him, the flood ceased;
18 By an everlasting sign was it made[2] with him, that he would not destroy all flesh.
19 Abraham was the father of a multitude of nations, he put no blemish[3] upon his glory;
20 Who kept the commandment of the Most High, and entered into a covenant with him:
20c In his flesh he made him an ordinance, and when he was proved he was found faithful.
21 Therefore he promised him with an oath, that he would bless the nations in his seed,
21e To cause them to inherit [from se]a to sea, and from the River unto the ends of the earth.
22 To Isaac also did he raise up a son[4], for the sake of Abraham his father;
22c He gave him (?)[5] the covenant of every ancestor,
23 and the blessing rested on the head of Israel;
23b And he confirmed him in the blessing[6], and gave him his inheritance;
23d And he set him in tribes, in twelve parts.
23f [And he brought ou]t of him a man, who[7] found favour in the sight of all living,
XLV. 1 [A man beloved of] God and men, (even) Moses, whose memory is unto good[8].
2 [And G]od[9] glorified him, and strengthened him in the heights[10] (of heaven).
3 By [his words[11]] . . . ., and gave him boldness before the king;
3c And gave him a charge unto [his people], and sh[ewed him of his glory].
4 For his faithfulness and meekness, he chose him out of all [flesh];

[1] See Glossary. [2] Marg. he made (it). [3] Marg. spot. [4] Marg. did he confirm it likewise. [5] For נתן לו.
[6] Marg. titled him with the birthright. [7] Marg. and one who found. The other MS. probably read איש חסד in the first half
[8] *Or* whom he remembered (וְזָכְרוּ) unto good; cf. Neh. 5, 19. 13, 31. [9] Marg. and the Lord glorified him. [10] Marg. with terrors (Deut. 4, 34. 34, 12). [11] Marg. word.

17 Νῶε εὑρέθη τέλειος δίκαιος, ἐν καιρῷ ὀργῆς ἐγένετο ἀντάλλαγμα·
17c διὰ τοῦτο ἐγενήθη κατάλιμμα τῇ γῇ, διὰ τοῦτο ἐγένετο κατακλυσμός·
18 διαθῆκαι αἰῶνος ἐτέθησαν πρὸς αὐτόν, ἵνα μὴ ἐξαλειφθῇ κατακλυσμῷ πᾶσα σάρξ.
19 Ἀβραὰμ μέγας πατὴρ πλήθους ἐθνῶν, καὶ οὐχ εὑρέθη ὅμοιος ἐν τῇ δόξῃ,
20 ὃς συνετήρησεν νόμον Ὑψίστου, καὶ ἐγένετο ἐν διαθήκῃ μετ' αὐτοῦ,
20c καὶ ἐν σαρκὶ αὐτοῦ ἔστησεν διαθήκην, καὶ ἐν πειρασμῷ εὑρέθη πιστός·
21 διὰ τοῦτο ἐν ὅρκῳ ἔστησεν αὐτῷ ἐνευλογηθῆναι ἔθνη ἐν τῷ σπέρματι αὐτοῦ,
21c πληθῦναι αὐτὸν ὡς χοῦν τῆς γῆς, καὶ ὡς ἄστρα ἀνυψῶσαι τὸ σπέρμα αὐτοῦ,
21e καὶ κατακληρονομῆσαι αὐτοὺς ἀπὸ θαλάσσης ἕως θαλάσσης καὶ ἀπὸ ποταμοῦ ἕως ἄκρου γῆς.
22 καὶ ἐν τῷ Ἰσαὰκ ἔστησεν οὕτως δι' Ἀβραὰμ τὸν πατέρα αὐτοῦ
22c εὐλογίαν πάντων ἀνθρώπων καὶ διαθήκην,
23 καὶ κατέπαυσεν ἐπὶ κεφαλὴν Ἰακώβ·
23b ἐπέγνω αὐτὸν ἐν εὐλογίαις αὐτοῦ, καὶ ἔδωκεν αὐτῷ ἐν κληρονομίᾳ·
23d καὶ διέστειλεν μερίδας αὐτοῦ, ἐν φυλαῖς ἐμέρισεν δέκα δύο·
23f καὶ ἐξήγαγεν ἐξ αὐτοῦ ἄνδρα ἐλέους, εὑρίσκοντα χάριν ἐν ὀφθαλμοῖς πάσης σαρκός
XLV. 1 ἠγαπημένον ὑπὸ θεοῦ καὶ ἀνθρώπων Μωυσῆν, οὗ τὸ μνημόσυνον ἐν εὐλογίαις·
2 ὡμοίωσεν αὐτὸν δόξῃ ἁγίων, καὶ ἐμεγάλυνεν αὐτὸν ἐν φόβοις ἐχθρῶν·
3 ἐν λόγοις αὐτοῦ σημεῖα κατέπαυσεν, ἐδόξασεν αὐτὸν κατὰ πρόσωπον βασιλέων·
3c ἐνετείλατο αὐτῷ πρὸς λαὸν αὐτοῦ, καὶ ἔδειξεν αὐτῷ τῆς δόξης αὐτοῦ·
4 ἐν πίστει καὶ πρᾳύτητι αὐτοῦ ἡγίασεν, ἐξελέξατο αὐτὸν ἐκ πάσης σαρκός·

(fol. 5 verso.)

	5 וישמיעהו את קולו	ויגישהו לערפל :	
ויתן	5[c] וישם בידו מצוה	תורת חיים ותבונה :	
לי'	5[e] ללמד ביעקב חקיו	ועדותיו ומשפטיו לישראל :	
	6 וירם קדוש את אהרן למטה לוי	7 וישימהו לחק עולם :	
לו הודו	7[b] ויתן עליו הוד	וישרתהו בכבודו :	בברכה
תואר	7[d] ויאזרהו בתועפות ראם[1]	וילבישהו פעמונים :	התוצה
האזרהו	8 וילבישהו כליל תפארת	ויפארהו בכבוד ועוז :	
	8[c] מכנסים כתנות ומעיל	9 ויקיפהו פעמונים[2] :	
	9[b] ורמונים המון סביב	לתת נעימה בצעדיו :	
	9[d] להשמיע בדביר קולו	לזכרון לבני עמו :	
	10 בגדי קדש זהב תכלת וארגמן	מעשה חשב[3] :	
	10[c] חשן משפט אפוד ואזור	11 ושני תולעת מעשה אורג[4] :	
	11[b] אבני חפץ[5] על החשן	פתוחי חותם במלא[ים][6] :	
	11[d] כל אבן יקרה לזכרון בכתב חרות[7]	למספר . . . . [יש]ראל :	
	12 עטרת פז מעיל ומצנפת	ציץ . . . . קדש[8] :	
	12[c] הוד כבוד ותהלת עז	מחמ[ד] . . . . . . [וי]ופי :	
	13 ל[פנ]י[הם] ל[א] . . . . ן	[ו]ל[א] ל . . . .[9] זר :	
	13[c] הא . ן . . . לבניו כוה[10]	וכן בניו לדורותם :	

[1] Num. 23, 22. 24, 8. [2] Exod. 28, 33. [3] Exod. 28, 6. 15. [4] Exod. 39, 22. [5] Is. 54, 12. [6] Exod. 25, 7, &c. [7] Exod. 32, 16. [8] Exod. 28, 36. [9] Probably ל[נצח יעבם]; see 40, 4 and 47, 6. The MS. does not seem to permit of ילבשם. [10] From the traces remaining of the bottoms of letters, this may be האמין לו ולבניו כוה.

	5[b] ܘܩܪܒܗ ܠܥܪܦܠܐ.
5[c] ܘܝܗܒ ܦܘܩܕܢܘܗܝ	ܢܡܘܣܐ ܕܚܝܐ ܘܕܣܘܟܠܐ.
5[e] ܠܡܠܦܘ ܠܝܥܩܘܒ ܢܡܘܣܘܗܝ.	ܘܦܘܩܕܢܘܗܝ ܘܕܝܢܘܗܝ ܠܐܝܣܪܝܠ.
6 ܘܐܪܝܡ ܠܐܗܪܘܢ ܩܕܝܫܐ ܐܚܘܗܝ ܡܢ ܫܒܛܐ ܕܠܘܝ.	7 ܘܣܡܗ ܠܩܝܡܐ ܕܥܠܡ.
7[b] ܘܝܗܒ ܠܗ ܡܢ ܐܝܩܪܗ ܘܫܡܫܗ.	ܘܫܒܚܗ ܒܝܩܪܐ ܕܐܝܩܪܗ.
8 ܘܐܠܒܫܗ ܢܚܬܐ ܕܐܝܩܪܐ.	ܘܣܡܗ ܒܡܐܢܐ ܕܫܘܒܚܐ.

(fol. 5 verso.)

5 And made him to hear his voice,	and caused him to draw near into the thick darkness;
5c And set[1] a commandment in his hand,	even the law of life and understanding;
5e To teach in[2] Jacob his statutes,	and his testimonies and judgements unto Israel.
6 And he exalted a holy man, even Aaron of the tribe of Levi,	7 and set him for an everlasting ordinance;
7b And put majesty upon him[3],	and he ministered unto him in his glory[4].
7d And he girded him about (as) with the towering horns of a wild-ox[5],	and clothed him with bells[6].
8 And he clothed him with the perfection of adornment[7],	and adorned him with glory and strength;
8c The breeches, the coats, and the robe,	9 and [compassed him] with bells,
9b And pomegranates, a multitude round about,	to make music with his steps;
9d To make the sound[8] of him to be heard in the inmost temple,	for a memorial to the children of his people.
10 Holy garments, of gold, blue, and purple,	the work of the designer:
10c The breastplate of judgement, the ephod, and the waist-cloth,	11 and scarlet, the work of the weaver;
11b Pleasant stones upon the breast-plate,	the engravings of a signet with settings;
11d Every precious stone for a memorial with graven writing,	according to the number of [the tribes of Is]rael;
12 The crown of pure gold, the robe, and the mitre,	and the plate[9], [having engraven on it, as on a signet,] Holiness;
12c Majesty, glory, and the praise of strength,	the desire [of the eyes, and the perfection of b]eauty.
13 Be[fore them were no]t [any such,	and no] stranger [should put them on for ever].
13c He [trusted him and] his sons after this manner,	and thus (should) his sons (do) throughout their generations;

[1] Marg. and gave. [2] Marg. unto. [3] Marg. gave him his majesty. [4] Marg. in blessing. [5] So text; but the idea seems incongruous. ? תפארת רום, with lofty adornment, *or* (marg.) with beauteous adornment; cf. 𝔊. [6] So text; but 'bells' seems a faulty anticipation of verse 9a. Marg. חשטח is obscure. [7] Marg. his adornment. [8] Exod. 28, 35. At verse 9a the margin has in Persian : این نوسخت تا آورد بود 'This MS. reached thus far.' [9] Exod. 28, 36.

5 ἠκούτισεν αὐτὸν τῆς φωνῆς αὐτοῦ,	καὶ εἰσήγαγεν αὐτὸν εἰς τὸν γνόφον,
5c καὶ ἔδωκεν αὐτῷ κατὰ πρόσωπον ἐντολάς, .	νόμον ζωῆς καὶ ἐπιστήμης,
5e διδάξαι τὸν Ἰακὼβ διαθήκην	καὶ κρίματα αὐτοῦ τὸν Ἰσραήλ.
6 Ἀαρὼν ὕψωσεν ἅγιον ὅμοιον αὐτῷ ἀδελφὸν αὐτοῦ ἐκ φυλῆς Λευεί·	7 ἔστησεν αὐτὸν διαθήκην αἰῶνος,
7b καὶ ἔδωκεν αὐτῷ ἱερατίαν λαοῦ·	ἐμακάρισεν αὐτὸν ἐν εὐκοσμίᾳ,
7d καὶ περιέζωσεν αὐτὸν περιστολὴν δόξης·	
8 ἐνέδυσεν αὐτὸν συντέλειαν καυχήματος,	καὶ ἐστερέωσεν αὐτὸν σκεύεσιν ἰσχύος,
8c περισκελῆ καὶ ποδήρη καὶ ἐπωμίδα·	9 καὶ ἐκύκλωσεν αὐτὸν ῥοίσκοις,
9b χρυσοῖς κώδωσιν πλείστοις κυκλόθεν,	ἠχῆσαι φωνὴν ἐν βήμασιν αὐτοῦ,
9d ἀκουστὸν ποιῆσαι ἦχον ἐν ναῷ	εἰς μνημόσυνον υἱοῖς λαοῦ αὐτοῦ·
10 στολῇ ἁγίᾳ, χρυσῷ καὶ ὑακίνθῳ	καὶ πορφύρᾳ, ἔργων ποικιλτοῦ,
10c λογίῳ κρίσεως, δήλοις ἀληθείας,	11 κεκλωσμένῃ κόκκῳ, ἔργῳ τεχνίτου,
11b λίθοις πολυτελέσιν γλύμματος σφραγῖδος,	ἐν δέσει χρυσίου, ἔργων λιθουργοῦ,
11d εἰς μνημόσυνον ἐν γραφῇ κεκολαμμένῃ	κατ' ἀριθμὸν φυλῶν Ἰσραήλ·
12 στέφανον χρυσοῦν ἐπάνω κιδάρεως,	ἐκτύπωμα σφραγῖδος ἁγιάσματος,
12c καύχημα τιμῆς, ἔργον ἰσχύος,	ἐπιθυμήματα ὀφθαλμῶν κοσμούμενα.
13 ὡραῖα πρὸ αὐτοῦ οὐ γέγονεν τοιαῦτα,	ἕως αἰῶνος οὐκ ἐνεδύσατο ἀλλογενὴς
13c πλὴν τῶν υἱῶν αὐτοῦ μόνον,	καὶ τὰ ἔκγονα αὐτοῦ διὰ παντός.

(fol. 6 recto.)

14 [מנ]חתו כליל תקטר[1] וכל יום תמיד פעמים:
15 [וי]מלא משה את ידו[2] וימשחהו בשמן הקדש:
15c ותהי לו ברית עולם ולזרעו כימי שמים[3]:
15e לשרת ולכהן לו ולברך את עמו בשמו:
16 ויבחר בו מכל חי להגיש עלה וחלבים:
16c ולהקטיר ריח ניחח ואזכרה[4] ולכפר על בני ישראל:
17 ויתן לו מצותיו וימשילהו בחוק ומשפט:
17c וילמד את עמו חק ומשפט את בני ישראל:
18 ויחרו[5] בו זרים ויקנאו בו במדבר:
18c אנשי דתן ואבירם ועדת קרח בעזוז אפם:
19 וירא ייי ויתאנף ויכלם בחרון אפו:
19c ויבא להם אות ויאכלם בשביב[6] אשו:
20 ו . . . . לאהרן כבודו ויתן לו נחלתו:
20c ר[7] . . . . קדש נתן לו לחם 21a אשי ייי יאכלון[8]:
20d . . . . . . [י]חלקו 21b ומתנה לו ולזרעו:
22 אך . . . . . . לא ינחל ובתוכם לא יחלק נחלה:
22c אשי יי[י] . ל . . . . ל . . . .[9] . . . . . ישראל:
23 וגם פינחס [ב]ן אלעזר בגבורה . ה . . . .

[1] Lev. 6, 15. [2] Lev. 8, 33. [3] Ps. 89, 30. [4] Lev. 2, 2. [5] Is. 41, 11. 45, 24. [6] Job 18, 5. [7] Or possibly ה or ח. [8] Deut. 18, 1[b]. [9] Deut. 18, 1. Jos. 13, 14.

15 ܘܡܠܐ ܒܟܗܢܘܬܗ ܡܘܫܐ ܐܝܕܘܗܝ: ܘܡܫܚܗ ܡܫܚܐ ܕܩܘܕܫܐ.
15c ܘܗܘܬ ܠܗ ܠܡܫܚܐ ܕܠܥܠܡ. ܘܠܒܢܘܗܝ ܐܝܟ ܝܘܡܬܐ ܕܫܡܝܐ.
15e ܠܡܫܡܫܘ ܘܠܡܒܪܟܘ ܠܥܡܗ ܒܫܡܗ.
16 ܘܓܒܝܗ ܡܢ ܟܠܗܘܢ ܚܝܐ. ܠܡܩܪܒܘ ܩܘܪܒܢܐ
16c ܘܒܣܡܐ ܘܒܣܡܐ. ܘܠܡܚܣܝܘ ܥܠ ܒܢܝ ܐܝܣܪܝܠ.
17 ܘܝܗܒ ܠܗ ܦܘܩܕܢܐ ܘܐܫܠܛܗ ܒܢܡܘܣܐ ܘܕܝܢܐ.

18 ܘܐܬܚܣܡܘ ܒܗ ܢܘܟܪܝܐ. ܘܩܢܘ ܒܗ ܒܡܕܒܪܐ
18c ܐܢܫܐ ܕܕܬܢ ܘܐܒܝܪܘܡ. ܘܟܢܘܫܬܐ ܕܩܘܪܚ ܒܚܘܡܬܐ.
19 ܘܚܙܐ ܐܠܗܐ ܘܪܓܙ. ܘܐܘܒܕ ܐܢܘܢ ܒܚܡܬܗ.
19c ܘܐܝܬܝ ܥܠܝܗܘܢ ܡܚܘܬܐ. ܘܐܘܩܕ ܐܢܘܢ ܒܫܠܗܒܝܬܐ ܕܢܘܪܗ.
20 ܘܐܘܣܦ ܥܠ ܐܗܪܘܢ ܐܝܩܪܐ. ܘܝܗܒ ܠܗ ܝܪܬܘܬܗ.
20c ܩܘܕܫܐ ܕܩܘܕܫܐ ܘܡܝܬܪܐ ܕܠܚܡܐ
21b ܠܗ ܘܠܒܢܘܗܝ.
22 ܒܠܚܘܕ ܒܐܪܥܗܘܢ ܠܐ ܢܐܪܬ ܝܪܬܘܬܐ. ܘܠܐ ܦܠܓܘ ܦܠܓܘܬܐ ܒܝܢܝܗܘܢ.
22c ܡܛܠ ܕܡܪܝܐ ܦܠܓܗ ܘܝܪܬܘܬܗ ܒܝܬ ܐܝܣܪܝܠ܀
23 ܘܐܦ ܦܝܢܚܣ ܒܪ ܐܠܥܙܪ. ܒܓܢܒܪܘܬܗ ܢܣܒ ܬܠܬܐ ܐܝܩܪܝܢ:

(fol. 6 recto.)

14 His meal-offering should be wholly burnt, and every day twice continually.
15 And Moses filled his hand[1], and anointed him with the holy oil.
15c And it was unto him an everlasting covenant, and to his seed as the days of heaven,
15e To minister and to execute the priest's office unto him, and to bless his people in his name.
16 And he chose him out of all living, to bring near the burnt-offering and the fat pieces;
16c And to burn a sweet savour and a memorial[2], and to make atonement for the children of Israel.
17 And he gave him his commandments, and made him to have authority over statute and judgement.
17c So he taught his people statutes, and judgements unto the children of Israel.
18 But strangers were incensed against him, and were jealous of him in the wilderness;
18c The men of Dathan and Abiram, and the congregation of Korah in the violence of their [anger.
19 And the Lord saw it and was angered, and consumed them in the heat of his anger:
19c And he brought upon them a sign, and devoured them with his flaming fire.
20 And [he increased] to Aaron his glory, and gave him his inheritance;
20c The holy f[irst-fruits[3]] he gave to him for bread,
21a that they should eat the fire-offerings of the Lord;
20d . . . . they should divide,
21b and (they should be) a gift to him and to his seed;
22 Only [in the land of his people] he should not inherit, and amongst them he should not divide an inheritance;
22c The fire-offerings of the Lord [should be their portion and their inheritance] . . . . Israel.
23 Moreover Phinehas, the son of Eleazar, in might . . . . .

[1] i.e. consecrated him; see Exod. 28, 41. Lev. 8, 33, R.V. [2] Lev. 2, 2, &c. [3] Supplying ר[אשית].

14 θυσίαν αὐτοῦ ὁλοκαρπωθήσονται καθ' ἡμέραν ἐνδελεχῶς δίς.
15 ἐπλήρωσεν Μωυσῆς τὰς χεῖρας καὶ ἔχρισεν αὐτὸν ἐν ἐλαίῳ ἁγίῳ·
15c ἐγενήθη αὐτῷ εἰς διαθήκην αἰώνιον, καὶ ἐν τῷ σπέρματι αὐτοῦ ἐν ἡμέραις οὐρανοῦ,
15e λειτουργεῖν αὐτῷ ἅμα καὶ ἱερατεύειν, καὶ εὐλογεῖν τὸν λαὸν αὐτοῦ ἐν τῷ ὀνόματι.
16 ἐξελέξατο αὐτὸν ἀπὸ παντὸς ζῶντος, προσαγαγεῖν κάρπωσιν Κυρίῳ,
16c θυμίαμα καὶ εὐωδίαν εἰς μνημόσυνον, ἐξιλάσκεσθαι περὶ τοῦ λαοῦ σου.
17 ἔδωκεν αὐτὸν ἐν ἐντολαῖς αὐτοῦ, ἐξουσίαν ἐν διαθήκαις κριμάτων,
17c διδάξαι τὸν Ἰακὼβ τὰ μαρτύρια, καὶ ἐν νόμῳ αὐτοῦ φωνῆσαι Ἰσραήλ.
18 ἐπισυνέστησαν αὐτῷ ἀλλότριοι καὶ ἐζήλωσαν αὐτὸν ἐν τῇ ἐρήμῳ,
18c ἄνδρες οἱ περὶ Δαθὰν καὶ Ἀβειρὼν καὶ ἡ συναγωγὴ Κόρε ἐν θυμῷ καὶ ὀργῇ·
19 εἶδεν Κύριος καὶ οὐκ εὐδόκησεν, καὶ συνετελέσθησαν ἐν θυμῷ ὀργῆς·
19c ἐποίησεν αὐτοῖς τέρατα, καταναλῶσαι ἐν πυρὶ φλογὸς αὐτοῦ.
20 καὶ προσέθηκεν Ἀαρὼν δόξαν, καὶ ἔδωκεν αὐτῷ κληρονομίαν·
20c ἀπαρχὰς πρωτογενημάτων ἐμέρισεν αὐτοῖς, ἄρτον πρώτοις ἡτοίμασεν πλησμονήν·
21 καὶ γὰρ θυσίας Κυρίου φάγονται, ἃς ἔδωκεν αὐτῷ τε καὶ τῷ σπέρματι αὐτοῦ.
22 πλὴν ἐν γῇ λαοῦ οὐ κληρονομήσει, καὶ μερὶς οὐκ ἔστιν αὐτῷ ἐν λαῷ,
αὐτὸς γὰρ μερίς σου, κληρονομία.
23 καὶ Φινεὲς υἱὸς Ἐλεαζὰρ τρίτος εἰς δόξαν,

(fol. 6 verso.)

23c בקנאו לאלוה כל ויעמד בפרץ[1] עמו:
23e אשר נדבו לבו ויכפר על בני ישראל[2]:
24 לכן גם לו הקים חק ברית שלום[3] לכלכל מקדש:
24c אשר תהיה לו ולזרעו כהונה גדולה עד עולם:
25 וגם בריתו עם דוד בן ישי למטה יהודה:
25c נחלת איש לפני כבודו נחלת אהרן לכל זרעו:
25e ועתה ברכו נא את ייי הטוב המעטר אתכם כבוד:
26 ויתן לכם חכמת לב 26c למען לא ישכח טובכם [וגב]ורתכם לדורות עולם:

XLVI. 1 גבור בן חיל יהושע בן נון משרת משה בנבואה:
1c אשר נוצר להיות בימיו תשועה גדלה לבחיריו:
1e להנקם נקמי אויב ולהנחיל את ישראל:
2 מה נהדר בנטותו יד בהניפו כידון[4] על עיר:
3 מי הוא לפניו יתיצב כי מלחמות ייי נל[חם:]
4 הלא בידו עמד השמש יום אחד . . . . . . :
5 כי קרא אל אל עליון כאכפה ל[ו] . . . .
5c ויענהו אל עליון באבני . . . . . . ל . . שׁ:
6 . . . . ל . . . . . זבֿ . . . .
6c למען [דע]ת כל גוי חרם כי צופה ייי מלחמתם:

[1] Ps. 106, 23. [2] Num. 25, 7-13. [3] Num. 25, 12. [4] Jos. 8, 18. 26.

23c ܒܛܢܢܐ ܕܠܗ ܠܡܪܝܡܐ ܘܟܕ ܐܝܣܪܐܝܠ. ܘܩܡ ܒܬܘܪܥܬܐ ܕܥܡܐ
23f ܘܚܣܐ ܥܠ ܐܝܣܪܐܝܠ.
24 ܡܛܠ ܗܢܐ ܒܟܘܡܪܘܬܐ ܩܝܡܐ ܠܗ ܐܠܗܐ. ܕܢܗܘܐ ܠܗ ܡܕܒܪܢܐ.
24c ܘܬܗܘܐ ܠܗ ܘܠܒܢܘܗܝ ܟܘܡܪܘܬܐ ܪܒܬܐ ܠܥܠܡ.
25 ܘܐܦ ܕܘܝܕ ܒܪ ܐܝܫܝ.
25c ܝܘܪܬܢܐ ܕܡܠܟܘܬܐ ܠܒܢܘܗܝ ܒܠܚܘܕ. ܘܝܘܪܬܢܐ ܕܐܗܪܘܢ ܠܗ ܘܠܒܢܘܗܝ.
25e ܡܟܝܠ ܒܪܟܘ ܠܐܠܗܐ
26 ܕܢܬܠ ܠܟܘܢ ܚܟܡܬܐ ܕܠܒܐ. ܠܡܕܢ ܠܥܡܗ ܒܩܘܫܛܐ. 26c ܡܛܠ ܕܠܐ ܢܬܛܥܐ ܛܒܬܗܘܢ. ܘܫܘܠܛܢܗܘܢ ܠܕܪܗܘܢ ܕܪܐ ܕܕܪܐ.

XLVI. 1 ܓܢܒܪܐ ܒܪ ܚܝܠܐ ܝܫܘܥ ܒܪ ܢܘܢ. ܡܫܡܫܢܐ ܐܬܒܚܪ ܒܢܒܝܘܬܐ ܐܝܟ ܡܘܫܐ ܢܒܝܐ.
1c ܕܢܗܘܐ ܒܝܘܡܘܗܝ ܦܘܪܩܢܐ ܠܓܒܝܘܗܝ.
1e ܘܠܡܬܦܪܥܘ ܡܢ ܒܥܠܕܒܒܐ. ܘܠܡܘܪܬܘ ܠܒܢܝ ܐܝܣܪܐܝܠ ܐܪܥܐ ܕܡܘܠܟܢܐ.
2 ܡܐ ܫܦܝܪ ܗܘܐ ܟܕ ܡܪܝܡ ܚܢܝܬܐ ܕܐܝܕܗ. ܘܟܕ ܡܚܝܐ ܥܠ ܡܕܝܢܬܐ.
3 ܡܢܘ ܡܨܐ ܠܡܩܡ ܩܕܡܘܗܝ. ܡܛܠ ܕܩܪܒܗ ܕܡܪܝܐ ܗܘ ܩܪܒ.
4 ܡܛܠ ܕܒܐܝܕܗ ܩܡ ܫܡܫܐ. ܘܝܘܡܐ ܚܕ ܗܘܐ ܐܝܟ ܬܪܝܢ.
5 ܡܛܠ ܕܩܪܐ ܩܕܡ ܡܪܝܐ ܘܥܢܝܗ. ܘܫܡܥ ܒܩܠܗ ܠܬܘܩܦܐ
5c ܘܥܢܝܗ ܒܟܐܦܐ. ܕܒܪܕܐ ܘܒܪܩܐ ܡܢ ܫܡܝܐ ܐܬܐ.
6 ܘܢܦܠ ܥܠ ܥܡܐ ܥܘܠܐ ܘܐܘܒܕ ܠܟܠܗܘܢ.
6c ܘܝܕܥܘ ܟܠܗܘܢ ܥܡܡܐ ܚܪܡܐ. ܕܐܠܗܐ ܗܘ ܐܪܒ ܩܪܒܗܘܢ.

(fol. 6 verso.)

23c In his jealousy for the God of all, and stood in the breach of his people.
23e Whose heart made him willing, and he made atonement for the children of Israel.
24 Therefore for him also did he establish an ordinance, a covenant of peace to maintain the sanctuary;
24c Which should be to him and to his seed, an high priesthood for ever.
25 Also his covenant (was) with David the son of Jesse, of the tribe of Judah.
25c An inheritance of fire in presence of his glory was the inheritance of Aaron unto all his seed.
25e And now bless ye the Lord, the good, who hath crowned you with glory;
26 And given you wisdom of heart, 26c that your goodness [and] your [mig]ht be not forgotten through perpetual generations.
XLVI. 1 A mighty man of valour was Joshua the son of Nun, the minister of Moses in prophecy,
1c Who was formed that there might be in his days a great salvation to his chosen ones;
1e To execute vengeance upon the enemy, and to give Israel his inheritance.
2 How glorious was he when he stretched out his hand, when he swung the javelin against the city!
3 Who was he that could stand before him? for he fou[ght] the battles of the Lord.
4 Did not the sun stand still by his hand, so that one day [became two]?
5 For he called unto God Most High, when he was pressed upon [round about].
5c And God Most High answered him with stones of [hail and coa]ls [of fir]e;
6 . . . . and in [the descent[1]] . . . . . .
6c That every banned nation[2] [might kn]ow that the Lord watched their battles.

[1] Jos. 10, 11. [2] For the idea, see Deut. 7, 2. Jos. 10, 40. 11, 12. 20, &c.; for the expression, cf. Is. 34, 5.

23c ἐν τῷ ζηλῶσαι αὐτὸν ἐν φόβῳ Κυρίου καὶ στῆσαι αὐτὸν ἐν τροπῇ λαοῦ
23e ἐν ἀγαθότητι προθυμίας ψυχῆς αὐτοῦ· καὶ ἐξιλάσατο περὶ τοῦ Ἰσραήλ.
24 διὰ τοῦτο ἐστάθη αὐτῷ διαθήκη εἰρήνης, προστάτην ἁγίων καὶ λαῷ αὐτοῦ,
24c ἵνα αὐτῷ ᾖ καὶ τῷ σπέρματι αὐτοῦ ἱερωσύνης μεγαλεῖον εἰς τοὺς αἰῶνας.
25 καὶ διαθήκην τῷ Δαυεὶδ υἱῷ ἐκ φυλῆς Ἰούδα,
25c κληρονομία βασιλέως υἱοῦ ἐξ υἱοῦ μόνου, κληρονομία Ἀαρὼν καὶ τῷ σπέρματι αὐτοῦ.

26 δῴη ὑμῖν σοφίαν ἐν καρδίᾳ ὑμῶν, κρίνειν τὸν λαὸν αὐτοῦ ἐν δικαιοσύνῃ,
26c ἵνα μὴ ἀφανισθῇ τὰ ἀγαθὰ αὐτῶν, καὶ τὴν δόξαν αὐτῶν εἰς γενεὰς αὐτῶν.
XLVI. 1 κραταιὸς ἐν πολέμοις Ἰησοῦς Ναυή, καὶ διάδοχος Μωσῆ ἐν προφητείαις,
1c ὃς ἐγένετο κατὰ τὸ ὄνομα αὐτοῦ μέγας ἐπὶ σωτηρίᾳ ἐκλεκτῶν αὐτοῦ,
1e ἐκδικῆσαι ἐπεγειρομένους ἐχθρούς, ὅπως κληρονομήσῃ τὸν Ἰσραήλ.
2 ὡς ἐδοξάσθη ἐν τῷ ἐπᾶραι χεῖρας αὐτοῦ καὶ τῷ ἐκκλῖναι ῥομφαίαν ἐπὶ πόλεις.
3 τίς πρότερον αὐτοῦ οὕτως ἔστη; τοὺς γὰρ πολεμίους Κύριος αὐτὸς ἐπήγαγεν
4 οὐχὶ ἐν χειρὶ αὐτοῦ ἀνεπόδισεν ὁ ἥλιος, καὶ μία ἡμέρα ἐγενήθη πρὸς δύο;
5 ἐπεκαλέσατο τὸν ὕψιστον δυνάστην ἐν τῷ θλίψαι αὐτὸν ἐχθροὺς κυκλόθεν·
5c καὶ ἐπήκουσεν αὐτῶν μέγας Κύριος ἐν λίθοις χαλάζης δυνάμεως κραταιᾶς·
6 κατέρραξεν ἐπ' ἔθνος πόλεμον, καὶ ἐν καταβάσει ἀπώλεσεν ἀνθεστηκότας,
6c ἵνα γνῶσιν ἔθνη πανοπλίαν αὐτῶν, ὅτι ἐναντίον Κυρίου ὁ πόλεμος αὐτοῦ·

(fol. 7 recto.)

6e [גם] כי מלא[1] אחרי אל   7 ובימי משה עשה חסד:
7b [הו]א וכלב בן יפנה   להתיצב בפרע[2] קהל:
7d להשיב חרן מעדה   ולהשבית דבה רעה[3]:
8 לכם גם הם בשנים נאצלו   מישש מאות אלף רגלי:
8c להביאם אל נחלתם ארץ זבת חלב ודבש:
9 ויתן לכלב עצמה   ועד שיבה עמדה עמו:
9c להדריכם[4] על במתי ארץ   וגם זרעו ירש נחלה:
10 למען דעת כל זרע יעקב   כי טוב למלא אחרי ייי:
11 והשופטים איש בשמו   כל אשר לא נשא לבו:
11c ולא נסוג[5] מאחרי אל   יהי זכרם לברכה 12b ושמם תחליף לבניהם:
13 אוהב עמו ורצוי[6] עשהו   המשואל מבטן אמו:
13c נזיר ייי בנבואה   שמואל שופט ומכהן:
13e נ[ביא] אל הבין ממלכת   וימשח נגידים על עם:
14 ב . . . . [צ]וה עדה   ויפקד אלהי יעקב:
15 ב . . . [ק]ורש חוה   וגם בדברו נאמן רועה:
16 וגם ה[וא] . . . [א]ל [א]ל   . . . ל[ו אי]ביו מסביב:
16c בעלתו . . . . ל .   17 ויר[עם] . . . .
17b בפקע אדיר נשמע קולו   18 ויכנע[7] נציבי[8] צר ויא[בד את] כל סרני[9] פלשתים:

[1] Num. 14, 24. [2] Prov. 29, 18. Exod. 32, 25. [3] Num. 14, 37. [4] Cf. Jos. 14, 9 (דרכה). [5] Ps. 44, 18. [6] Deut. 33, 24. [7] 1 Sam. 7, 13. [8] 1 Sam. 10, 5. 13, 3. 4. [9] 1 Sam. 7, 7, &c.

6e ܘܐܦ ܗܘ ܫܠܡ ܒܬܪ ܐܠܗܐ.   7 ܘܒܝܘܡܝ ܡܘܫܐ ܥܒܕ ܛܝܒܘܬܐ:
7b ܗܘ ܘܟܠܒ ܒܪ ܢܘܢ.   ܠܡܩܡ ܒܬܘܪܥܬܐ ܕܥܡܐ.
7d ܠܡܗܦܟܘ ܚܘܡܬܐ   ܘܠܡܫܬܩܘ ܡܘܬܐ ܡܢ ܐܪܥܐ ܕܡܘܠܟܢܐ.
8 ܘܬܪܝܗܘܢ ܒܠܚܘܕܝܗܘܢ ܐܬܦܨܝܘ   ܡܢ ܫܬܡܐܐ ܐܠܦܝܢ
8c ܠܡܥܠܘ ܐܢܘܢ ܠܝܪܬܘܬܗܘܢ   ܠܐܪܥܐ ܕܡܪܕܝܐ ܚܠܒܐ ܘܕܒܫܐ.
9 ܘܝܗܒ ܠܟܠܒ ܚܝܠܐ   ܘܩܝܡܐ ܠܣܝܒܘܬܗ ܐܠܡܐ ܠܥܡܗ
9c ܠܡܥܠܝܘܬܗ ܥܠ ܪܘܡܗ ܕܐܪܥܐ   ܘܐܦ ܙܪܥܗ ܝܪܬ ܝܪܬܘܬܐ.
10 ܡܛܠ ܕܢܕܥ ܙܪܥܗ ܕܝܥܩܘܒ   ܕܛܒ ܢܣܒܘܗܝ ܕܐܠܗܐ ܘܢܬܒܥܘܢܗ.
11 ܓܒܪ ܓܒܪ ܒܫܡܗ   ܟܠ ܕܠܐ ܛܥܐ ܠܒܗܘܢ
11c ܘܠܐ ܗܦܟܘ ܡܢ ܒܬܪܗ ܕܐܠܗܐ   ܢܗܘܐ ܕܘܟܪܢܗܘܢ ܠܒܘܪܟܬܐ.
12 ܘܓܪܡܝܗܘܢ ܢܦܪܚܘܢ ܐܝܟ ܡܘܫܐ   ܘܫܡܗܘܢ ܢܥܒܪ ܥܠ ܒܢܝܗܘܢ ܘܠܒܢܝ ܒܢܝܗܘܢ ܠܬܫܒܚܬܗܘܢ.
13 ܘܪܚܝܡ ܠܒܪܝܗ   ܗܘ ܕܐܬܫܐܠ ܡܢ ܟܪܣܐ ܕܐܡܗ
13c ܢܙܝܪܐ ܒܢܒܝܘܬܐ   ܫܡܘܐܝܠ ܕܝܢܐ ܘܟܗܢܐ
13e ܕܒܡܠܬܗ ܩܝܡ ܡܠܟܘܬܐ   ܘܡܫܚ ܡܠܟܐ ܘܫܠܝܛܢܐ ܠܥܡܐ.
14 ܒܢܡܘܣܗ ܕܝܢ ܟܢܘܫܬܐ   ܐܠܗܐ ܕܥܩܒ ܡܢܗ ܕܝܥܩܘܒ.
16 ܘܐܦ ܗܘ   ܩܪܐ ܠܐܠܗܐ ܡܢ ܟܠܗܘܢ ܚܕܪܘܗܝ
16c ܒܡܩܪܒܘܬܗ ܐܡܪܐ ܕܚܠܒܐ.   17 ܘܐܪܥܡ ܡܢ ܫܡܝܐ ܡܪܝܐ
17b ܘܒܩܠܐ ܥܫܝܢܐ ܐܫܡܥ ܩܠܗ.   18 ܘܐܒܕ ܟܠܗܘܢ ܫܠܝܛܢܐ ܕܨܘܪ ܘܐܘܒܕ ܟܠܗܘܢ ܫܠܝܛܢܐ ܕܦܠܫܬܝܐ.

(fol. 7 recto.)

6c [Yea], because he followed fully after God, 7 and in the days of Moses wrought godliness,
7b [H]e, and Caleb the son of Jephunneh, in standing fast when the assembly cast off restraint,
7d To turn away wrath from the congregation, and to still the evil report;
8 Therefore[1] they also, two alone, were reserved[2], out of six hundred thousand men on foot,
8c To bring them into their inheritance, a land flowing with milk and honey.
9 And he gave strength unto Caleb, and even unto old age it remained with him;
9c To make him[3] to tread upon the high places of the land, and that his seed also should possess an inheritance;
10 That all the seed of Jacob might know that it was good to follow fully after the Lord.
11 Also the judges every one by his name, every one whose heart had not turned aside[4],
11c And who drew not back from (following) after God— may their memory be blessed, 12b and their name succeed to their sons.
13 The lover[5] of his people, & acceptable to his Maker, (was) he who was lent[6] from his mother's womb,
13c A nazirite of the Lord in prophecy, Samuel, who was judge and priest.
13e [The pro]phet of God established a kingdom, and anointed leaders[7] over the people.
14 By [his law he com]manded the congregation, and the God of Jacob visited (them).
15 By . ... . he was [san]ctified a gazer (prophet), and by his word also he was confirmed as a shepherd[8].
16 He also [called] unto God, [when] his [ene]mies [pressed hi]m[9] round about,
16c When he offered up [a sucking lamb[10]], 17 and [the Lord] thun[dered out of heaven];
17b With a mighty crash his voice was heard, 18 and he subdued the garrisons of the foe, and des[troy]ed all the lords of the Philistines.

[1] Reading לכן. [2] ? נצלו were delivered (𝔊 𝔖). [3] Reading להדריכו, or (Jer. 39, 14) הו–. [4] נסוה for נשא; cf. 𝔊 𝔖. [5] ? אהוב beloved by. [6] המשואל for המשואל, with a play on the name Samuel; cf. 1 Sam. 1, 28. [7] 1 Sam. 9, 16. 2 Sam. 5, 2, R.V. *marg.* [8] Or perhaps רואה (as a seer); cf. 𝔊, and 1 Sam. 3, 20. 9, 19. [9] Perhaps בהצר. [10] 1 Sam. 7, 9.

6c καὶ γὰρ ἐπηκολούθησεν ὀπίσω Δυνάστου. 7 καὶ ἐν ἡμέραις Μωυσέως ἐποίησεν ἔλεος,
7b αὐτὸς καὶ Χαλὲβ υἱὸς Ἰεφοννή, ἀντιστῆναι ἔναντι ἐχθροῦ,
7d κωλῦσαι λαὸν ἀπὸ ἁμαρτίας καὶ κοπάσαι γογγυσμὸν πονηρίας.
8 καὶ αὐτοὶ δύο ὄντες διεσώθησαν ἀπὸ ἑξακοσίων χιλιάδων πεζῶν,
8c εἰσαγαγεῖν αὐτοὺς εἰς κληρονομίαν, εἰς γῆν ῥέουσαν γάλα καὶ μέλι.
9 καὶ ἔδωκεν ὁ κύριος τῷ Χαλὲβ ἰσχύν, καὶ ἕως γήρους διέμεινεν αὐτῷ,
9c ἐπιβῆναι αὐτὸν ἐπὶ ὕψος τῆς γῆς, καὶ τὸ σπέρμα αὐτοῦ κατέσχεν κληρονομίαν·
10 ὅπως ἴδωσιν πάντες οἱ υἱοὶ Ἰσραὴλ ὅτι καλὸν τὸ πορεύεσθαι ὀπίσω Κυρίου.
11 καὶ οἱ κριταί, ἕκαστος τῷ αὐτοῦ ὀνόματι, ὅσων οὐκ ἐξεπόρνευσεν ἡ καρδία
11c καὶ ὅσοι οὐκ ἀπεστράφησαν ἀπὸ Κυρίου, εἴη τὸ μνημόσυνον αὐτῶν ἐν εὐλογίαις·
12 τὰ ὀστᾶ αὐτῶν ἀναθάλοι ἐκ τοῦ τόπου αὐτῶν, καὶ τὸ ὄνομα αὐτῶν ἀντικαταλλασσόμενον ἐφ' υἱοῖς δεδοξασμένων αὐτῶν.
13 ἠγαπημένος ὑπὸ κυρίου αὐτοῦ

13c προφήτης Κυρίου κατέστησεν βασιλέα, καὶ ἔχρισεν ἄρχοντας ἐπὶ τὸν λαὸν αὐτοῦ·
14 ἐν νόμῳ Κυρίου ἔκρινεν συναγωγήν, καὶ ἐπεσκέψατο Κύριος τὸν Ἰακώβ.
15 ἐν πίστει αὐτοῦ ἠκριβάσθη προφήτης, καὶ ἐγνώσθη ἐν πίστει αὐτοῦ πιστὸς ὁράσεως.
16 καὶ ἐπεκαλέσατο τὸν κύριον δυνάστην, ἐν τῷ θλίψαι ἐχθροὺς αὐτοῦ κυκλόθεν,
16c ἐν προσφορᾷ ἀρνὸς γαλαθηνοῦ· 17 καὶ ἐβρόντησεν ἀπ' οὐρανοῦ Κύριος,
17b καὶ ἐν ἤχῳ μεγάλῳ ἀκουστὴν ἐποίησεν τὴν φωνὴν αὐτοῦ, 18 καὶ ἐξέτριψεν ἡγουμένους Τυρίων καὶ πάντας ἄρχοντας Φυλιστιείμ.

(fol. 7 verso.)

19 ועת נוחו על משכבו[1] העיד ייי ומשיחו 19ᶜ כופר ונעלם ממ[י לקח]תי[2] וכל אדם לא ענה בו:

19ᵉ וגם עד עת קצו נבון נמצא בעיני ייי ובעיני כל חי:

20 וגם אחרי מותו נדרש ויגד למלך דרכיו: 20ᶜ וישא מארץ קולו בנבואה:

XLVII.	1 וגם אחריו עמד נתן	להתיצב לפני דוד:	
	2 כי כחלב מורם[3] מקדש	בן דויד מישראל:	
	3 לכפירים שחק כנדי	ולדובים כבני בשן[4]:	
	4 בנעוריו הכה [ג]בור	ויכר . . . . עולם:	
	4ᶜ בהניפו ידו על קלע	וישבר ת[פא]רת גלית:	
	5 כי קרא אל אל עליון	ויתן בימינו עז:	
	5ᶜ להרף את איש יודע מלחמות	ולהרים את קרן עמו:	
	6 על כן ענו לו בנות	ויכנוהו ברבבה:	
	6ᶜ בעטותו צניף נלחם	7 ומסביב הכניע צר:	
	7ᵇ ויתן בפלשתים ערים	ועד היום שבר קר[נם:]	
	8 בכל מעשהו נתן הודות	לאל עליון . . . . [כ]בוד:	
דויד	8ᶜ בכל לבו אוהב עשהו	ובכל . . . . . ב̄:	
הכין	9 נגינות שיר ל	וקול ה̄ . . . [נב]לים תיקן:	נבל
	10 . . ל	. . . . נ̄ה:	
	10ᶜ בהל[לם] א̄ת שם קדשו	לפני בק[ר] ירנן משפט[5]:	

9ᵇ קול מזמור הנבלים

[1] Is. 57, 2. [2] 1 Sam. 12, 3. [3] Lev. 4, 8. 10. 19. [4] Deut. 32, 14. [5] Above משפט is written מקדש.

19 ܘܒܥܕܢܐ ܕܡܫܟܒܗ ܥܠ ܥܪܣܗ. ܐܣܗܕ ܩܕܡ ܡܪܝܐ ܘܩܕܡ ܡܫܝܚܗ: 19ᶜ ܕܡܘܗܒܐ ܘܡܣܐܢܐ ܡܢ ܐܢܫ ܠܐ ܢܣܒ.
ܘܟܠ ܒܗܢ ܠܐ ܐܣܗܕ ܒܒܝܫܘ.

20 ܘܡܢ ܒܬܪ ܕܡܝܬ. ܐܬܢܒܝ. ܘܚܘܝ ܠܡܠܟܐ ܐܘܪܚܗ. 20ᶜ ܘܐܪܝܡ ܡܢ ܐܪܥܐ ܩܠܗ ܒܢܒܝܘܬܐ ܠܡܚܦܝܘ ܚܛܗܐ ܀

XLVII.	1 ܘܒܬܪܗ ܩܡ ܢܬܢ ܢܒܝܐ	ܠܡܫܡܫܘ ܩܕܡ ܕܘܝܕ
	2 ܐܝܟ ܬܪܒܐ ܕܦܪܫ ܠܐܠܗܐ ܡܢ ܩܘܪܒܢܐ.	ܗܟܢܐ ܦܪܫ ܕܘܝܕ ܡܢ ܐܝܣܪܝܠ.
	3 ܐܪܝܘܬܐ ܐܝܟ ܓܕܝܐ ܚܐܟ	ܘܕܒܐ ܐܝܟ ܐܡܪܐ.
	4 ܒܛܠܝܘܬܗ ܩܛܠ ܓܢܒܪܐ.	ܘܐܥܒܪ ܚܣܕܐ ܕܥܡܗ.
	4ᶜ ܐܪܝܡ ܐܝܕܗ ܒܩܠܥܐ	ܘܬܒܪ ܒܩܠܥܐ ܪܘܪܒܘܬܗ ܕܓܘܠܝܬ.
	5 ܡܛܠ ܕܩܪܐ ܩܕܡ ܐܠܗܐ	ܘܝܗܒ ܠܐܝܡܢܗ ܬܘܩܦܐ.
	5ᶜ ܠܡܩܛܠ ܠܓܢܒܪܐ ܕܝܕܥ ܩܪܒܐ	ܠܡܪܡܘ ܩܪܢܐ ܕܥܡܗ ܐܝܣܪܝܠ.
	6 ܡܛܠ ܗܢܐ ܡܫܒܚܝܢ ܒܢܬܐ	ܒܪܒܘܬܐ.
	6ᶜ ܡܛܠ ܐܬܓܒ.	7 ܘܐܒܕ ܒܥܠܕܒܒܐ ܡܢ ܟܠܗܘܢ ܚܕܪܘܗܝ.
	7ᵇ ܘܐܬܒܪ ܡܢ ܦܠܣܛܝܐ.	ܘܗܘ ܒܝܘܡܐ ܒܫܘܦܪܐ ܠܥܠ ܩܪܢܗܘܢ.
	8 ܡܛܠ ܗܢܐ ܗܘܐ ܗܘܐ ܡܠܐ	ܒܟܠܐ ܕܐܘܕܝܬ ܘܬܫܒܘܚܬܐ.
	8ᶜ ܘܒܟܠܗ ܠܒܗ ܪܚܡ ܒܪܝܗ.	ܘܒܟܠ ܝܘܡ ܐܫܬܒܚ.
	9 ܠܡܫܡܫܘ ܐܩܝܡ ܗܘܐ ܩܕܡ ܡܕܒܚܐ.	
	10 ܘܝܗܒ ܠܡܫܡܫܐ ܬܫܒܚܬܐ	ܟܠ ܫܢܐ ܒܫܢܐ.

(fol. 7 verso.)

19 And at the time of his resting upon his (last) bed, he called the Lord and his anointed to witness, (saying,)
19c From [whom] have I [taken] a ransom or a secret gift[1]? and no man answered against him.
19e Also till the time of his end he was found prudent in the sight of the Lord and in the sight of all living.
20 And even after his death he was sought, and declared to the king his ways, 20c and lifted up his voice from the earth in prophecy.

XLVII. 1 Moreover after him rose up Nathan,   to stand before David.
2 For like fat separated[2] from the holy (offering),   so was David (separated) from Israel.
3 He mocked at lions as at a kid,   and at bears as at the herds of Bashan.
4 In his youth he smote a mighty man,   and took away an everlasting [reproach],
4c When he swung his hand upon the sling,   and brake the pr[id]e of Goliath.
5 For he called unto God Most High,   and he put strength in his right hand,
5c To thrust away the man skilled in battles,   and to exalt the horn of his people.
6 Therefore the daughters sang of him,   and titled him with ten thousand[3].
6c When he had put on the diadem he fought,   7 and subdued the adversary round about;
7b And set nakedness[4] among the Philistines,   and brake [their h]orn in pieces unto this day.
8 In all his works he gave thanks   to God Most High [with words of gl]ory,
8c With his whole heart loving him that made him,   and every [day] . . . .
9 Stringed instruments of song (he set[5]) be[fore the altar],   and the sound of [. . . . and of har]ps[6] he set in order.
10 . . . . [year by y]ear.
10c While [they pr]aised his holy name,   the sanctuary[7] resounded before the morning.

[1] Perhaps נעלים a pair of sandals; cf. 𝔊 here, and in 1 Sam. 12, 3. [2] *Lit.* lifted off; see Lev. 4, 8. 10. 19, &c. [3] See 1 Sam. 18, 7. [4] עלים (?) for ערים. [5] So the marg. adds. [6] Marg. harp. The vertical note has, He made a sweet sound of melody. [7] This is written above the word judgement.

19 καὶ πρὸ καιροῦ κοιμήσεως αἰῶνος ἐπεμαρτύρατο ἔναντι Κυρίου καὶ χριστοῦ 19c Χρήματα καὶ ἕως
ὑποδημάτων ἀπὸ πάσης σαρκὸς οὐκ εἴληφα· καὶ οὐκ ἐνεκάλεσεν αὐτῷ ἄνθρωπος.

20 καὶ μετὰ τὸ ὑπνῶσαι αὐτὸν προεφήτευσεν καὶ ὑπέδειξεν βασιλεῖ τὴν τελευτὴν αὐτοῦ, 20c καὶ ἀνύψωσεν
ἐκ γῆς τὴν φωνὴν αὐτοῦ ἐν προφητείᾳ, ἐξαλεῖψαι ἀνομίαν λαοῦ.

XLVII. 1 καὶ μετὰ τοῦτον ἀνέστη Ναθὰν   προφητεύειν ἐν ἡμέραις Δαυείδ.
2 ὥσπερ στέαρ ἀφωρισμένον ἀπὸ σωτηρίου,   οὕτως Δαυεὶδ ἀπὸ τῶν υἱῶν Ἰσραήλ.
3 ἐν λέουσιν ἔπαιζεν ὡς ἐν ἐρίφοις,   καὶ ἐν ἄρκοις ὡς ἐν ἄρνασι προβάτων.
4 ἐν νεότητι αὐτοῦ οὐχὶ ἀπέκτεινεν γίγαντα,   καὶ ἐξῆρεν ὀνειδισμὸν ἐκ λαοῦ
4c ἐν τῷ ἐπᾶραι χεῖρα ἐν λίθῳ σφενδόνης   καὶ καταβαλεῖν γαυρίαμα τοῦ Γολιάθ;
5 ἐπεκαλέσατο γὰρ Κύριον τὸν ὕψιστον,   καὶ ἔδωκεν ἐν τῇ δεξιᾷ αὐτοῦ κράτος,
5c ἐξᾶραι ἄνθρωπον ἐν πολέμῳ·   ἀνυψῶσει κέρας λαοῦ αὐτοῦ.
6 οὕτως ἐν μυριάσιν ἐδόξασεν αὐτόν,   καὶ ᾔνεσεν αὐτὸν ἐν εὐλογίαις Κυρίου
6c ἐν τῷ φέρεσθαι αὐτῷ διάδημα δόξης.   7 ἐξέτριψεν γὰρ ἐχθροὺς κυκλόθεν,
7b καὶ ἐξουδένωσεν Φυλιστιεὶμ τοὺς ὑπεναντίους   ἕως σήμερον συνέτριψεν αὐτῶν κέρας.
8 ἐν παντὶ ἔργῳ αὐτοῦ ἔδωκεν ἐξομολόγησιν   ἁγίῳ Ὑψίστῳ, ῥήματι δόξης·
8c ἐν πάσῃ καρδίᾳ αὐτοῦ ὕμνησεν   καὶ ἠγάπησεν τὸν ποιήσαντα αὐτόν.
9 καὶ ἔστησεν ψαλτῳδοὺς κατέναντι τοῦ θυσιαστηρίου,   καὶ ἐξ ἤχους αὐτῶν γλυκαίνειν μέλη·
10 ἔδωκεν ἐν ἑορταῖς εὐπρέπειαν,   καὶ ἐκόσμησεν καιροὺς μέχρι συντελείας,
10c ἐν τῷ αἰνεῖν αὐτοὺς τὸ ἅγιον ὄνομα αὐτοῦ   καὶ ἀπὸ πρωὶ ἠχεῖν τὸ ἁγίασμα.

(fol. 8 recto.)

11	. . ײ העביר פשעו	וירם לעולם קרנו:
11c	[וית]ן לו֗ חקת מלכת	וכסאו הבין על ירושלם:
12	[ו]בֿעֿםֿ אין עמד אחריו	בן משכיל[1] שוכן לבטח:
13	שלמה מלך בימי שלוה	ואל הניח לו מסביב:
13c	אשר הכין בית לשמו	ויצב לעד מקדש:
14	מה חכמת בנעריך	ותצף כיאר מוסר:
15	ארץ . . . . ךֿ	ותקל[ס ב]מרום שירה:
17	בשיר מ[ש]ל חידה ומליצה	עמים הסערתה:
18	נקראת בשם הנכבד	הנקרא על ישראל:
18c	ותצבר כברזל זהב	וכעפרת הרבית כסף:
19	ותתן לנשים כסליך	ותמשילם בגויתך:
20	ו[ת]תן מום בכבודך	ותחלל את יצועיך[2]:
20c	. . . . אף על צאצאיך	ואנחה על משכבך:
21	לֿ . . . . . לשני שבטים	ומאפרים ממלכת חמס:
22	. . . [א]ל לא ימוש חסד	ולא יפיל מדבריו ארצה:
22c	לא . . . . . . ו נין ונכד	[ואוה]ביו לא ישמיד:
22e	ויתן ל	ול . . . .
23	וישכב שלמה מֿיֿוֿ . ש[3]	ויעזב אחֿ[ריו] . . . . ו֗:

[1] Prov. 10, 5. [2] Gen. 49, 4. [3] The whole word looks most like מיושש (? מְיֻשָּׁשׁ made aged), or מיואש (מְיֹאָשׁ in despair), but no verb ישש is quoted, and מיואש seems unsuited to the context.

11	ܘܐܦ ܐܠܗܐ ܫܒܩ ܠܗ ܚܛܗ̈ܘܗܝ	ܘܐܪܝܡ ܠܥܠܡ ܩܪܢܗ.
11c	ܘܝܗܒ ܠܗ ܩܝܡܐ ܕܡܠܟܘܬܐ	ܥܠ ܐܝܣܪܝܠ ܠܥܠܡ.
13	ܘܡܢ ܒܬܪܗ ܩܡ ܡܠܟܐ ܚܟܝܡܐ ܒܪܐ ܒܫܝܢܐ ܫܠܝܡܘܢ.	ܘܐܠܗܐ ܐܢܝܚ ܠܗ ܡܢ ܟܠܗܘܢ ܣܚܪ̈ܢܘܗܝ.
13c	ܡܠܟ ܕܢܒܢܐ ܒܝܬܐ ܠܫܡܗ ܠܥܠܡ܀	
14	ܟܡܐ ܚܟܝܡ ܗܘܝܬ ܒܛܠܝܘܬܟ ܫܠܝܡܘܢ..	ܘܐܬܢܦܫܬ ܐܝܟ ܢܗܪܐ ܣܘܟܠܐ ܒܣܘܟܠܟ. ܘܥܘܡܩܐ ܕܐܪܥܐ ܕܡܬ̈ܠܐ.
16	ܠܓܙܪ̈ܬܐ ܪ̈ܚܝܩܬܐ ܢܦܩ ܫܡܟ.	ܘܡܠܝܬ ܒܡܬ̈ܠܝܟ.
17	ܥܦܪ ܡܬ̈ܠܐ ܕܫܡܥܬܐ ܒܒܒܠ.	ܘܒܢܒܝܘܬܐ ܐܬܚܒܬ ܒܥܡ̈ܡܐ.
18	ܘܐܬܩܪܝܬ ܒܫܡܗ ܕܐܠܗܐ. ܕܡܠܟܗ ܗܘ ܐܠܗܐ	ܕܐܬܩܪܝ ܥܠ ܐܝܣܪܝܠ.
18c	ܘܟܢܫܬ ܐܝܟ ܐܒܪܐ ܕܗܒܐ.	ܘܣܓܝܬ ܐܝܟ ܥܦܪܐ.
19	ܘܝܗܒܬ ܠܢܫ̈ܐ ܠܒܟ.	ܘܐܫܠܛܬ ܐܢܝܢ ܒܦܓܪܟ.
20	ܘܝܗܒܬ ܡܘܡܐ ܒܐܝܩܪܟ.	ܘܛܢܦܬ ܠܙܪܥܟ.
20c	ܠܡܫܡܠܘ ܪܘܓܙܐ ܥܠ ܒܢ̈ܝ ܒܝܬܟ.	ܕܢܐܬܘܢ ܥܠ ܡܫܟܒܟܘܢ.
21	ܠܡܬܦܠܓܘ ܠܬܪܝܢ ܫܒܛ̈ܝܢ.	ܡܢ ܕܒܝܬ ܐܦܪܝܡ ܡܠܟܘܬܐ ܚܛܝܬܐ.
22	ܘܐܦ ܐܠܗܐ ܠܐ ܫܒܩ ܛܝܒܘܬܗ.	ܘܠܐ ܢܦܠ ܡܠ̈ܘܗܝ ܥܠ ܐܪܥܐ.
22c	ܘܠܐ ܢܘܒܕ ܙܪܥܐ ܕܪ̈ܚܡܘܗܝ.	ܘܒ̈ܢܝ ܕܪ̈ܚܡܘܗܝ ܠܐ ܢܘܒܕ.
22e	ܘܝܗܒ ܠܝܥܩܘܒ ܡܫܘܙܒܢܘܬܐ	ܘܠܕܘܝܕ ܝܗܒ ܡܠܟܘܬܐ ܟܠܗ.
23	ܘܫܟܒ ܫܠܝܡܘܢ.	ܘܩܡ ܒܪܗ ܒܬܪܗ܀

(fol. 8 recto.)

11 . . . . the Lord took away his transgression, and exalted his horn for ever,
11c [And ga]ve him the ordinance of the kingdom, and established his throne over Jerusalem.
12 [And] among the people there arose none after him, an understanding son, dwelling securely.
13 Solomon reigned in days of prosperity, and God gave rest to him round about,
13c Who established an house for his name, and set up a sanctuary for ever.
14 How wast thou wise in thy youth! and didst make instruction to overflow[1] like the Nile:
15 The earth . . . . and thou didst celebrate song in the height (?):
17 With songs, proverbs, dark sayings, and figures, thou didst greatly move[2] the nations:
18 Thou wast called by the glorious name, which is called over[3] Israel,
18c And thou didst heap up gold as iron, and didst multiply silver like lead;
19 But thou gavest thy loins unto women, and lettest them have dominion over thy body;
20 So [thou] didst put a blemish upon thy glory[4], and didst profane thy couch,
20c [To bring] wrath upon thy issue, and sighing upon thy bed; [arise).
21 That [they should become] two tribes, and that out of Ephraim a kingdom of violence (might
22 [Nevertheless] God forsaketh not mercy, nor letteth any of his words fall to the ground.
22c He will not [cut off from his chosen] progeny and offspring, nor destroy them that [lo]ve him;
22e So he gave unto [Jacob a remnant], and to [David] . . . .
23 And Solomon slept . . . . and left of his [seed] af[ter him].

[1] i.e. וַתָּצֶף, as 𝔖. *Or* וַתֵּצֶף didst overflow with instruction, as 𝔊. [2] *Lit.* move as with a tempest (cf. 2 Kings 6, 11).
[3] Deut. 28, 10, &c. See 1 Kings 8, 43, R.V. *marg.*; and cf. Sir. 36, 12 𝔖. [4] Cf. 44, 19 and 33, 22 𝔖𝔊.

11 Κύριος ἀφεῖλεν τὰς ἁμαρτίας αὐτοῦ, καὶ ἀνύψωσεν εἰς αἰῶνα τὸ κέρας αὐτοῦ,
11c καὶ ἔδωκεν αὐτῷ διαθήκην βασιλέων καὶ θρόνον δόξης ἐν τῷ Ἰσραήλ.
12 μετὰ τοῦτον ἀνέστη υἱὸς ἐπιστήμων, καὶ δι' αὐτὸν κατέλυσεν ἐν πλατυσμῷ·
13 Σαλωμὼν ἐβασίλευσεν ἐν ἡμέραις εἰρήνης, ᾧ ὁ θεὸς κατέπαυσεν κυκλόθεν,
13c ἵνα στήσῃ οἶκον ἐπ' ὀνόματι αὐτοῦ καὶ ἑτοιμάσῃ ἁγίασμα εἰς τὸν αἰῶνα.
14 ὡς ἐσοφίσθης ἐν νεότητί σου, καὶ ἐνεπλήσθης ὡς ποταμὸς συνέσεως.
15 γῆν ἐπεκάλυψεν ἡ ψυχή σου, καὶ ἐνέπλησας ἐν παραβολαῖς αἰνιγμάτων·
16 εἰς νήσους πόρρω ἀφίκετο τὸ ὄνομά σου, καὶ ἠγαπήθης ἐν τῇ εἰρήνῃ σου·
17 ἐν ᾠδαῖς καὶ παροιμίαις καὶ παραβολαῖς καὶ ἐν ἑρμηνίᾳ ἀπεθαύμασάν σε χῶραι·
18 ἐν ὀνόματι Κυρίου τοῦ θεοῦ, τοῦ ἐπικεκλημένου θεοῦ Ἰσραήλ,
18c συνήγαγες ὡς κασσίτερον τὸ χρυσίον, καὶ ὡς μόλιβον ἐπλήθυνας ἀργύριον.
19 παρανέκλινας τὰς λαγόνας σου γυναιξίν, καὶ ἐνεξουσιάσθης ἐν τῷ σώματί σου·
20 ἔδωκας μῶμον ἐν τῇ δόξῃ σου, καὶ ἐβεβήλωσας τὸ σπέρμα σου,
20c ἐπαγαγεῖν ὀργὴν ἐπὶ τὰ τέκνα σου, καὶ κατενύγην ἐπὶ τῇ ἀφροσύνῃ σου,
21 γενέσθαι δίχα τυραννίδα καὶ ἐξ Ἐφράιμ ἄρξαι βασιλείαν ἀπειθῆ.
22 ὁ δὲ Κύριος οὐ μὴ καταλίπῃ τὸ ἔλεος αὐτοῦ, καὶ οὐ μὴ διαφθαρῇ ἀπὸ τῶν ἔργων αὐτοῦ,
22c οὐδὲ μὴ ἐξαλείψῃ ἐκλεκτοῦ αὐτοῦ ἔκγονα, καὶ σπέρμα τοῦ ἀγαπήσαντος αὐτὸν οὐ μὴ ἐξάρῃ·
22e καὶ τῷ Ἰακὼβ ἔδωκεν κατάλιμμα, καὶ τῷ Δαυεὶδ ἐξ αὐτοῦ ῥίζαν.
23 καὶ ἀνεπαύσατο Σαλωμὼν μετὰ τῶν πατέρων, καὶ κατέλιπεν μετ' αὐτὸν ἐκ τοῦ σπέρματος αὐτοῦ

(fol. 8 verso.)

23c רחב אולת וחסר בינה — רחבעם הפריע[1] בע[צתו ע]ם:

23e עד אשר קם אל יהי לו זכר — ירבעם בן נבט אשר ה[חטי]א א[ת] . . .

23g ויתן לאפרים מכשול — 24b להריחם [מ]ארמתם:

24a ותגדל חטאתו מאד — 25 ולכל רעה התמכר[2]:

XLVIII. 1 עד אשר קם נביא כאש — ודבריו כתנור בוער:

2 וישבר להם מטה לחם — ובקנאתו המעיטם:

3 בדבר אל ע[צ]ר שמים — . . . . אשות:

4 מה נורא את[ה] אליהו — אשר כ[מו]ך יתפאר:

5 המקים גוע ממות — ומשאול ברצון ייי:

6 המוריד מלכים על שחת — ונכבדים [מ]מטותם:

8 המושח מלא תשלומות — ונביא תחליף תחתיך:

7 והשמיע בסיני תוכחות — ובחורב משפטי נק[ם]:

9 הנלקח בסערה מעלה — ובגדודי איש . . . . :

10 הכתוב נכון לעת[3] — להשבית אף לפנ[י] . . .

10c להשיב לב אבות על בנים — ולהכין ש[בטי ישרא]ל:

11 אשר ראך ומת . . — . . . ד[4] . . . . . . יה:

12 [א]ל[יהו] . . . . — [וא]ל[ישע] . . . .

12c פי ש[נים] אתות הרבה — ונלמד בכל מוצא פיהו:

[1] Exod. 32, 25. [2] 1 Kings 21, 20. 25; 2 Kings 17, 17. [3] Mal. 4, 5 sq. [4] Only the tail of the letter remains.

23c ܣܓܝܐ ܫܛܝܘܬܐ ܘܚܣܝܪ ܣܘܟܠܐ — ܪܚܒܥܡ. ܕܦܪ ܒܡܠܟܘܬܗ ܠܥܡܗ.

23e ܘܠܐ ܢܗܘܐ ܠܗ ܕܘܟܪܢ — ܠܝܪܒܥܡ ܒܪ ܢܒܛ ؛ ܕܚܛܐ ܘܐܚܛܝ ܠܐܝܣܪܝܠ.

23g ܘܝܗܒ ܬܘܩܠܬܐ ܐܦܪܝܡ ܠܡܬܬܩܠܘ. — 24b ܠܡܓܠܝܘܬܗ ܐܝܟ ܡܢ ܐܪܥܗܘܢ.

24a ܘܐܣܓܝ ܣܟܠܘܬܗܘܢ ܛܒ. — 25 ܘܒܟܠ ܟܠ ܒܝܫܬܐ ܐܙܕܒܢܘ.

XLVIII. 1 ܥܕܡܐ ܕܩܡ ܢܒܝܐ ܕܕܡܐ ܠܢܘܪܐ. — ܘܡܠܘܗܝ ܝܩܕܐ ܐܝܟ ܬܢܘܪܐ ܕܡܫܓܪ.

2 ܘܐܝܬܝ ܥܠܝܗܘܢ ܟܦܢܐ. — ܘܒܛܢܢܗ ܙܥܪ ܐܢܘܢ.

3 ܒܡܠܬܗ ܕܐܠܗܐ ܟܠܐ ܫܡܝܐ. — ܘܐܚܬ ܬܠܬ ܙܒܢܝܢ ܢܘܪܐ ܡܢ ܫܡܝܐ. ܟܠ ܡܟܝܟܐ ܘܟܠ ܐܢܫ ܕܫܡܥܗ

4 ܡܐ ܕܚܝܠ ܐܢܬ ܐܠܝܐ.. — ܘܡܢ ܕܐܟܘܬܟ. ܗܘ ܢܫܬܒܚ.

5 ܕܐܚܝ ܡܝܬܐ — ܡܢ ܫܝܘܠ ܐܝܟ ܨܒܝܢܗ ܕܡܪܝܐ.

6 ܡܚܬܝܢ ܡܠܟܐ ܡܢ ܡܪܟܒܬܗܘܢ.

7 ܘܐܫܡܥ ܒܣܝܢܝ ܡܟܣܢܘܬܗܘܢ.

8 ܘܡܫܚ ܡܠܟܐ ܠܡܬܦܪܥܘ ܢܩܡܬܐ. — ܘܢܒܝܐ ܕܢܗܘܐ ܚܠܦܝܟ.

9 ܘܐܬܕܒܪ ܒܥܠܥܠܐ ܠܥܠ — ܒܪܟܒܐ ܕܢܘܪܐ ܠܫܡܝܐ.

10 ܗܘܐ ܠܗܘ ܥܬܝܕܐ — ܡܢ ܕܠܐ ܢܐܬܐ ܝܘܡܐ ܕܡܪܝܐ.

10c ܠܡܦܢܝܘ ܒܢܝܐ ܥܠ ܐܒܗܐ. — ܘܠܡܬܩܢܘ ܠܫܒܛܝ ܝܥܩܘܒ.

11 ܛܘܒܘܗܝ ܠܡܢ ܕܚܙܟ. ܘܡܝܬ. — ܒܪܡ ܠܐ. ܡܝܬ ܐܠܐ ܡܚܝܐ ܢܚܐ.

12 ܐܠܝܐ ܒܥܠܥܠܐ ܐܬܟܣܝ ܠܫܡܝܐ. — ܘܦܠܓ ܪܘܚܗ ܐܬܪܝܢ ܐܠܝܫܥ.

12c ܘܣܓܝ ܢܝܫܐ ܘܐܬܘܬܐ — ܡܠܠ ܦܘܡܗ.

(fol. 8 verso.)

23d Ample[1] in foolishness and lacking understanding, Rehoboam by [his coun]sel let loose [the peo]ple;
23e Until there arose—let him have no memorial!—Jeroboam, the son of Nebat, who made [Israel to si]n.
23g And he gave unto Ephraim a stumbling-block, 24b to drive them out [of] their land.
24a And his sin was great exceedingly, 25 and he sold himself to all evil.
XLVIII. 1 Till there arose a prophet like fire, whose words were like a burning furnace.
2 And he brake for them the staff of bread, and by his jealousy[2] made them few in number.
3 By the word of God he shut up the heavens, ... fires.
4 How terrible wast thou, O Elijah! he who is like thee may glory!
5 Who didst raise up one that expired from death, and from Sheol, according to the will of the Lord;
6 Who broughtest down kings to the pit, and honourable men [from] their beds;
8 Who anointedst one filled with retribution, and a prophet to succeed in thy place;
7 Who heardest[3] reproofs in Sinai, and judgements of vengeance in Horeb;
9 Who wast taken up by a whirlwind on high, and by troops of fire [into heaven];
10 Who art written down[4] as ready for a season, to make anger to cease before . . . .
10c To turn the heart of the fathers to the children, and to give understanding to the tr[ibes of Isra]el.
11 Happy[5] he that saw thee and died (?) . . . .
12 Elijah . . . . and Elisha . . . .
12c With a do[uble] measure[6] he multiplied signs, and he was learned in every utterance of his mouth.

[1] In the Hebrew with a play on the name Rehoboam. [2] 1 Kings 19, 10. 14. [3] Reading תוכחות, as 𝔊. [4] Mal. 4, 5 seq. [5] Reading אשרי, as 𝔊 𝔖. [6] With allusion to 2 Kings 2, 9, where the same phrase is rendered 'double portion:' *lit.* a mouth—i. e. a portion—of two.

23c λαοῦ ἀφροσύνην καὶ ἐλασσούμενον συνέσει Ῥοβοάμ, ὃς ἀπέστησεν λαὸν ἐκ βουλῆς αὐτοῦ,
23f καὶ Ἱεροβοὰμ υἱὸν Ναβάτ, ὃς ἐξήμαρτεν τὸν Ἰσραὴλ
23g καὶ ἔδωκεν τῷ Ἐφράιμ ὁδὸν ἁμαρτίας.
24 καὶ ἐπληθύνθησαν αἱ ἁμαρτίαι αὐτῶν σφόδρα,
24b ἀποστῆσαι αὐτοὺς ἀπὸ τῆς γῆς αὐτῶν·
25 καὶ πᾶσαν πονηρίαν ἐξεζήτησαν, ἕως ἐκδίκησις ἔλθῃ ἐπ' αὐτούς.
XLVIII. 1 καὶ ἀνέστη Ἠλίας προφήτης ὡς πῦρ, καὶ ὁ λόγος αὐτοῦ ὡς λαμπὰς ἐκαίετο·
2 ὃς ἐπήγαγεν ἐπ' αὐτοὺς λιμόν, καὶ τῷ ζήλῳ αὐτοῦ ὠλιγοποίησεν αὐτούς·
3 ἐν λόγῳ Κυρίου ἀνέσχεν οὐρανόν, κατήγαγεν οὕτως τρὶς πῦρ.
4 ὡς ἐδοξάσθης, Ἠλεία, ἐν τοῖς θαυμασίοις σου· καὶ τίς ὅμοιός σοι καυχᾶσθαι;
5 ὁ ἐγείρας νεκρὸν ἐκ θανάτου καὶ ἐξ ᾅδου ἐν λόγῳ Ὑψίστου·
6 ὁ καταγαγὼν βασιλεῖς εἰς ἀπωλίαν καὶ δεδοξασμένους ἀπὸ κλίνης αὐτῶν·
7 ἀκούων ἐν Σεινὰ ἐλεγμὸν καὶ ἐν Χωρὴβ κρίματα ἐκδικήσεως·
8 ὁ χρίων βασιλεῖς εἰς ἀνταπόδομα, καὶ προφήτας διαδόχους μετ' αὐτόν·
9 ὁ ἀναλημφθεὶς ἐν λαίλαπι πυρὸς ἐν ἅρματι ἵππων πυρίνων·
10 ὁ καταγραφεὶς ἐν ἐλεγμοῖς εἰς καιρούς, κοπάσαι ὀργὴν πρὸ θυμοῦ
10c καὶ ἐπιστρέψαι καρδίαν πατρὸς πρὸς υἱὸν καὶ καταστῆσαι φυλὰς Ἰακώβ.
11 μακάριοι οἱ ἰδόντες σε καὶ οἱ ἐν ἀγαπήσει κεκοσμημένοι, καὶ γὰρ ἡμεῖς ζωῇ ζησόμεθα.
12 Ἠλείας ὃς ἐν λαίλαπι ἐσκεπάσθη· καὶ Ἐλεισαῖε ἐνεπλήσθη πνεύματος αὐτοῦ,

(fol. 9 recto.)

12e מימיו לא זע[1] מכל ולא משל ברוחו כל בשר :
13 כל דבר לא נפלא ממנו ומתחתיו[2] נברא בשרו :
14 בחייו עשה נפלאות ובמותו תמהי מעשה :
15 בכל זאת לא שב העם ולא חדלו מחטאתם :
15c עד אשר נסחו מארצם ויפצו בכל הארץ :
15e וישאר ליהודה מזער ועוד לבית דוד קצין :
16 יש מהם עשו יושר ויש מהם הפליאו מעל :
17 יחזקיהו חזק עירו בהטות אל תוכה מים :
17c ויחצב בנחשת צורים ויחסום הרים מקוה :
18 בימיו עלה סנחריב וישלח את רב שקה :
18c וים ידו על ציון וינדף אל בגאונו :
19 . . [נ]מונו בנאון לבם ויחילו כיולדה :
20 וי[קר]או אל אל עליון ויפרשו אליו כפים :
20c וי. . . . . קול*תפלתם ויושיעם ביד ישעיהו :
21 ו . . . [מ]חנה אשור ויהמם במגפה :
22 . . . . [יחז]קיהו את הטו[ב] [ו]יחזק בדרכי דוד :
22c . . . .
23 . . . .

[1] Est. 5, 9.

[2] Zech. 6, 12.

12e ܡܢ ܝܘܡܘܗܝ ܠܐ ܙܥ ܡܢ ܩܕܡ ܐܢܫ. ܘܠܐ ܫܠܛ ܒܗ ܟܠ ܒܣܪ.
13 ܘܟܠ ܡܕܡ ܠܐ ܐܬܟܣܝ ܡܢܗ.
14 ܒܚܝܘܗܝ ܥܒܕ ܬܕܡܪܬܐ. ܘܒܡܘܬܗ ܐܚܝ ܡܝ̈ܬܐ.
15 ܘܒܟܠܗܝܢ ܗܠܝܢ ܠܐ ܬܒ ܥܡܐ. ܘܠܐ ܦܪܩܘ ܡܢ ܚܛܗ̈ܝܗܘܢ ܕܣܓܝܐ.
15c ܥܕܡܐ ܕܓܠܘ ܡܢ ܐܪܥܗܘܢ. ܘܐܬܒܕܪܘ ܒܟܠ ܡܕܝܢ̈ܬܐ.
15e ܘܫܪܐ ܗܘܐ ܠܒܝܬ ܝܗܘܕܐ. ܐܠܐ ܫܘܠܛܢܐ ܠܒܝܬ ܕܘܝܕ.
16 ܐܝܬ ܡܢܗܘܢ ܕܥܒܕܘ ܫܦܝܪܬܐ. ܘܐܝܬ ܡܢܗܘܢ ܕܐܘܣܦܘ ܚܛܗ̈ܐ ܥܠ ܚܛܗ̈ܐ.
17 ܚܙܩܝܐ ܚܝܠ ܡܕܝܢܬܐ. ܘܐܥܠ ܠܓܘܗ ܡܝ̈ܐ.

18 ܒܝܘܡܘܗܝ ܣܠܩ ܠܘܬܗܘܢ ܣܢܚܪܝܒ: ܘܫܕܪ ܠܘܬܗܘܢ ܠܪܒ ܫܩܐ.
18c ܘܐܪܝܡ ܐܝܕܗ ܥܠ ܨܗܝܘܢ. ܘܓܕܦ ܒܫܘܒܗܪܗ ܥܠ ܐܠܗܐ.

20b ܘܦܪܣ ܚܝܠܐ ܗܘ ܡܪܐ ܐܝܩܪܗ.
20c ܘܫܡܥ ܐܠܗܐ ܒܩܠ ܨܠܘܬܗܘܢ. ܘܦܪܩ ܐܢܘܢ ܒܝܕ ܐܫܥܝܐ ܢܒܝܐ.
21 ܘܡܚܐ ܡܫܪܝܬܗ ܕܐܬܘܪ. ܘܚܒܠ ܐܢܘܢ ܡܚܘܬܐ ܪܒܬܐ.
22 ܡܛܠ ܕܥܒܕ ܚܙܩܝܐ ܕܫܦܪ: ܘܗܠܟ ܒܐܘܪܚܬܗ ܕܕܘܝܕ:
22c ܕܦܩܕܗ ܐܫܥܝܐ ܢܒܝܐ ܡܗܝܡܢܐ ܕܚܙܘܐ.
23 ܡܛܠܗ ܕܨܠܝܗ ܡܢ ܫܡܫܐ. ܘܐܬܘܣܦ ܥܠ ܚܝܘܗܝ ܕܡܠܟܐ.

(fol. 9 recto.)

12e All his life long he quaked before none, and no flesh had dominion over his spirit;
13 No matter was too hard for him, and from its place his flesh prophesied[1];
14 In his life he did wonders, and in his death marvellous works.
15 For all this the people turned not, and ceased not from their sins,
15c Till they were rooted up from their land, and were scattered through all the earth.
15e But there were left to Judah a few, and still a judge to the house of David.
16 There were of them that dealt uprightly, and there were of them that trespassed wondrously.
17 Hezekiah strengthened[2] his city, when he turned aside waters into the midst of it,
17c And hewed the rocks with[3] brass, and stopped up mountains for a pool.
18 In his days came up Sennacherib, and sent Rabshakeh;
18c And he stretched out his hand against Sion, and blasphemed God in his pride.
19 [Then were] they melted in the pride of their heart, and were in anguish as a woman in travail;
20 So they ca[lled] unto God Most High, and spread forth their hands unto him;
20c And he [heard] the voice of their prayer, and saved[4] them by the hand of Isaiah;
21 And [he smote the c]amp of the Assyrian, and discomfited them with the plague.
22 [For Heze]kiah [did] that which was go[od, and] was strong[2] in the ways of David.
22c . . . .
23 . . . .

[1] Reading נבא, as 𝔊; see 2 Kings 13, 21.
[2] In the Hebrew with a play on the name Hezekiah.
[3] Reading בנח״.
[4] In the Hebrew with a play on the name Isaiah.

12e καὶ ἐν ἡμέραις αὐτοῦ οὐκ ἐσαλεύθη ὑπὸ ἄρχοντος, καὶ οὐ κατεδυνάστευσεν αὐτὸν οὐδείς.
13 πᾶς λόγος οὐχ ὑπερῆρεν αὐτόν, καὶ ἐν κοιμήσει ἐπροφήτευσεν τὸ σῶμα αὐτοῦ·
14 καὶ ἐν ζωῇ αὐτοῦ ἐποίησεν τέρατα, καὶ ἐν τελευτῇ θαυμάσια τὰ ἔργα αὐτοῦ.
15 ἐν πᾶσιν τούτοις οὐ μετενόησεν ὁ λαός, καὶ οὐκ ἀπέστησαν ἀπὸ τῶν ἁμαρτιῶν,
15c ἕως ἐπρονομεύθησαν ἀπὸ τῆς γῆς αὐτῶν καὶ ἐσκορπίσθησαν ἐν πάσῃ τῇ γῇ,
15e καὶ κατελείφθη ὁ λαὸς ὀλιγοστός καὶ ἄρχων τῷ οἴκῳ Δαυείδ.
16 τινὲς μὲν αὐτῶν ἐποίησαν τὸ ἀρεστόν, τινὲς δὲ ἐπλήθυναν ἁμαρτίας.
17 Ἑζεκίας ὠχύρωσεν τὴν πόλιν αὐτοῦ, καὶ εἰσήγαγεν εἰς μέσον αὐτῶν τὸν Γώγ·
17c ὤρυξεν σιδήρῳ ἀκρότομον, καὶ ᾠκοδόμησεν κρήνας εἰς ὕδατα.
18 ἐν ἡμέραις αὐτοῦ ἀνέβη Σενναχηρείμ καὶ ἀπέστειλεν Ῥαψάκην, καὶ ἀπῆρεν·
18c καὶ ἐπῆρεν ἡ χεὶρ αὐτοῦ ἐπὶ Σειών, καὶ ἐμεγαλαύχησεν ὑπερηφανίᾳ αὐτοῦ.
19 τότε ἐσαλεύθησαν καρδίαι καὶ χεῖρες αὐτῶν, καὶ ὠδίνησαν ὡς αἱ τίκτουσαι·
20 καὶ ἐπεκαλέσαντο τὸν κύριον τὸν ἐλεήμονα, ἐκπετάσαντες τὰς χεῖρας αὐτῶν πρὸς αὐτόν.
20c καὶ ὁ ἅγιος ἐξ οὐρανοῦ ταχὺ ἐπήκουσεν αὐτῶν, καὶ ἐλυτρώσατο αὐτοὺς ἐν χειρὶ Ἠσαίου·
21 ἐπάταξεν τὴν παρεμβολὴν τῶν Ἀσσυρίων, καὶ ἐξέτριψεν αὐτοὺς ὁ ἄγγελος αὐτοῦ.
22 ἐποίησεν γὰρ Ἑζεκίας τὸ ἀρεστὸν Κυρίῳ, καὶ ἐνίσχυσεν ἐν ὁδοῖς Δαυεὶδ τοῦ πατρὸς αὐτοῦ,
22c ἃς ἐνετείλατο Ἠσαίας ὁ προφήτης ὁ μέγας καὶ πιστὸς ἐν ὁράσει αὐτοῦ.
23 ἐν ταῖς ἡμέραις αὐτοῦ ἀνεπόδισεν ὁ ἥλιος, καὶ προσέθηκεν ζωὴν βασιλεῖ·

(fol. 9 verso.)

24 ברות גבורה חזה אחרית   וינחם אבלי ציון[1]:

25 עד עולם הגיד נהיות   ונסתרות לפני בואן:

XLIX. 1 שם יאשיהו בקטרת סמים   הממלח מעשה רוקח[2]:

1c בחך כדבש ימתיק זכרו   ובמזמור על משתה היין:

2 כי נחל על משובתינו   וישבת[3] תועבות הבל:

3 ויתם אל אל לבו   ובימי חמס עשה חסד:

4 לבד מדויד יחזקיהו   ויאשיהו בלם השחיתו:

4c ויעזבו תורת עליון   מלכי יהודה עד תמם:

5 ויתן קרנם לאחור   וכבודם לגוי נבל[4] נכרי:

6 ויציתו קרית קדש   וישמו ארחתיה:

6c ביד ירמיהו 7 כי ענוהו   והוא מרחם[5] נוצר נביא:

7b לנתוש ולנתוץ ולהאביד להרס וכן לבנות לנטע[6] ולהשיב:

8 יחזקאל ראה מראה   ויגד זני מרכבה:

9 וגם הזכיר את איוב   המכלכל כל ד[רכי צ]דק:

10 וגם שנים עשר הנביאים   תהי עצמתם פר[חת ממקומו]תם:

10c אשר החלימו את יעקב   וישיבוהו בֿרֿ . . . .

11 . . . . . ל[7] . . . . ל . . . .

12 . . . .

[1] Is. 61, 3. [2] Exod. 30, 35. 31, 11. [3] 2 Kings 23, 5. 11, 5. [4] Deut. 32, 21.
[5] Jer. 1, 5. [6] Jer. 1, 10. [7] Perhaps ל[איך נגר].

24 ܘܒܪܘܚܐ ܓܢܒܪܬܐ ܚܙܐ ܐܚܪܝܬܐ.   ܘܒܝܐ ܠܐܒܝܠܐ ܕܨܗܝܘܢ.

25 ܘܥܕ ܠܥܠܡ ܗܘ. ܚܙܐ ܐܬܝܬܐ   ܘܟܣܝܬܐ ܥܕ ܠܐ ܢܐܬܝܢ ܀

XLIX. 1 ܫܡܗ ܕܝܘܫܝܐ ܐܝܟ ܒܣܡܐ ܕܒܣܡܐ   ܕܡܬܒܣܡ ܒܥܒܝܕܬܐ ܕܒܣܡܐ.

1c ܐܝܟ ܕܒܫܐ ܒܚܟܐ ܚܠܐ ܕܘܟܪܢܗ.   ܘܐܝܟ ܙܡܘܪܬܐ ܥܠ ܡܫܬܝܐ ܚܡܪܐ.

2 ܡܛܠ ܕܐܬܟܪܝ ܡܢ ܬܝܒܘܬܢ.   ܘܒܛܠ ܦܬܟܪܐ ܕܗܒܠܐ.

3 ܘܐܫܠܡ ܠܐܠܗܐ ܠܒܗ.   ܘܒܝܘܡܝ ܚܛܝܐ ܥܒܕ ܛܝܒܘܬܐ.

4 ܒܠܚܘܕ ܒܪ ܡܢ ܕܘܝܕ ܘܚܙܩܝܐ ܘܝܘܫܝܐ   ܟܠܗܘܢ ܚܒܠܘ.

4c ܘܫܒܩܘ ܢܡܘܣܐ   ܡܠܟܐ ܕܒܝܬ ܝܗܘܕܐ ܥܕܡܐ ܠܐܚܪܝܬܐ.

5 ܘܝܗܒܘ ܚܝܠܗܘܢ ܠܐܚܪܢܐ   ܘܐܝܩܪܗܘܢ ܠܥܡܐ ܢܘܟܪܝܐ.

6 ܘܓܡܪܘ ܩܪܝܬܐ ܩܕܝܫܬܐ.   ܘܐܚܪܒܘ ܟܠܗܝܢ ܫܒܝܠܝܗ.

6c ܒܐܝܕܝ ܐܪܡܝܐ   7b ܕܗܘܐ ܡܢ ܟܪܣܐ ܕܐܡܗ ܢܒܝܐ.

8 ܘܚܙܩܝܐܝܠ   ܚܙܐ ܚܙܘܐ ܕܡܪܟܒܬܐ ܘܚܘܝ ܚܝܘܬܐ.

9 ܘܐܦ ܥܠ ܐܝܘܒ ܐܡܪ.   ܕܢܛܪ ܐܘܪܚܬܐ ܕܙܕܝܩܘܬܐ ܟܠܗܝܢ ܀

10 ܘܐܦ ܬܪܥܣܪ ܢܒܝܐ.   ܢܗܘܘܢ ܓܪܡܝܗܘܢ ܡܦܪܥܝܢ ܠܐܬܪܗܘܢ.

10c ܕܐܚܝܘ ܠܝܥܩܘܒ   ܘܐܫܬܘ ܐܢܘܢ ܕܡܫܪܪܝܢ ܀

11 ܐܝܟܢܐ ܢܫܒܚ ܠܙܘܪܒܒܠ.   ܕܗܘܐ ܐܝܟ ܚܬܡܐ ܥܠ ܐܝܕܐ ܕܝܡܝܢܐ ܀

12 ܘܐܦ ܝܫܘܥ ܒܪ ܝܘܨܕܩ.   ܕܒܝܘܡܝܗܘܢ ܐܬܒܢܝ ܡܩܕܫܐ

(fol. 9 verso.)

24 By a spirit of might he saw the end, and comforted the mourners of Sion.
25 For ever he declared things that should be, and hidden things before they came.
XLIX. 1 The name of Josiah is like incense of sweet spices, salted, the work of the perfumer:
1c His memory is sweet as honey on the palate, and as music at the banquet of wine.
2 For he was grieved for[1] our backslidings, and he made the abominations of vanity to cease;
3 And he made his heart perfect toward God, and in days of violence he wrought godliness.
4 Except David, Hezekiah, and Josiah, they all did corruptly;
4c And forsook the law of the Most High, the kings of Judah, till they were ended.
5 So he turned their horn backward, and (gave) their glory to a foolish, foreign nation;
6 And they set on fire the holy city, and made her ways desolate.
6c By the hand[2] of Jeremiah, 7 for they afflicted him, yet from the womb he was formed (to be) a prophet,
7c To pluck up and to break down and to destroy (and) to overthrow, and in like manner to build up, to plant, and to make strong.
8 Ezekiel saw the vision, — and declared divers kinds of chariot.
9 Also he made mention of Job, who maintained all the w[ays of righ]teousness.
10 Moreover the twelve prophets, may their strength[3] flou[rish out of their pla]ces.
10c Who recovered Jacob to health, and restored him by . . . . . .
11 [How shall we magni]fy [Zerubbabel]? . . . . . .
12 . . . .

[1] נחלו (Amos 6, 6) for נחל. Text, perhaps: inherited the yoke (על) of our backslidings. [2] ? בימי *in the days of*, as 𝔖. [3] ? bones, as 𝔊 𝔖.

24 πνεύματι μεγάλῳ ἴδεν τὰ ἔσχατα, καὶ παρεκάλεσεν τοὺς πενθοῦντας ἐν Σειών·
25 ἕως τοῦ αἰῶνος ὑπέδειξεν τὰ ἐσόμενα καὶ τὰ ἀπόκρυφα πρὶν ἢ παραγενέσθαι αὐτά.
XLIX. 1 μνημόσυνον Ἰωσείου εἰς σύνθεσιν θυμιάματος, ἐσκευασμένον ἔργῳ μυρεψοῦ·
1c ἐν παντὶ στόματι ὡς μέλι γλυκανθήσεται, καὶ ὡς μουσικὰ ἐν συμποσίῳ οἴνου.
2 αὐτὸς κατευθύνθη ἐν ἐπιστροφῇ λαοῦ, καὶ ἐξῆρεν βδελύγματα ἀνομίας·
3 κατεύθυνεν πρὸς Κύριον τὴν καρδίαν αὐτοῦ, ἐν ἡμέραις ἀνόμων κατίσχυσεν τὴν εὐσέβειαν.
4 παρὲξ Δαυεὶδ καὶ Ἐζεκίου καὶ Ἰωσείου πάντες πλημμελίαν ἐπλημμέλησαν·
4c κατέλιπον γὰρ τὸν νόμον τοῦ ὑψίστου, οἱ βασιλεῖς Ἰούδα ἐξέλιπον.
5 ἔδωκαν γὰρ τὸ κέρας αὐτῶν ἑτέροις καὶ τὴν δόξαν αὐτῶν ἔθνει ἀλλοτρίῳ·
6 ἐνεπύρισεν ἐκλεκτὴν πόλιν ἁγιάσματος, καὶ ἠρήμωσαν τὰς ὁδοὺς αὐτῆς
6c ἐν χειρὶ Ἱερεμίου· 7 ἐκάκωσαν γὰρ αὐτόν, καὶ αὐτὸς ἐν μήτρᾳ ἡγιάσθη προφήτης,
7c ἐκριζοῦν καὶ κακοῦν καὶ ἀπολλύειν, ὡσαύτως οἰκοδομεῖν καὶ καταφυτεύειν.
8 Ἰεζεκιήλ, ὃς εἶδεν ὅρασιν δόξης — ἣν ὑπέδειξεν αὐτῷ ἐπὶ ἅρματος χερουβείμ·
9 καὶ γὰρ ἐμνήσθη τῶν ἐχθρῶν ἐν ὄμβρῳ, καὶ ἀγαθῶσαι τοὺς εὐθύνοντας ὁδούς.
10 καὶ τῶν ιβʹ προφητῶν τὰ ὀστᾶ ἀναθάλοι ἐκ τοῦ τόπου αὐτῶν.
10c παρεκάλεσεν δὲ τὸν Ἰακώβ, καὶ ἐλυτρώσατο αὐτοὺς ἐν πίστει ἐλπίδος.
11 πῶς μεγαλύνωμεν τὸν Ζοροβαβέλ; καὶ αὐτὸς ὡς σφραγὶς ἐπὶ δεξιᾶς χειρός.
12 οὕτως Ἰησοῦς υἱὸς Ἰωσεδέκ· οἳ ἐν ἡμέραις αὐτῶν οἰκοδόμησαν οἶκον.

www.ingramcontent.com/pod-product-compliance
Lightning Source LLC
Chambersburg PA
CBHW031451270326
41930CB00007B/951
9783337415389